D0276637

Emotional Capital

Emotional Capital

Capturing Hearts and Minds to
Create Lasting Business Success

KEVIN THOMSON

CAPSTONE

First Published 1998 by
Capstone Publishing Limited
Oxford Centre for Innovation
Mill Street
Oxford OX2 0JX
United Kingdom
http://www.capstone.co.uk

British Library Cataloguing in Publication Data
A CIP catalogue record for this book is available from the British Library

ISBN 1-900961-62-8

Typeset in 11/15 pt Garamond by
Sparks Computer Solutions, Oxford
http://www.sparks.co.uk
Printed and bound by
T.J. International Ltd, Padstow, Cornwall

This book is printed on acid-free paper

To my family, who waited through long days and long nights for me to finish this book and who are boundless contributors to the emotional capital of my life

Contents

Preface

'It's not enough to imagine the future – you also have to build it. You need a blueprint for building future businesses.'

– C.K. Prahalad

I believe the blueprint for building businesses in the future will go well beyond the focus on traditional financial assets into new territory using two critical and interrelated assets, knowledge *and* emotions.

Information and knowledge management will be vital. Yet even more importantly, the blueprint for the future will manage feelings, beliefs, perceptions and values – the asset of emotional capital – as the hidden resources that matter most.

Managing emotions will be the essential core competence for organizations of the future, achieved by treating the old 'employee' as the new 'internal customer'; the old divisions and functions as the new 'internal markets' and by applying what we call internal marketing, or marketing from within. I see a future in which organizations take an integrated approach to managing knowledge and emotions in business and around their stakeholders.

This is the blueprint for the next millennium, and it is also what this book is about: how to build and capitalize on your organization's emotional capital, and leverage your intellectual capital. It sets out a strategic framework for emotional capital management, defines the terms and tools you'll want and explains how you can start to apply them in your organizations.

Two caveats. First, this book concentrates on how to *manage* emotional capital rather than how to *measure* it. I believe that the first priority for organizations is to understand what this vital asset is and how to manage it. Then we can afford to focus on creating and implementing quantitative measures of it. In fact, all of this applies to not-for-profit organizations as much as companies and businesses (and I use the terms interchangeably throughout the book).

Second, this book is written the way I am, and our consulting firm is, for our core value is that 'we are passionate about everything we do'. I want you to feel this book has stirred your emotions as well as appealed to your intellect.

One goal is also to help as many people as we can to achieve better business results. I am proud of our achievements and the outcomes we achieve for our clients. And I am passionate about helping other organizations and individuals to do the same.

Part of my passion is to develop these concepts, and to explore ways that you can put them into practice in your own organizations. This book is the result of a lifetime of dedication to the profession of marketing and communication, and I want to share this learning and experience with you.

Kevin Thomson
Chairman
The Marketing and
Communication Agency
Ltd (MCA)
January 1998

About My Notes

At the end of each chapter, I have included a set of 'My notes' and in some places a model of emotional capital under the title 'Building the blueprint.' These short and at times highly visual sections are intended to deliver a number of benefits:

- Provide 'one liners' on each chapter as a summary and quick reference guide
- Show how the big picture of soft and hard measures in business provides an integrated whole
- Allow visually orientated people to see the picture 'that tells a thousand words'
- Illustrate as we go along how each of the pieces is linked to all of the others
- Stimulate debate on the 'what, where, why, when, how and who' of emotional capital with some 'Thought Provokers For the Future'
- Give those people who love to scribble notes in the margin some space for their own memory joggers, questions and ideas.

These notes are distinguishable by the informal 'script' style used.

Acknowledgments:
A Heartfelt
Thank-you

'A good business novel or business biography is not about business. It is about love, hate, craftsmanship, jealousy, comradeship, ambition, pleasure. These have been, and will continue to be, man's central concerns.'
– H.A. Simon

I believe the quote above could read *'any* good business book ... is about love, hate, craftsmanship, jealousy, comradeship, ambition, pleasure' for these are the stuff businesses are truly made of.

Businesses *are* people and people are shaped as much by their emotions as they are by their intellect. So, here is one of my emotions: my heartfelt thanks to those who have helped and to those whose passion for what we do and want to achieve makes it sometimes painful, always worthwhile, a lot of fun, and most of all very exciting:

- To everyone at MCA who gave their thinking and a lot of emotion to developing the concepts of emotional capital and the philosophy of internal marketing – especially Kathy Whitwell, Virginia Merritt, Kathryn Carnegie, Andrew Flint, Adrian Lenard and Anne Gilbert.
- To Lorrie Arganbright who gave her all in the development of MCA and as one of the editors and researchers who helped

put this book together, as well as Marion Devine, Louise Berkye, Michelle Gagnon, and Liz Young.

- To the contributors of material to the book including colleagues and clients from KPMG, Price Waterhouse, BNFL, the Royal Mail, Walkers Snack Foods (part of PepsiCo), NatWest, the Automobile Association, Ernst and Young, Steve Robinson of Ashridge Management College and all of our many other clients who allow us to learn and grow together, as we apply our principles and practices.

- Our strategic partners who work alongside us, and add value to our business and our thinking, especially Mark Allin and Richard Burton of Capstone Publishing for their great enthusiasm for both *Emotional Capital* and its self-development sister book *Passion at Work*; and Ralph Jackson and Alan Reid of Jackson Communications, our PR agency, who have helped with my thinking and also prompted me to coin the phrase 'emotional capital' to describe what we do.

- My friends in the IABC (International Association of Business Communicators) for their support, including Colin Ringrose, IABC UK Secretary and joint founder of our venture into 'touring workshops' and Veronica Pollard and Gloria Walker, IABC UK Past Presidents, for encouraging me to become embroiled in (and accredited by) this terrific organization.

Finally my thanks to you for investing your time, thinking, and emotions in reading this. So now, as they say, 'over to you!'

Introduction

Overview

This chapter provides you with:

- a summary of what emotional and intellectual capital are
- why emotional capital matters to you and to your business.

Introduction

In the next millennium, emotional capital will be an asset on the balance sheet of any major business. Business leaders will be working to a blueprint for their organizations that will go well beyond the focus on traditional assets. They will be exploring new territory – how to build upon two critical and interrelated assets, knowledge *and* emotions.

Knowledge will be the new stock of the future. This is the intellectual capital. It is what organizations know and use to create wealth. Managing information and knowledge will be vital. Leading thinkers such as Peter Drucker and Warren Bennis already say so. Drucker asserts that knowledge is 'taking the place of capital as the driving force in organizations world-wide' while Bennis predicts: 'The problem facing almost all leaders in the future will be how to develop their organizations' social architecture so that it actually generates intellectual capital.'

Yet knowledge will only be the first of the two greatest assets of any organizations. Even more importantly, the hidden resources of feelings, beliefs, perceptions and values that make up an organization's 'emotional capital' will be harnessed and help drive every person and every organization forward. Emotional assets are the ones truly capable of adding untold wealth to organizations, or, as has happened time and again, of destroying them.

This book was written in the belief that more and more business leaders want to tap into the emotional assets of their organizations. At long last, passion, obsession, drive, motivation, inspiration, innovation, belief, values, visions, spirit, and many, many more positive emotions, are finding a place alongside the knowledge, intellectual property, best practice and information base within successful organizations.

Intellectual and emotional capital are two driving forces that are ready to begin working together to build and sustain the businesses, the brands, and the corporate reputations and personalities of the future.

When people understand what needs to be done, when it needs to be done, how, and most importantly *why*, we can begin to get *everyone* delivering against the same goals. It is then that we can begin to receive the greatest gift of all – an organization with a heart that is racing with all the emotions it needs to live and breathe for a long time to come; an organization that has the ability to generate success from limitless reserves of something that almost everyone will give, if we only knew how to tap into it.

In order to maximize its emotional and intellectual assets, business can now look to develop the internal marketing and communication strategies, processes and tools to allow the data, information knowledge and emotions to flow. It is knowledge, driven by emotions, that creates the basis for business success. This is the focus of the chapters you are about to read: to chart a new journey exploring what goes on in the heart and mind of organizations to deliver better business results.

C H A P T E R   1

Intellectual versus Emotional Capital

Overview

In this chapter we'll explore:

- the difference between intellectual and emotional capital
- why knowledge on its own isn't valuable
- what the most expensive letter is in the business world
- what makes up emotional capital
- the benefits of taking more accurate stock of *all your* assets.

Intellectual versus
Emotional Capital

Intellectual capital and emotional capital are very different yet very related. In many ways, 'hearts and minds' are two sides of the same coin. Commentators, like Thomas Stewart in his book on intellectual capital, talk of one of the three types of intellectual capital being 'human capital' (the other two are 'structural capital' and 'customer capital'). But human capital is just one concept to describe two unique phenomena – what we think and what we feel. These both need defining and assessing as to the added value they bring organizations.

Intellectual capital: what's in people's heads

Intellectual capital is made up of the time, money, training, data bases, manuals, formulae, processes, policies, procedures, etc., that an organization has invested in the development of information *and* the translation of that information into knowledge.

It is easy to confuse the facts and figures, or the raw information, with knowledge, or intellectual capital. Information or data may be held in three very different places: in print, in PCs and in people's heads. Knowledge, however, can only be held in people's heads and it is they who will use it to add to or create wealth.

In many traditional organizations information has been managed in an autocratic 'top down' mode of telling and instructing people to 'do as I say'. Information has also been seen as power

– and for two centuries managers have protected this power by keeping the information to themselves. The 'permafrost layer' of middle management is well documented.

Truth is, information without knowledge is pretty meaningless. Information becomes useful when it is transformed – through understanding and integration with people's experiences – into knowledge and used to leverage some advantage for the business. It is this process that distinguishes pure information from intellectual capital.

Box 1.1 shows how Ernst & Young is developing its knowledge process. What is extremely powerful is that this process is documented in the annual report and accounts.

Box 1.1   Making knowledge work

'Our clients are under great pressure constantly to enhance their performance. To do this, they need to understand current and emerging "best practice" (i.e. knowledge) and performance benchmarks across industry sectors. We are investing significant resources, both internationally and in the UK, to capture knowledge by industry and by key business processes.

'Our considerable investment in knowledge over the last two years is now starting to bear fruit. The challenge will be to ensure that our people make the sharing of knowledge a real priority – another key part of the Ernst & Young process of change.'

Source: *Ernst & Young Report and Accounts.*

Knowledge is a vital part of the firm's vision. It must therefore form a vital part of the firm's value.

Technology does not equal 'techknowledgy'

How will organizations like Ernst & Young share knowledge? By technology? Yes of course, but there is a really big problem here. Technology does *not* equal 'techknowledgy'.

This is what Peter Drucker says when he warns: 'It is all too easy to confuse data with knowledge, and information technology with information.'

When does information become valuable? Many managers think information is made valuable simply by making it accessible. This myth has made untold millions for the computer industry.

The premise is that the better the communicationS (i.e. the system or tools required to access information), the more it can be turned into knowledge that then generates revenue, cuts costs, or makes a profit. The trouble with this is that better communicationS does *not* mean better communicatioN (i.e. the exchange of ideas and creation of understanding that helps turn information into knowledge).

And so an erroneous belief has been accepted around the world that communicationS = communicatioN. This letter 'S' at the end of the communication has become the most expensive letter in the world. Why? Because this misunderstanding between communicationS and communicatioN has led businesses across the globe to spend literally billions of dollars on electronic communicationS, on both hardware and the software like e-mail, groupware and Intranets. This is in addition to the paper-based products, such as guides, manuals, and instructions. Did they deliver? Well … the paper-based manuals are often used to prop open the door!

Would Boards have invested so much in communicationS had they known that, without communicatioN, the level of understanding would go up by exactly nothing, or even worse could go down? Did they realize that stress, poor morale, high staff turnover, low productivity, and our other ills would not improve just because we put electronic communicationS systems in place?

Investing in communicationS will not deliver the results, without the investment of communicatioN. But, herein lies another truth: Just as communicationS does not equal communicatioN, knowledge without positive emotion can be equally useless!

Emotions: the fuel to fire your intellectual capital

In the past, knowledge was not treated as an asset. The first shift in attitude occurred when organizations began to protect their intellectual property through patents and copyrights. Information became property on which organizations could put a price. Just think of the invaluable Coca-Cola formula, or the (now lapsed) patent rights of Zantac, the ulcer drug.

Managers began to believe that they could safeguard all of their intellectual property. This is yet another myth. Certainly many trade secrets can be locked away behind fire walls or in a safe. They can be copyrighted, trademarked, and patented. But an invaluable form of intellectual property, knowledge, walks out the door when your people do.

Once again, this proves that information is useful, yet it is knowledge that is vital. It is knowledge which is used to increase and leverage the value of business. And knowledge held in people's heads is only valuable when they want to use it.

This may seem like strikingly obvious stuff. However, management theorists have made some stunningly naive assumptions that based the management of information and knowledge around function and business processes, rather than around motivating people and harnessing their passion and drive.

Emotional capital: what's in people's hearts

So what exactly is emotional capital? At this stage, emotional capital can be simply described as being made of two core elements (the next chapter will break down these components still further):

- **External emotional capital.** This is held in the hearts of the customer and the external stakeholder. This is the capital sometimes described as, and included in, brand value and goodwill, and is being seen by more and more companies as critical to their success and as a core part of their asset base.
- **Internal emotional capital.** This is held in the hearts of people within the business. I believe that this is the capital soon to be accounted for.

External emotional capital is beginning to be valued as brand and corporate capital. The value of brands is going on the books. Of course, it should! It results in sales, repeat sales through customer loyalty, and, at the top of the customer loyalty ladder, lifetime relationships *and* recommendations and referrals to potential future customers. This makes good business sense.

Internal emotional capital can also be described as the feelings, beliefs and values held by everyone in the business. It results in behaviors and actions which generate products and services. What a company produces and how it produces them propels revenue or cost savings that drive the top and bottom line. Emotional capital, held in the hearts of employees or 'internal customers,' is in fact the internal equivalent of the brand value held in the hearts of external customers.

Internal corporate and brand values are just as powerful emotional tools as external brand values. They also require investment. The results of doing so are obvious in every successful organization in the world. Internal emotional capital centered on a passion (or otherwise) for the corporate business and external brands, is the driver of intellectual capital, which in turn uses business capital to make and deliver the goods. Obvious, yes. Measured? Not yet … but all of that is about to change.

You can't see it or touch it ... can you measure it?

Skandia is one company taking an explicit stand on the oversight of valuing intellectual and emotional assets. In its 1994 annual report and accounts, the company uses a section on *Visualising intellectual capital at Skandia* to comment:

> *'Commercial enterprises have always been valued according to their financial assets and sales, their real estate holdings, or other tangible assets.*
>
> *'These views of the industrial age dominate our perception of businesses to this day – even though the underlying reality began changing decades ago.*
>
> *'Today, it is the service sector which stands for dynamism and innovation ... The service sector has few visible assets, however. What price does one assign to creativity, service standards or unique computer systems?'*

What price indeed does one assign to knowledge, and more importantly, the emotions needed to use knowledge for business advantage? These days, the contribution derived from people's intellectual and emotional capital is highlighted only in the front half of their Annual Reports. Is this a problem? Yes it is, given that they are seen as such vital assets to a business. Why aren't they listed in the back as measurable assets? How long will it be before these new assets *are* measured and put in the back half? Not long.

The winds of change are already starting to move through the accounting profession. Some of the world's biggest accountancy firms are beginning to express their belief in the importance of emotional and intellectual assets. For example, Ellen Knapp, Vice Chairman and Chief Knowledge Officer of Coopers &

Lybrand, New York, says, 'All our assets are knowledge assets'. Allen Frank, Chief Technology Officer of KPMG, New York, speaks in similar terms: 'We're basically a giant brain. For us, the knowledge management environment is the core system to achieve competitive advantage.'

If individuals like Knapp and Frank say that their organization's asset base only consists of knowledge, then it won't be long before all the accountants are placing a value on the intellectual and emotional assets held by their client's businesses. They become champions of this philosophy, not only in their organizations, but within their industry.

Another of the (currently) Big Six accounting firms has discovered you can also measure your intellectual and emotional assets when you are losing them. Price Waterhouse has developed a simple measurement process called the *K Factor* which assesses the loss of knowledge (see Box 1.2). We will assume that implicit in the loss of knowledge (the K in *K Factor*) they also mean a loss of emotions (an *E Factor*).

Wouldn't you want to know the *K Factor* in an organization if you were buying the business? Wouldn't you want to compare it to industry standards? Would you value the business as highly if

---

Box 1.2　K Factor: A knowledge management measure used by Price Waterhouse

'… It relates to the amount of knowledge entering and leaving the organization. Measured crudely, it is the number of employees in their first or last year of employment with the organization, as a percentage of the total employee population. This K Factor percentage presents an eye-opening reality of the importance of Knowledge Management.

Source: *Strategic Communication Management*, May 1997

you knew that a large percentage of the brains, knowledge and emotional capital were leaving or joining the organization every year!

Other accountancy firms are moving towards a more accurate description of their assets as well. KPMG's annual report, for instance, has a section about people, about relationships and how together they create value, wealth and add to the worth of its clients (see Box 1.3). It believes that its ability to do this makes it one of the most successful companies in the world. Colin Sharman, now the International Chairman of KPMG, states his commitment to increasing the emotional and intellectual assets of his business, through people 'working together, delivering value'.

Box 1.3   Working together, delivering value

'KPMG is a people business. Through outstanding teamwork and excellent client relationships, our people are vital to our competitive advantage as highly professional business advisers. Some of the key challenges facing the firm are people issues. Against a background of ever increasing and changing demands from clients, KPMG has broadened its intake of skills by recruiting and training the brightest and best from universities, industry and the professions.

'UK senior partner Colin Sharman has said, "We must fully develop the talents and potential of our people, for if we are to be leaders we must look to leaders to join us". This philosophy of high expectation and unlimited career potential is at the heart of our message to people joining the firm.'

Source: *KPMG UK Annual Report,* 1996

Forging a new relationship with its employees and so tapping into the emotional and intellectual assets was also the goal of Ernst & Young when it introduced a program called *Achieving our Vision* for thousands of employees in the UK. The program provided the 'big picture' and all the pieces of its direction and the processes needed to achieve its vision.

Nick Land, Ernst & Young's UK senior partner, described this new communication process as part of the firm's on-going commitment to 'expand the knowledge base' of the firm. In the 1996 Annual Report, he wrote:

> *'Our commitment to provide maximum value to our clients is underpinned by our firm-wide commitment to enhance our knowledge, expertise and ability. In the past year, our investment in people, technology, knowledge management and product development reached record levels.*
>
> *'We are continually extending our use of technology, and investing to achieve leading-edge capabilities both in client service processes and in capturing and communicating knowledge throughout our world-wide firm ... but, above all, I should like to thank all our people for their continuing commitment to the success of Ernst & Young.'*

A giant brain needs a giant heart

During a recent British Telecom (BT) Forum conference in London, Daniel Goleman, author of *Emotional Intelligence*, supplied a powerful illustration of how heart and mind work together. He described a famous case where what could best be described as the seat of the emotional brain (the amygdala) was severed during an operation on a bright lawyer. The lawyer retained all his intellectual capability but lost everything else – his job, his wife and his friends. Why? Because he lost his emotional capability. Goleman's analogy leads to an inevitable conclusion, which intuitively is obvious too (with hindsight of course): 'It is emotional intelligence that creates successful businesses.'

Knowledge on its own is as useless as a factory with no one to work in it and no one to decide what to manufacture. It is equally useless to measure only the value, for example, an accountancy firm's office blocks and equipment. Attempting to measure the knowledge of the accountants within a firm is a step in the right direction, but it is only one step. Although Coopers and Lybrand's Ellen Knapp is right, she is only partly right – yes, their assets are their knowledge assets, *and* their assets are also their emotional assets. KPMG's Allen Frank is also right; knowledge is competitive advantage, and competitive advantage is the real value of a business. Yes, and that 'giant brain' will *only* function if it is driven by a giant heart! Hearts *and* minds produce thriving, driving, competitive business.

Here are just some of the emotional drivers that exist within businesses (these will be summarized and described in Chapter 2 as either the *dynamic emotions*, or the *deadly emotions* in organizations): let's make them big and bold – they deserve it! With a few exclamation marks thrown in for good measure! Who needs a book about emotional capital that does not go 'over the top'?

Obsession, pride, fear, anger, apathy, stress, passion! anxiety, trust, guts!, determination, commitment, grit!, belief, enthusiasm, as well as hostility, greed, envy, hatred, selfishness, the list is as endless as what we feel in our heads, hearts and in our guts. For this is what emotions are; literally feelings that move you, that you actually can sense. Powerful!

Emotional capitalism at work

Look up accounting in a number of books and you'll find that there aren't any accounting procedures to measure emotions like these. Accounting (but not accountants who can sometimes be an emotional bunch) seems to be devoid of emotion! Yet isn't this list of emotions the same list of emotions that gave the USA its freedom of spirit and made it the economic center of the world for centuries? Didn't these emotions put the Great into Britain, the Russians in space and Japanese technology into the electrical sockets of every household in the world? Doesn't this list make capitalism what it is – a force living off the emotions of people?

Capitalism as we know it would be better described as 'emotional capitalism'. And this is what makes us all emotional capitalists – our success comes from our hearts and our heads and our will to make business succeed. When we trade off positive emotional capital, our chances of success far outweigh the advantages of trading off tangible issues around a product or service.

The bottom line: emotional capital is the stuff of dreams. It is the energy, drive and commitment invested and held in hearts of everyone connected with the business. Emotional capital is expressed not in terms of data, process or guides, but in such wonderful, emotive words as passion and obsession. Now is the time for these words to become a part of the language of business, not just the world of marketing, and not a hidden extra, or something to be ignored.

Building the blueprint: intellectual versus Emotional capital

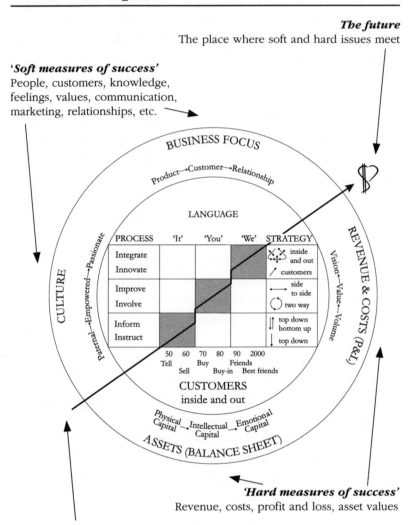

The future
The place where soft and hard issues meet

'Soft measures of success'
People, customers, knowledge,
feelings, values, communication,
marketing, relationships, etc.

'Hard measures of success'
Revenue, costs, profit and loss, asset values

The 'emotional capital timeline' (Chapter 3)
We will explore how to place yourself along here:
1   to assess your approach to external customers
2   to assess your approach to internal customers

My notes on intellectual versus emotional capital

This model for creating and sustaining both intellectual and emotional capital has two different and interlocking parts. There is an 'outer wheel' giving us business measures of success like revenue, or culture (i.e. both 'hard' and 'soft' measures) that come from the 'inner hub' of marketing and communication principles and practices (like strategy, process and language). The 'marketing and communication timeline' covered in Chapter 3 integrates the two and shows how organizations have moved onward and upward over the last half century — and where they can now go into the next millennium. There are four interlocking parts for each of the hub and wheel, so the questions we can begin to ask, and answer in Emotional Capital are:

Inner hub — the driving forces

1   Strategy: How does your organization want to talk to itself and everyone around it? How will an integrated communication and marketing strategy — inside and out — deliver the business strategy?

2   Customers: How does the organization deal with its customers — inside and out? Why does 'tell and sell' of the past produce lower returns than the other modes of later years?

3   Language: How does the focus of a business impact on the language, i.e. the words people use? Do they talk more about 'it' — the product; 'you' — the customers; 'we' — the relationship? Does it matter?

4   Process: What do people actually do when they communicate? Are giving instructions different to say innovation? How do these processes work?

Outer wheel — the business results

1   *Business focus:* Does the organization concentrate on what it makes, who it is targeting, or the relationships it has?

2   *Culture:* Is the organization paternalistic, empowered, or passionate, and how do these impact on its financial results?

3   *Revenue and costs:* How does the organization maximize its profitability, through concentrating on volume, value or a vision of the future?

4   *Assets:* Are the assets on the books purely physical like plant, land, cash or are they intangible like knowledge and emotions, e.g. those which add up to brand value?

Thought provokers for the future

• Are your 'soft' measures treated as 'touchy feely'; maybe necessary, but not quite related to the 'hard' measures, i.e. those seen as 'the real business of making money'?

• How many initiatives do you have — not related in any real big picture?

• How successful is 'change' in your organization? Does it seem to get stuck around the 'soft' issues?

Your notes

Elements of Emotional Capital, Inside and Out

Overview

This chapter explains:

- the link between emotional capital and corporate personality
- 10 dynamic and deadly emotions in business
- the four elements of emotional capital and personality
- how organizations are using personality as a sustainable competitive advantage.

Elements of Emotional Capital, Inside and Out

If the people in and around an organization are communicating, using their hearts and minds, and if they are successful in reaching the hearts and minds of their customers, then something unique begins to happen. By applying intellect and emotion, the organization becomes more 'human' in the most amazing and positive sense of the word.

Many of today's business leaders are striving to create such human organizations. They are places where, as Arie de Geus describes in *The Living Company*, 'People naturally think and speak about a company as if they were speaking about an organic, living creature with a mind and character of its own'. Yet the traditional language used in the working world actively discourages such thinking. The definition of a company seems to mean a 'business' – and that means the profit-and-loss statement (P&L) and balance sheet, doesn't it? But a company is not just a commercial entity; it cannot be described simply in terms of facts and figures.

Even the most cold-hearted businesses have, whether they like it or not, 'corporate personalities'. Personalities are not new; they have always been there. Many are good, some may be 'hard-hearted', autocratic and even malevolent, but they are still personalities. They were created simply because people are the lifeblood of every organization.

We need to return to the true meaning of a company – a society or collective *of people*. Emotions are entwined with everything an organization does and produces; in its products, services, brands and identity. And it is the hearts and minds of everyone in that company that create its personality. Emotional capital therefore involves the responses of employees to the company brand *and* their feelings about the company as a whole.

If a company and its personality are about people, then it is the communication process between people that really matters. It is the internal and external communication process between employees, customers and stakeholders that allows an organization's distinct and unique characteristics – or personality – to develop. Company personality becomes richer and more apparent when robust communication is taking place.

Emotional capital: creating and sustaining personality

Companies can only show their uniqueness by harnessing the positive emotions, perceptions and personality of people in and around the organization. Companies that have succeeded in capturing the hearts and minds of their people demonstrate a personality filled with emotions like passion, obsession and motivation, which has tremendous appeal for customers. Many of these companies exhibit what I call the *ten dynamic emotions in business*, and it is the varying degree and mix of these emotions that help create unique personalities (see Box 2.1).

Perhaps your business exhibits very few of these positive emotions, and perhaps this does not worry you. Well, start worrying! Companies are living entities with emotions just below the surface – and not necessarily good ones. Is your business full of the *ten deadly emotions*, the ills and woes of low emotional

---

Box 2.1   Ten Dynamic Emotions in Business

- *Obsession* – persistent idea that constantly forces its way into consciousness
- *Challenge* – desire to rise up, fight and win – especially against the odds
- *Passion* – strong affection or enthusiasm for a product, service, personality, concept or idea
- *Commitment* – the dedication or involvement with a particular action or cause
- *Determination* – unwavering mind, firmness of purpose
- *Delight* – the act of receiving pleasure like fun, laughter, amusement
- *Love* – great affection or attachment, to want to 'give'
- *Pride* – feeling of honor and self-respect, a sense of personal worth and organizational worth
- *Desire* – wish to have, own or be
- *Trust* – confidence in the integrity, value or reliability of a person or entity, such as a team or organization.

---

capital? Have you become used to hearing people around you whining that 'half the company doesn't know what the other half is doing', or, 'You can talk all you want but your views won't be listened to'? Or worse, 'I hate working here'.

These type of comments are symptomatic of the *ten deadly emotions* listed in Box 2.2 and are the opposite of the *ten dynamic emotions*. Just imagine living and working with a list like these – or perhaps you don't have to imagine.

What if some of the *ten deadly emotions* took hold in your organization? How productive would your people be? How willing to take risks? How committed to making improvements? How likely to stay with you? The answer: not very. So, how much would this wipe off a company's P&L or add to its costs? (Hint: think in terms of millions of dollars.)

Box 2.2   Ten Deadly Emotions in Business

- **Fear** – feeling of distress, apprehension or alarm caused by a sense of impending danger
- **Anger** – feeling of great annoyance or antagonism as the result of some real or supposed grievance
- **Apathy** – lack of motivation (give me anger any day. Anger can be turned around; apathy is much worse!)
- **Stress** – mental, physical or emotional strain or tension
- **Anxiety** – state of uneasiness or tension caused by apprehension of a possible misfortune
- **Hostility** – antagonistic and/or 'oppositional' behavior
- **Envy** – discontent, a begrudging feeling or resentful admiration aroused by the possessions, achievements or qualities of another
- **Greed** -excessive desire for wealth and power
- **Selfishness**- lack of consideration of others actuated by self-interest
- **Hatred** – feeling of intense dislike.

It is surely not rocket science to realize that the value of a company suffering from such emotional malaise *must* be lower, yet how do managers or investors know the cost or value of negative or positive emotional capital? If negative emotional capital is adversely affecting the value of their investment then they would surely want to know exactly what the organization is doing to improve the situation. They would be looking for the emotional capital to be improved or created, if it does not yet exist.

Many organizations today outwardly appear to be paying greater attention to the emotional capital within their organizations through such initiatives as customer service and culture change programs. Yet in reality, are they merely paying lip service for the benefit of investors? These businesses may say that these programs are running in order to increase share value, but how often do they measure or publicize the results? The *ten dynamic or deadly emotions* in business affect the emotional capital of any organization. My question is whether businesses or investors really look at this issue seriously – as seriously as the hard numbers in a financial statement. My belief is they soon will.

Personality – the only competitive point of difference

Emotions are powerful drivers of personality in humans, and the same is true in business. Externally, emotions help the brand and the corporate identity to come alive and take on human characteristics. The brand and the business reflect the wonderful variety of emotions that create personality. Why? Because humans have created it.

Ironically, the growing recognition of this elusive thing called corporate personality is coming not just from company directors and managers but also from employees, customers and the advertising industry.

In today's society employees are no longer willing to be part of a rigid, unfeeling bureaucracy. People want to work in organizations they like, and are like them. Customers want to buy from organizations they like, and are like them. This is the real essence of corporate personality.

The advertising industry has already begun to recognize the value of corporate personality as a more sophisticated way to differentiate a product or brand or service or organization. In reality, the only differentiation point, the final USP (Unique Selling Point), the only sustainable advantage is an organization's personality. It shines through in everything that is said or done.

Everything else about your business can be replicated: your product, your service, your added value, the imagery that you use to express your company identity such as sexy logos and the like. What can't be replicated, what makes you different, what guides you forward is personality.

Because personality is unique, it is too tough to copy (how many people do you know have the same personality?). Besides, is there commercial advantage in being a 'me too' personality? Of course some companies try to emulate or blatantly copy. Their attempts are pointless when, for the sake of short-term gain, they are eventually perceived to be fooling customers or even 'rip-off artists'? Neither too can they demand a premium price without a unique proposition. This is the essence of strategy.

Other companies try to project a forced personality, but this is also a strategy doomed to fail. In this sophisticated world of ours, personality appeal needs to be real and sincere. Gone are the days of generating a hyped image or fictitious personality of a business. You can have fun with a brand, but if you try to fabricate your business personality, it is at your peril.

Customers respond to a company's personality. They are thinking, feeling people who give their loyalty to organizations because they increasingly recognize the importance and value of a long-term relationship. The dynamic of this relationship is that loyalty repays loyalty.

If this is becoming true then the individuality of every organization will be important – to everyone. Having a 'me too' product is fine but the personality around the people who made it must shine through.

We are moving to a world where a focus on what the organization makes and does is less important than the way it is, and the way it does it. Growing numbers of customers already *are* asking questions such as does this company dump things in the sea or rivers? Does it care for minorities, its staff, its suppliers, its pensioners? Is it fun, or easy, or simple, or straightforward, or no nonsense to deal with? Do I like the people in it and are they like me?

All these questions and a whole lot more are the stuff of corporate personality. Integrity, fun, caring, seriousness, passion will begin to take center stage. This cannot be manufactured by advertising. It has to be real to have appeal.

Stirring emotions from the inside out

This is indeed the lesson being learned by organizations around the world, as the examples of NatWest Bank, the Saturn car and Daewoo cars illustrate (see Boxes 2.3, 2.4 and 2.7). It is a lesson that is particularly vivid in the ascent of the Automobile Association in the UK. The AA ran during the early 90s a 'hype' campaign around the advertising strapline 'He's a very nice man'. In the ads, this catch phrase was said by people (obviously actors and actresses) who had just been helped by the AA patrol attendant. The campaign was successful for its day – but needed changing by the mid 90s.

The AA's advertising agency did some research within the organization by talking with staff responsible for rescuing people and fixing breakdowns. The agency discovered that when staff were helping customers who were stranded alone, perhaps in the dark or pouring rain, they saw themselves as an 'emergency service' just like the police or fire services – and so did their relieved customers!

The AA campaign went out under the banner: *To our members, we are the 4th Emergency Service.* The ads depict the other police, fire and ambulance services at an accident scene, with the AA as the fourth part of the picture. The result? Customers love it, and it works. The spin off? As well as sending a message to the outside world, a campaign like this has massive potential to communicate a message from the 'outside-in', as staff watch the ads and get involved in the launch.

With such an inspirational message, AA staff now see themselves as more than just 'very nice people,' and a part of something deeper, more passionate, more inspired. They see themselves as another vital emergency service. This is what I call capturing the high ground!

The campaign worked because the internal research revealed the real personality of the AA. This is a campaign that can run and run. The execution of the ads may change, but the deep psychological connection with the core essence of the business produces real, sustainable, competitive advantage.

An advertising campaign does not automatically have to show real people doing real things. That is not the point of the various examples provided in this chapter. Personality can be put across in many ways. These examples show how the essence of

---

Box 2.3   Saturn Cars: field of dreams

In the US the conceptual thinking around the Saturn car was one of involving everyone – customers and employees.

From the campaign's inception, this tremendous involvement process was apparent from building a completely new site to creating and developing the cars, and culminated in an extraordinary birthday party. Saturn invited the nation to come to the factory for its birthday party and to meet the workers featured making cars in the ads.

The campaign created a huge resonance with everyone. The ads of the party had a feel of the film 'Field of Dreams' in which actor Kevin Costner watched as thousands of people came to see his 'imaginary' team of (long dead) superstar baseball players. Through maximizing the company's emotional capital, an admittedly 'average' car has taken on a personality of its own, a slice of the market, and a place in history.

a business lies in what it is like, as much as what it makes. Sponsorship by Coke of the Olympic games and other sporting events around the globe show the company's sporty nature, a 'gutsy' appeal to those who love competitiveness, people, outdoors, winning, etc. After all 'Coke is it!'

Emotional capital creates and drives company personality, which in turn drives everything the company is and does; its brands, products, services, processes, identity and reputation. Let's now look at the four elements of emotional capital, which will help explain the relationship among the different components of a business.

The four elements of emotional capital

Emotional capital can be separated into four key elements: external corporate personality; external brand personality; internal corporate personality; and internal brand personality. In other words, what the business as a whole is like, from the inside and out; and the perceptions of what it makes and labels as its brands, both inside and out.

1. External corporate personality

What is the organization like in the eyes of the customers, consumers, external stakeholders and other influencers? How does this come across?

Pick up any newspaper and see what sort of image is being created by organizations as a result of their local policies, environmental concerns, staff relations, trade union relations, race relations, etc. Are directors being criticized for taking pay-rises when they are laying off workers at the same time? Does a 'share price' mentality seem to grip the organization? Is the company well known for its excellent staff training or skill in handling its relationships with suppliers?

Organizations are now being viewed as living entities within a larger, global community. Corporate governance, how you act as a responsible member of the community, is taking hold. Growing numbers of companies now see themselves as having a responsibility to add value to the community of which they are a part. Part of their identity within this community stems from their reputation, built over years of saying and doing things that people now see as 'good' or 'bad'. Yet, surely a more important issue is what the company is doing *now*, what it is like – and of course, how it acts now is driven by its character and personality.

Box 2.4   That'll be the Daewoo!

Daewoo also took a 'personality' based advertising campaign when they launched and sold their cars in the UK. Their campaign ran with the advertising strapline, *That'll be the Daewoo* (a play on the rock 'n' roll classic *That'll be the day*). Through having 'no commission' sales people (a unique strategy in the UK) who were there to help you, not 'relieve you of your money,' Daewoo captured an amazing share of the market – and all this by starting off with second-hand designs from other manufacturers.

How did Daewoo achieve their results? They presented themselves as ordinary people, just like their customers. They stopped frightening customers with high-powered sales techniques. Daewoo's sales rooms allowed you to let the kids play, to browse around as if in your own home, and to play on computers. The company's free after-sales care freed customers from worrying about service ... and so it went on.

Daewoo's personality said: 'We know you, we are like you, please get to like us.' And people did!

Corporate personality is the element that attracts customers who think, 'I like the way they are' and ' I like the way they do business with me' and 'They are *my* kind of people'.

We are not talking about manufacturing a personality, or giving the organization's image some 'spin'. We are talking about something so tangible that every customer can feel it and describe it in a similar way. Personality comes out of everything that an organization is and does. What it makes, designs, sells, promotes; how it deals with customers, suppliers, the community, its internal customers. All this must add up to something special.

Just think of the personalities of the following organizations:

- Benetton versus Ralph Lauren
- Harley Davidson versus Yamaha
- Macys versus Harrods
- McDonalds versus Wendy's
- British Airways versus Virgin Atlantic.

How different are their corporate personalities and reputations? As the examples of British Airways and Virgin Atlantic reveals (see Box 2.5), their difference is their strength. Advertising, design, public relations, packaging, promotion can all use this personality. We will explore this in the middle section of the book in depth. It is the most important part of every company's future.

Personality rules, but who is responsible?

Who holds responsibility for corporate personality'? This is the same role that marketing plays with the brand – but practiced with all stakeholders. Traditionally this has been the remit of corporate communication and has mostly focused on the reputation of the organization, not its personality. But while the spin doctors can cook up short-term stories and hype, they cannot

Box 2.5   A tale of two tails

British Airways spent over £50 million in 1997 to change its British personality to a more global one. Claiming that BA is 'the world's favourite airline,' the company decided it was time to prove its global personality. The old logo reflecting the angular British flag was changed to become a user-friendly, squiggly shape. And the tail-fins featured pictures of British artist David Hockney and other artists from around the globe.

As a result, BA is seen as building on its world class service and dedication to safety by providing a new global personality. More precisely, according to Kevin Murray, Corporate Communication Director, the new corporate identity is a personality based on a global formula and local flavor. The net result? Masses of free publicity and the ability to drive the project on the back of such a high profile external launch. I even met external suppliers who were all choked up at the launch across BA sites.

So what does 'cheeky chappy' Richard Branson do with his Virgin Atlantic airline – he grabs the 'British' personality by painting the tail-fins of his planes with the suddenly acquired British Union Jack flag! A double whammy ensues. Virgin is seen once again as the David fighting the Goliath. Its personality is enhanced as clever, crafty, fun and it gets all the emotional capital tied up in the Union Jack. And both organizations build their reputation by trading off their personality.

Yet look how easy it is to begin to erode a powerful reputation and brand. Within a month of the launch of BA's corporate identity came 'the world's prettiest picket line' as dubbed by one journalist. Much work is now being done to build and restore the emotional capital in BA as a result of a damaging strike over terms, conditions and the running of the airline in the future.

hide the personality of an organization for long. Indeed, the secret weapon is to use personality not as an image maker's rabbit pulled out of a hat, but as something real, observable, measurable and unique.

Then who *delivers* corporate personality? The answer is *everyone*. Great reputations are built not on erratic or inconsistent behaviors with some employees displaying some but not all of the company's positive personality traits and characteristics. Reputations are built on consistent behaviors by everyone. How is this achieved? By building up the right type and amount of emotional capital in everyone so that they can all deliver against the desired behaviors.

A Harley Davidson employee, a Benetton employee, a Harrods employee will be expected to behave in a certain way – no, not clones – but if they join the band then they will be expected to play the same tune. If not? On your bike! (A British expression applied to a Harley ...)

Living up to the corporate personality is critical if all the stakeholders externally are to remain loyal. But it doesn't stop at just corporate personality. If only it were so simple as just the personality of the organization. It isn't. The products and services every organization delivers take on a life – and value – of their own while retaining the characteristics of the parent. This brings us to the second key element of emotional capital.

2. External brand personality

What are the perceptions and feelings of external customers to the products and services?

Brands will display the traits of the parent organization, and yet like children, they will always have their own unique characteristics and personality. This is created internally by the people in the organization who give the 'baby' their traits. It is then nurtured and developed in the minds of the customer by marketing.

Managed by marketing, created by advertising and the imagemakers, the brand personality is created not for its own sake but to attract people. How? Simple: brand personality is created to reflect the customer's personality or aspirations. It leads to customers purchasing for reasons as simple as, 'I like this,' or 'I like this because it is like me,' or in a more complex way 'I like this and I want to be like it'. This is the 'personality fit' of the customer and their emotions to the brand.

Stuart Crainer, author of *The Real Power of Brands*, vividly describes the emotional power of brands. 'We are in a new era, where brands are positioned as having emotional and lifestyle benefits ... In this new era, brands are driven by consumers. They are psychological, as well as physical; brands are about hearts and minds. To look at the product in isolation from the overall package is no longer possible – the simple purchase is perceived as an experience.'

What value can be placed on the beliefs and feelings for a product, service, corporate identity or brand identity?

The answer is measured in almost innumerable billions of dollars. It is the value placed on the brands and the corporate reputation of every organization across the globe. For proof, look to the work done by Interbrand, which now puts brand value on balance sheets; or to *Superbrands*, the book on the world's leading brands, written by Marcel Knobil of Creative and Commercial Communications. My thanks to him for allowing me to list (see Box 2.6) several brands that have been identified by the Superbrands Council, a body comprising people with extensive experience in the world of marketing and advertising.

Brands are emotional and psychological. They are born from emotional capital. Just how valuable is this to external customers?

Box 2.6   The value of superbrands

What value the emotional capital of American Express?

'American Express is an exclusive brand. It is an achievement in itself to own one. It is a global brand which maintains a prestigious appeal throughout the world. American Express also has a romantic history which has established itself as the undoubted Superbrand it is today.'

How valuable is the emotional capital in the American Express corporate and brand identities?

$_____million?

What value the emotional capital of BMW?

'BMW has used the expression *the ultimate driving machine* for over 15 years. This remark succinctly expresses BMW's brand position and is always played back by consumers in research as summarizing exactly what they feel about the brand.'

How valuable is the emotional capital in the BMW corporate and brand identities?

$_____million?

What value the emotional capital of British Airways?

'The pioneering spirit of British Airways has always shone through, and is a powerful driving force behind the brand. The airline has become particularly noted for its exceptional customer service, matched with the breadth of its network and total commitment to safety.'

How valuable is the emotional capital in the BA corporate and brand identities?

$_____million?

What value the emotional capital of Coca-Cola?
'*It's the real thing* and *Coke is it!* articulate perfectly the core elements of Coca-Cola. It's the first, authentic, truly genuine article. Coke is portrayed as a life-giving force.'
How valuable is the emotional capital in the Coca-Cola corporate and brand identities?
$_____million?

According to *Superbrands* research (and good old common sense), the answer to this question is beyond a doubt: 'More than three-quarters of consumers claim they would be more likely to purchase branded products than own label. Branded goods benefit strongly from their equity/reputation, and perceptions of superior quality'.

So there we have it. The blindingly obvious conclusion that investment in the emotional capital of a brand, as well as the intellectual capital to create it in the first place, far outweighs any business capital.

So it isn't just that you like the taste of Coke, the service of British Airways, or the drive in a BMW. It is all those emotions and sensations that create value to you the customer and to us the business.

Who is responsible for the brand?

Marketing has traditionally looked after brands, while corporate communication has tended to look after the organizational image. This is changing, with a move to integrate all marketing and communication in organizations. Some advertising agencies actually set out their stall as being totally integrated. This does not just mean that the ads, promotion and point-of-sale materials all bear the same design. It means that everything happening under the brand identity is seen as part of a whole.

Who is responsible for delivering the emotional capital of a brand? Increasingly, business leaders and marketing professionals are seeing that their brands are being made, delivered, sold, promoted, innovated and improved by internal people. Even more importantly, they see the reputation and personality of their brands as held in the hands of everyone in the organization. They recognize that the people ARE the brand. Simply put, the employee is no longer there to simply make or deliver the goods; the employee is a critical part of the brand.

This brings us to the next key element of emotional capital: an organization's internal brand personality.

3. Internal brand personality

This element could be summed up as, 'We are what we make; we make what we are'. The brand, just like the overall organization, contains the human characteristics and personality to which customers, consumers and stakeholders relate. It is the brand personality developed, nurtured and grown by everyone in the organization that creates the unique and sustainable advantage over other brands – or not.

In a letter to a management magazine, marketing expert David Yates expresses the concept of internal brand personality in these terms: 'The development of a brand needs to recognize that it is *a window to the view that an organization takes of itself,* its markets and the environments in which it operates. The foundation of the [brand] development process is the rigorous and systematic analysis of the organization's relations with its customers, shareholders, stakeholders and its suppliers.'

How do our perceptions of ourselves as living organizations come across in what we make and in the ways we make and deliver it?

Do your employees speak in similar terms as this employee: 'They featured some of us in an ad on TV making the product.

We're damn proud of the brand and everything it stands for.' Are words like these being said by everyone in your organization? Are employees proud of the brands in the company portfolio? Do they feel as though they have contributed to the brand? Or do they feel that everything happens outside their sphere of influence?

Pride may well be one of the deadly sins but it is one of the most powerful emotions to drive people to deliver results – pride in the personality of brands that are innovative, creative, fun, exciting, passionate, different, wacky, quirky, reserved, sophisticated, raw, zany and many, many other personality traits will increase the emotional drive to deliver the product, service and brand values.

Who is responsible for internal brand personality?

Brand personality is not the sole remit of the marketing or advertising function. The sooner it is realized that everyone creates brand personality, the sooner everyone will want to add their mark to the brand. In this way, ownership of everything from creating to delivering a product or service will devolve to where it belongs.

But who currently takes responsibility for the internal brand identity? In many organizations it is either Public Relations (PR) or Human Resources (HR). HR is responsible because they do what is commonly referred to as 'the touchy-feely stuff'. Alternatively, the PR department may get the job because 'they write magazines, don't they, and that is what internal communication is all about isn't it?'

Times are changing, and corporate communication professionals are taking over. Newly enlightened CEOs are taking responsibility for communication and reputation, and marketing professionals are waking up to the fact that their brands are being made, delivered, sold, promoted, innovated and improved by internal people.

Box 2.7   Brand values and personality at NatWest Bank

When we leverage positive emotional capital, our chances of success far outweigh the advantages of trading off tangible issues around a product or service. NatWest, one of the largest banks in the UK, recognizes this. Their people have defined their brand in terms of 'brand values' and 'brand personality.'

In the past, banks in the UK enjoyed high standing in the community simply as a matter of course. Today, the highly competitive nature of the banking industry has made the creation of brand values and personality a key goal for many UK financial institutions.

The following is an extract from a NatWest staff handbook about brands, which shows the value of emotional capital as well as the more tangible values of NatWest products and services. My thanks to Ian Schoolar for providing the material and insight into the marketing platform for NatWest.

Understanding the NatWest brand

'Qualitative research conducted during 1996 set out to explore what customers and non-customers expect from a financial organization which offers a broad range of financial products and services.

'The key advantages which were expected, can be separated into two categories: tangible and emotional. An organization offering both these advantages would be more likely to be considered for a range of products.

'As you can see from the chart, each of these brand values has both a tangible and an emotional aspect. In creating a strong brand it is essential that we consistently deliver against these values. They are intended to help us ensure we do the right things to make customers more likely to choose us first.

- *Reliability* – *efficient (tangible)*
  – *Dependable (emotional)*
- *Accessibility* – *easily available (tangible)*
  – *Easily understood (emotional)*
- *Appropriateness* – *right features and right service (tangible)*
  – *Feels right for many (emotional).'*

If no one is adequately communicating to these employees or tapping into their emotional capital, the brand personality will slowly wither and die. Suddenly, the organization will wake up to the fact that its brand no longer excites employees or customers and that its emotional message is outdated.

Only by talking to and challenging employees can the external marketing professionals do their job and help promote a living, dynamic brand. It has to be the responsibility of marketing to develop the people in the organization as a fundamental part of the brand. And it goes way beyond simply developing people to ensure they deliver good customer service, for example, or even a quality product. When all else is equal it must rest on the remaining USP – personality, to differentiate the organization and its brands from its competitors.

4. Internal corporate personality

Think of your internal corporate personality as the way we do things around here. Emotions around the brands like passion, obsession, motivation, morale, drive, creativity, dependability and a host of others create internal personality and drive perceptions about what the business makes and sell.

Corporate personality is difficult to recognize and harness, yet it has never been more vital to the success of a business. Today, business competitiveness relies on closely working with a host of external organizations such as suppliers and strategic alliance partners. So often, these partnerships involve an exchange of know-how or they require a pooling of creativity and expertise. Companies need strong internal personalities so that employees can communicate and market the needs, wants and desires of their organization to their partners.

A strong internal personality is also a vital magnet to employees, helping them to relate to the organization and have a personal stake in its success. All organizations need everyone on board if they are to deliver in today's competitive environment. So the personality of the organization and everyone in and around it becomes critical to the success of the whole business.

Companies have made innumerable attempts to harness the emotional capital of internal personality. The last decade has seen a variety of business models that attempt to define an organization's unique personality by analyzing its vision, mission, values, behaviors and style, etc. These models have formed the basis of 'cultural change' programs and have sprung from the desire of organizations to create the emotions that drive employees forward.

Who is responsible for internal corporate personality?

Often, internal corporate personality has tended to be described as corporate culture – and there lies the problem.

Despite all the work done on culture and culture change, organizations still struggle to maximize the emotional capital of their internal personalities. The catch phrase of 'culture change' has became universal and also fashionable as the panacea of all ills. However, the problem with pointing the finger at culture is that it is perceived as internally focused. Anything with an internal focus therefore has to be the responsibility of anyone *other* than marketing or corporate communication. Human resources becomes the focus for culture change programs.

The misunderstanding is that culture change is seen as the lever to affect issues such as quality, customer service, speed and innovation; yet something much more fundamental is at stake. This is the personality of the organization and the way it does business with everyone in and around it.

Very little attention has been paid to using communication as the lever to change culture. Yet it is communication in and around the business that can form the bedrock of an organization's personality. It is how employees talk, walk, live their brand, communicate with suppliers, partners and customers, that really determines the culture or personality of the business.

If you want to build on or change the personality of your organization, you need to discover which emotions fire people up and connect them with the business and its brand. It is the 'emotional mix' of these responses that creates the corporate personality in every business.

I have dubbed this term 'emotional mix' to illustrate how it is like the marketing mix. By altering one element of the 'mix' you will alter the output. It is the ability to communicate and manage the emotional mix so that everyone begins and continues to adopt the essence of the personality that will ensure a cohesive and powerful internal personality. Having the ability to alter the emotional mix will also determine the success or failure of any change to an organization's culture/personality.

Have you researched the emotions in your organization? Perhaps, but I would bet it was not done in a way that treats the business and the people as an integrated whole or approaches staff as internal customers. I predict it will be done this way, as emotional capital becomes understood to be a business and financial issue.

It is worth noting at this point that a lot of the work done so far on the emotions has been inconclusive. What has been noted though is that the relationship between job satisfaction and productivity and stress is a lot more complex and multi-faceted than even a casual glance might suggest. Yet studies on 'satisfaction' proliferate both inside and outside organizations and are very similar to marketing studies on customer satisfaction.

The real issue is not the causes of employee behavior like satisfaction, it is the business result. In the next few chapters, we will see where organizations have been in terms of their culture and how this has impacted on this business.

Reaching for a new synthesis

These then, are the components of emotional capital. Externally, emotional capital drives the brand. It results in sales, repeat sales through customer loyalty and, at the top of the customer loyalty ladder, lifetime relationships AND recommendations to future customers. This makes good business sense.

Internally, emotional capital is seen in the passion of employees' beliefs and values. It results in behaviors and actions that generate unique products and services. This makes good business strategy. Emotional capital held in the heart of your internal customers (your people) is the equivalent of the brand value held in external customers' hearts. Isn't it time that communication and marketing strategies were integrated so that the emotional capital of these two groups can be managed as a single, powerful asset? Isn't it time that a business' internal personality is merged with the personality of its brands?

The central tenet of this book is that the only way to achieve this new synthesis is through integrating internal and external marketing and communication functions and processes. Their job? To create and harness emotional capital so that people buy in to the brands and corporation AND to leverage intellectual capital so that people make the most of their knowledge.

The integration of external marketing with internal communication processes is leading to a new discipline – internal marketing. This concept will be explored thoroughly in the middle section of the book, but for now, here is a brief overview of its essence:

- *Goal:* Increase the emotional capital of a business and to increase its knowledge base.
- *Method:* Achieve buy-in to change by applying marketing principles and effective communication to all those relationships around the internal customer.

- **_Business result:_** Increase intellectual and emotional capital that drive revenue up, create cost savings and deliver measurable value to the business.
- **_Customer result:_** Customers perceive a personality that drives everything the company does and makes; it results in lifetime relationships with the company.

The next section of the book will explore the principles of internal marketing by first charting the development of external marketing and then showing how these approaches can be applied to a whole business. The challenge is to build a new picture of integration, successful communication and relationships that work as opposed to the current picture of disintegration, poor communication and dysfunctional relationships. We aim to create and sustain a big picture where emotions, knowledge and the assets of a business work together, not apart.

My notes on the elements of emotional capital

Marketing has always been about appealing to people on two levels — the intellectual (do they understand its attributes, features and benefits) and the emotional (do they feel good about what it does for them). Internal marketing however is much more complex than external marketing. Why? Because there is a physical as well as emotional contract. In short, people are paid to deliver. They do not have a free choice like an external customer. Yet the impact of living and working in an ever-changing organization creates much more complex challenges on marketing and communication than the simple employee contract would seem to suggest is needed. In addition, with an organization's personality as a key plank in creating its competitiveness, defining and using emotional capital will be a critical success factor. This is why concepts like the top ten dynamic and deadly emotions will be so important.

Building the blueprint: the elements of emotional capital

Corporate and brand personality
This creates and sustains competitive advantage

Culture
This comes about from what people do and say, creating and environment where they feel, believe and value the same things.

BUSINESS FOCUS

Product→Customer→Relationship

CULTURE

Paternal→Empowered→Passionate

LANGUAGE

PROCESS	'It'	'You'	'We'	STRATEGY
Integrate Innovate				inside and out / customers
Improve Involve				side to side ◯ two way
Inform Instruct				↕ top down / bottom up top down

50	60	70	80	90	2000
Tell		Buy		Friends	
	Sell		Buy-in	Best friends	

CUSTOMERS
inside and out

REVENUE & COSTS (P&L)

Vision→Value→Volume

Physical Capital→Intellectual Capital→Emotional Capital

ASSETS (BALANCE SHEET)

The dynamic and deadly emotions
Emotions like passion and obsession as well as anger and fear combine to create powerful drivers or destroyers of a business, its products and services. They all add up to create a personality.

Personality – the last USP
The last unique selling point is the personality that makes an organization different from its competitors. Personality creates and sustains brands and corporate reputation.

Thought provokers for the future

- *How is your emotional capital? Do you need more? Does your business need more? Do your customers need more? Do your strategic alliance partners and suppliers have the same levels as your business? The heat is on to deliver, but is the way to deliver through hearts and mind? Yes, it is. The question is simply how and by how much.*

- *How ready is your organization for internal marketing; for integrated approaches that will turn up the emotional heat and reveal the business' true personality? Consider these key questions:*

- *To what extent does your organization regard internal customers in the same way as your marketing department regards external customers?*

- *What data do you possess that will allow you to assess accurately your internal customers' needs now and in the future?*

- *What do your internal customers like and dislike about you and the organization?*

- *In the eyes of your internal customers, what differentiates your products and services from those of your external competitors?*

- *How involved are your internal customers with your long-term strategy?*

- *What are the top ten deadly and dynamic emotions driving your brand and corporate personality?*

Your notes

C H A P T E R 3

The Past, Present and Future of Emotional Capital: A Timeline

Overview

In this chapter, you'll discover:

- six distinct phases in the development of emotional capital through marketing and communication
- how these historical phases shape today's communication practices
- the link between marketing practices and media choices
- the potential and the pitfalls of new technology
- future trends for internal marketing and communication.

THREE

The Past, Present
and Future of
Emotional Capital:
A Timeline

Once upon a time life was easy for those who managed corporate communication. The external part was handled either by a
PR 'expert' whose job was to handle media relations, or by the
marketing 'experts' whose job was to handle customers. Responsibility for the third form of communication, to the employee,
was usually held somewhere down the chain of command, often in Human Resources. Generally, an editor was appointed to
produce a variety of media to cascade down the organization in
a one-way 'tell' mode. Every now and then, an outside supplier
of videos or events produced something 'motivational' like a
roadshow, or helped introduce business TV, or even provide
software to allow you to set up an intranet.

Oh if only life were as simple now! Today's external communication has undergone a fundamental paradigm shift, with huge
ramifications for internal communication strategies. The strategy
for customer communication in many organizations now goes
way beyond even the concept of 'relationship marketing' with
its idea of customers for life. The new strategy looks to make
the product or service a part of someone's life. Brand strategies
go beyond 'share of voice' in the media to 'share of mind' in the
customer's head.

Internal customers deliver the new thinking and feeling

Organizations around the world such as Disney, Levi Strauss and British Airways, are developing strategies for a 'total customer experience'. For example, 'the experience' of an airline flight today extends from the point of even thinking about a trip to returning and telling people about it. Did the chauffeur add to the experience? How about the ground staff and cabin crew?

Every 'moment of truth' along the way is not just a link in a very complex chain delivery of the product and service, it is a part of a critical link in the chain of communication. Get this wrong and the experience goes wrong. So who is the target audience? Everyone. Who gives this customer the experience? Everyone. Who needs to be targeted to get buy-in to wanting to give the customers this experience? Everyone.

This goes way beyond customer service programs. Delivering sophisticated, quality products and services to today's sophisticated, quality-conscious customer requires new thinking inside every organization. It is the new internal customer who is expected to deliver the new thinking and feeling. It is vital that organizations are 'connected' both to their external customers *and* to their internal customers – perhaps even more so. Influencing customers to buy a bar of soap, for example, requires a lot less emotional capital than getting internal people to invent, make, package, warehouse, distribute, improve, promote and sell the soap.

If organizations want their people to *want* to contribute to these processes, they need to connect with every part of the organization and encourage each part to communicate and market itself to other parts. This is what internal marketing and internal markets is all about. This is the only way to increase both intellectual capital and emotional capital and to deliver against the customer's ever changing needs.

This is where 'teams' and 'empowerment' and the work of management gurus comes in. Peter Senge, for example, declares: 'We have to develop a sense of "connectedness", a sense of working together as part of a system, where each part of the system is affecting and being affected by others, and where the whole is greater than the sum of its parts.'

Few organizations know how to achieve this connectedness or how to capture the drive, enthusiasm and emotions of their people, so instead they look to leverage just their knowledge. This is not enough. From all the *vision, mission and value* statements flying around, it isn't hard to see that many at senior levels believe that some new feeling is required! However, in many cases, the execution of the many vision, mission and values initiatives have badly failed.

When employees and different stakeholders in a business are asked to become 'brand ambassadors' during every moment of their working day, they need to be communicated with in a new and more powerful way. A company's communication strategy needs to ensure that all its brand ambassadors are on board and fully understand what they are doing, why, when, how, with whom and where.

Such a strategy is made highly complex when, in many organizations, the downsizing, 'rightsizing,' reorganizing (and fears of capsizing!) lead to complex problems of communication logistics. We used to have 'employees' for example. Now, however, some organizations have more people contracted out than those in the permanent work force. Who communicates with these key contractors? To whom are these contractors committed? How do you capture their hearts and minds?

Internal communication: the problem and the answer

Treating employees as internal customers is the way forward. By using marketing-based communication strategies that match the needs of employees and create a two-way flow between the organization and its people, businesses can get far greater degrees of buy-in to corporate messages.

Every part of an organization and every internal market like a department or function, and the people in and around it, can be fully functioning and working toward the business and customer goals, if, and only if, they are using minds *and* hearts.

Is traditional internal communication contributing towards this goal? Virtually every communication study suggests not. Why? Firstly traditional communication is seen to fail in its own right, by its own measure; secondly because it fails to produce hard, measurable results. Research carried out in 1996 with Dr Richard Varey of the BNFL Corporate Communication Unit at the University of Salford and my company, MCA, offers some insights into traditional communication's poor performance.

The research, an in-depth qualitative study on internal marketing and communication, revealed that many organizations are being seriously hampered by inadequate communication philosophies and practices. Salford found that the majority of organizations scored a pitiful 5.6 out of 10 for the effectiveness of current communication—and this is at the end of the 20th century! Other studies paint a similarly dismal picture (see Box 3.1).

How can an organization change hearts and minds if 40% of the time it fails to get through at all, or worse, is seen as putting out propaganda? This mitigates what the organization is trying to achieve, in a big way!

We are in a world of global product excellence when only 10 out of 10 in product quality is acceptable. However, when it

---

Box 3.1   Communication trends in business

- 64% of staff often don't believe their senior managers (Source: Council of Communication Management, US)
- 55% of staff say the relevance of information they receive has worsened (Source: Institute of Management, UK)
- Less than 50% of employees know their company's objectives (Source: Market and Opinion Research International)

---

comes to communicating and marketing to our key target audience – internal customers, and the internal markets they operate in – our performance is just plain lousy.

These various studies reveal some appalling statistics. Ask yourself:

- How can you get through to 'minds' if the relevance of information has got worse?
- How can employees be 'empowered' when they have no idea what it is they are empowered to do?
- How can anyone capture 'hearts and minds' if people think their leaders are liars?

Many organizations feel their external marketing and communication is now about as good as it can be. Many however, admit that they still have a long way to go with their internal communication processes. So, what do most do about it? They use the same old processes of the company newsletter and road-shows. And unfortunately, as we have seen with electronic communications, the new processes like e-mails or home pages on intranets merely mirror the old ones by giving even more 'top down' messages, or simply give untargeted and often unsolicited information. All that those initiatives do is simply increase the 'propaganda' factor, making communication worse, not better.

Marketing holds the key

Marketing has achieved considerable business success for one reason and one reason alone: It provides the principles and practices to achieve external customer buy-in, loyalty and brand retention. And, with a lot of help from the disciplines of human resources, psychology and total quality, the same principles and practices of marketing can be applied inside every organization.

By internally applying strategies, processes and tools of external marketing and external corporate communication, organizations will carry forward their internal customers into the next millennium.

This shift of thinking is being seen in academia and business. For example, Adrian Payne, Professor of Services Marketing at the UK's Cranfield School of Management, has helped pioneer the concept of relationship marketing. As the name implies, the focus is on relationships; this means doing things 'with' the customer *and* increasingly 'with' all the other stakeholders of the business. Professor Payne has developed a totally integrated approach showing 'three spotlights on the same stage' consisting of marketing, human resources and quality, which need to come together in today's organizations. Nice analogy.

In the book *Relationship Marketing,* Payne and his co-authors Martin Christopher and David Ballantyne, write: 'While the expression, "our employees are our greatest asset" is increasingly being heard among companies, it is clear that this statement is often a platitude. We believe that by recognizing the contribution of people to getting and keeping customers, within the overall marketing mix, the company's competitive performance will be substantially enhanced.'

Other business leaders agree. For example, Michael C. Brandon, Director of Global Employee Communication Platforms for Northern Telecom, wrote about a new approach to communication in *Communication World* magazine (May 1997). He said:

'The first generation of employee communication was an offshoot of industrial relations practices ... The new mission of employee communication became to inform employees about company "news." Employing the styles and techniques taught in schools of journalism, this new generation of employee communicators shifted the focus to reporting company events, activities and announcements ...

'The challenge to senior management [today] is to implement its strategy. The only function that can help do that effectively is employee communication...

'[For this reason] today's environment necessitates that employee communication evolve into an extension of the management process, helping an organization's executive leadership implement strategy more effectively.'

The evolution that we need is internal marketing. By adding marketing principles to internal communications we can secure buy-in to 'the big picture,' and get *everyone* in the organization to recognize how each part of the business wheel affects the other. Once this big picture is in place, we can show the new internal customers what it means, where they fit, and most important of all, what's in it for them. Then, and only then, will they want to know the part *they* can play in working with each other. (The next chapters of this book explore this in greater detail.)

Marketing and communication can enable organizations to propel themselves forward, yet many organizations are stuck using processes more appropriate for the 1950s. The model developed in the remainder of this chapter explains a history of marketing and communication over the last 50 years, and illustrates how, internally, many organizations are using the wrong elements of the marketing mix at the wrong time – and what they can do differently to succeed.

The marketing and communication timeline

Here we are approaching a new millennium with a change in everything from where we work to what we buy. Yet only 40 years ago we made our weekly rounds to the local butcher, grocer, and other local speciality shops. Now it is global choice, global businesses, global communication, global culture, global brands, global everything. Global choice with local customers looking for an exact fit with what they want and not what the business wants to give them.

We all live and work in a community; is our working life really so different to the old days when the butcher, baker and candle stick maker all did their bit for the village? The advent of the global village is leading us inexorably back to the simple truth – we are all in this together.

During these past 40 years businesses have gone through a lot and learned a lot. To create our future, we need to understand our past. Why? Because many organizations are stuck in it. Finding where they are stuck is the key to knowing what to do to move forward.

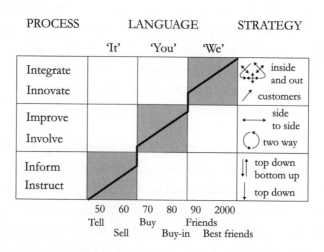

Fig. 3.1 The marketing and communication timeline.

1. Tell
1950s–1960s: the production economy

Manufacturers ruled supreme up to the second world war and immediately after. Customers were so hungry for anything the manufacturer could make that car producers like Henry Ford could say, 'You can have any color as long as it is black'. Imagine the reaction to the arrogance of a statement like that today!

Not only was there limited choice, but the chances of a quality product were sometimes pretty slim as well. There was even a time when the Japanese, desperate to create trade and establish a positive balance of payments after the war, were only able to deliver what was disparagingly referred to as 'junk'. Today Japanese quality is envied the world over.

With manufacturing far from able to create a total quality product, the manufacturer simply had to concentrate on the process of production. It was more a case of getting something made rather than getting it right first time. Whether they liked it or not, customers had to make do with guarantees and repairs rather than knowing they had a reliable, fault-free product.

During this period, mass markets began to emerge, shifting the focus to mass production. How did the manufacturer communicate with their customer? Easy! Tell them the product was available. Tell them what it contained, did, cost and needed in order to remain in working order. Most importantly, get them to buy it and then think perhaps about how to move them on to a repeat purchase.

Here is how Cadbury Schweppes, the UK chocolate manufacturer, recounts its own history: 'The early Cadbury labels were for the most part clear and dignified. Their designs reflected the "quality and superior style" which marked the Cadbury approach to business … Chocolate for eating was a novelty and the packs were designed to tempt the customers to taste this new product.'

Listen to the language, the labels were 'clear and dignified' and chocolate for eating was a novelty! Compare this to the company's sophisticated marketing and communication approach today where Cadbury Schweppes believes: 'Successful companies monitor their consumers' attitudes and lifestyle changes, then move quickly to respond to their demands'.

Manufacturers during the 1950s were simply in *tell* mode. Such was the lack of competition that if they came up with a snappy name, they could even sometimes manage to make their brand name into the generic product name. A Hoover became the generic word for a vacuum cleaner (now in the UK a Hoover all too often reminds people of a disastrous sales promotion offering Air Miles and holidays on which the company was unable to deliver).

What power the manufacturers had in the past and how they failed to make use of it! They saw little reason to develop the emotional capital of their customers as they had an almost automatic stranglehold on them. If they could make it the customers would buy it. Demand far exceeded supply. Apart from the seemingly inevitable boom and bust economic cycles created by insatiable demand over heating national economies, manufacturers could do no wrong.

Following the 1950s, where communication was relatively simple and it was so much easier to reach the customer, something new took hold. In the 1960s, competition became more intense; distribution became the key to success.

2. Sell

1960s–1970s: the distribution and sales-driven economy

Here we enter a new period, a time when supply and demand were almost equally balanced. The key to survival lay in establishing geographic markets and servicing the needs of those markets. In other words, the battle between manufacturers was volume-based. The name of the game internally was 'tell 'em to make more', and externally to 'sell, sell, sell' more.

The first part of selling your goods was to make as many of them as you could. Secondly, selling was about getting your goods into the marketplace; the goal here was to ensure distribution by developing the logistics to get goods to market. Distribution also occurred by developing the retail and wholesale outlets to ensure availability in the main street or out of town stores. Finally, distribution occurred by persuading customers at the point of sale to part with their money. Selling and promotional offers became the tools to leverage money out of an unsophisticated customer's wallet.

Organizations developed sales forces to ensure the customer bought their goods. Door-to-door salesman were trained in techniques to 'close that sale'. It often didn't matter whether the customer wanted, needed, or could afford the product – the name of the game was commission and volume. The same held true for the promotional offers to get the unwary customer to buy – hard selling and hard-driving offers were the order of the day. The communication mode was sell, sell, sell.

'Talking at' the customer

Public relations agencies also came into their own with another version of sell, which was hype, hype, hype. It was no longer good enough to tell the journalist that a product was now available. With competition for editorial space becoming intense, it became critical to spin new, brighter, bolder and more exciting stories around a product or service. This was the PR version of sell.

Both tell and sell have one thing in common: They 'talk at' the customer. Identifying customer needs was an incidental means to an end. Of course proficient sales people recognized the importance of customer needs and lifetime relationships. However, the era's sales literature was crammed with technique after technique for winning the order. Virtually every sales conference awarded prizes to staff winning the greatest sales volumes, not the greatest retention rates of customers.

The level of sophistication of sales, promotional and PR techniques was high. However the understanding of customers, markets and relationships, especially lifetime relationships, left a lot to be desired. Something else was needed. That something again was driven by competition.

As competition intensified and the customer became more sophisticated, something remarkable took place: a paradigm shift. Competition created a shift in the way organizations dealt with their customers which:

- led to the creation of new departments called marketing
- shifted the thinking away from *tell and sell*
- moved the thinking and communication strategies away from *push*
- began the processes that ensure customers want the product and are prepared to pay for it, look for it, remain loyal to it – in other words a *pull* strategy.

Organizations stopped focusing on how to shift the product, and started doing things for the now all-powerful customers in their target markets. They realized that to get the customer to buy from them, the product had to meet the customer's needs and be 'right first time'.

Marketing began to act as the interface between the business and the customer. Customer service programs kicked in to ensure maximization of any face-to-face contact in retail outlets and verbal communication on the phone.

By the end of the 1960s, the focus had changed from 'it', the product, to 'you', the customer. The next decade was to be very exciting.

3. Buy
1970s–early 1980s: the quality and mass marketing economy

The customer became king in the 1970s. In the new customer-driven economy, there was a reversal of the supply driven economy. Supply now exceeds demand and customers were faced with an increasingly sophisticated and diverse choice of products and services, all vying for their attention and wallet.

The door opened for the marketing professional to meet and create the need for their particular product and services. The way was clear for quality philosophies and practices to take hold, first in Japan, then in Western companies. The path was open for customer service initiatives to create the 'feel good factor' and sales in the retail outlets.

At first the steps taken by the new disciplines were tentative. For example, mass marketing was gradually developed as an art form through a heavy reliance on mass means of communication. Quality moved from being just another initiative to driving all the processes of a business. Customer service only gradually came to be seen as a 'way of life'.

Gung-ho marketing

Marketing was responsible for identifying target markets, identifying the products that would satisfy those markets and putting in place the plans to deliver the right product at the right price in the right place with the right promotions. And so the four Ps were born: product, price, place and promotion.

In a gung-ho fashion, with the advertising agencies happily recommending massive spends, marketing began to establish itself as the driver of organizations – externally.

Marketing directors took over from sales directors in importance in organizations. Advertising agencies grew and grew in importance and stature in the business world. Clever design and copy, jingles, themes, logos, brand names – all took hold as the way to promote products, services and occasionally corporate identity as well.

With this newly found power, marketing could fundamentally change the way of communicating with customers. Marketing's role was not one of telling customers what to do, or selling them something they may or may not want. Marketing's role was to find out what customers wanted and to meet their needs.

The central driving force of marketing became the development of the customer base using a strategy of creating awareness, purchase, repeat purchase and ultimately, a level of loyalty in the customer that extended to recommending the product. Marketing became responsible for developing the concept of the 'ladder' of customer loyalty.

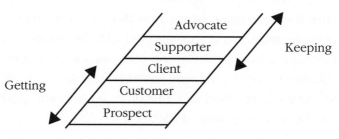

From *Relationship Marketing* (Payne *et al.*)

In the early days of marketing, it was enough to get the customers up the first few rungs of the ladder. Getting large groups of customers to buy the message was sufficient to generate enough interest for customers to want to purchase products or services.

Mass markets required mass marketing techniques. With large marketing budgets and the consequent hype around the advertising and promotional spend, the level of precise targeting was minimal. In hindsight, the heyday of big spends on big campaigns in big markets with big results did not last long. For perhaps only a decade, mass marketing ruled supreme.

4. Buy-in

Late 1980s–mid 1990s: the customer service and niche marketing economy

Throughout the 1980s, customers became more sophisticated, as products and services became more sophisticated. And quality had done such a good job in reducing time to market that the ever more demanding customer could ask for more 'new, new, new' products and services.

Caught in the trap of meeting ever more sophisticated tastes, marketing began to segment the target markets into smaller and smaller sections and to drive the development of products and services for these niche markets. However, with unsophisticated ways of identifying and reaching individual customers, niche marketing was seen as the best way of maximizing the spend and minimizing the impact of increasingly intense, often international, competition.

At the time, lumping customers together seemed like a logical way of communicating with them; however, try squeezing two individuals together. It's impossible. Individuals remain individuals, no matter how many labels are put on them. Whether based on social labels (for example blue collar, used by marketing in its early days) or even the lifestyle labels (like 'aspirers,' still used by the psychologists and advertising agencies today) these provide only crude methods to help marketing departments do a job of communication.

What is interesting is that the level of customer sophistication had been created through the very process of marketing and advertising. As marketing and advertising professionals plied their trade they became forced to concentrate on putting ever more sophisticated messages about their products to persuade customers to switch from competitors or to stay loyal.

Climbing the ladder of success

To overcome the shortfalls of niche marketing, organizations began the journey of taking their customers with them up the loyalty ladder. Customers were being seen as more, much more than the route to their wallet. They were being treated to ever increasing levels of 'friendly' service. The role models were retailers Nordstrom in the US and Marks and Spencer in the UK, both of whom are famed for their legendary stories of customer service.

Marketing changed its focus from the 1970s' short-term focus on getting customers to 'buy' the product (by trading on the imagery created by advertising and promotion) to a longer-term focus on getting them to 'buy-into' the brand and even the corporate identity (through building up brand values and corporate reputation).

Customer loyalty became the new buzzword and securing buy-in for the long-term became the goal. One of the most obvious new methods was the loyalty scheme. Whether free air miles every time you fly, or loyalty cards with various discount or bonus points every time you buy, the basic system didn't much vary. Visit a Toys 'R Us, fly any airline, shop in a supermarket or department store and there was likely to be a loyalty scheme in place. The basic idea was that if we look after you and reward you for staying with us, then you will look after us and choose to shop with us rather than a competitor.

However, everyone was offering loyalty schemes. And at the same time, customers' tastes, needs, wants and desires were being fueled by increasing choice on offer, increasing levels of technological sophistication, increasing levels of democracy throughout the world and with the global boom of the eighties. Politicians like Ronald Reagan and Margaret Thatcher were telling people that the power house economic conditions allowed them to operate in a 'me' culture. Gordon Gekko and Yuppies ruled.

So instead of 'keeping up with the Joneses', a customer wanted to be treated as a special one. And marketing moved beyond 'buy-in' to getting as close to a customer as a *friend*.

5. Friends
Late 1980s to Early 1990s: databases take over. Relationship marketing arrives

Just as mass markets had become niche markets, niche markets became ever smaller. Although this paradigm shift finally occurred in the 1990s, the concept actually originated in the late 80s with the relationship marketing model, based on databases of increasing sophistication and power. Ultimately, when tied to the ability to target customers with individually laser-printed letters, or talk to them on a 24 hour basis from call centres, database marketing moved to relationship marketing. Friends now become best friends or 'customers of one'.

6. Best Friends
1990 to 2000 and beyond: 'customers of one' has arrived and is here to stay

Don Peppers and Martha Rogers led the way with the 'one-to-one future', published in 1994. It painted a whole new world based on creating lifetime relationships. It showed the immense benefits of 'life time value' (LTV) of keeping a customer. It showed how to use database information to target specific messages to a customer who was happy to give you their needs and wants so you the supplier could make their life easier. And making life easy is the goal of all organizations according to the one-to-one relationship theory.

Marketing to customers of one is fine as a concept. The reality is that we live in a global village of billions of people. If marketers were to treat every individual as a critical target market, they need new tools which technology can provide. The advances in this area enable marketing to achieve levels of sophistication and specialization unimagined only a few years before. Database marketing can yield an amazing amount of detail about individuals, their addresses, needs, purchases, desires, credit ratings and almost anything else you could think, yet this is still only a very young science.

According to Andrew Wileman and Michael Jary, authors of *Retail power plays – From trading to brand leadership*, we've only just begun to tap the full benefit that technology can bring; 'Compared with producers, retailers have frequent direct contact with customers multiplied across a wide range of shopping transactions. With advances in in-store and central database management technology, one of their most valuable assets is the ability to understand shopping behavior, target marketing investment and build loyalty down at the level of type customer groups and even at the level of individual customers.

'Many product retailers now have much of the technology in place and are awash with customer data, but using the data in an effective way is still in its infancy.'

Think global, act local

This now-overused catch phrase sums up the incredible shift that has taken place from national, international and even multinational companies to truly global companies, global alliances and global supply and distribution, all linked to serving individual customers in specific geographic locations. And again, technology has had a major part to play.

What does acting local mean if not looking after people who have specific needs, wants and desires? Thanks to the incredible power and sophistication of technology to create one–to–one interfaces, companies became able to 'mass customize'. Here's how Dr Martha Rogers, who coined this expression, illustrated the concept at an international communication conference (IABC) in 1997: 'I want a pair of jeans that actually fit ME. And I got them, made especially to fit my measurements, made just for me by Levis. And they come with my brand name on – a label saying Martha Rogers! The great thing is I can actually sit down in them. And if I want another pair I don't have to go through the whole shopping thing again.'

Technology will keep Martha's measurements and probably remind her when the next new design is available and make them in her size. All this global complexity and incredible customer sophistication often boils down to needs and wants, clear and simple. The more you know about your customers' needs, the more likely they are to be friends with you and stay friends with you for life.

The emotional capital that can build over the lifetime of an *external* customer relationship can create financial value for organizations that often exceeds the wildest dreams of managers at all levels and all functions. Now let's look at how this timeline relates to *internal* customers.

The missing link: external marketing and internal communication

The marketing timeline reveals how over the decades marketing and corporate communication have worked together successfully to alter the way customers think, feel, believe and act.

While external marketing has become ever more sophisticated, internal communication has lagged far behind. Yet the employee, the internal customer, has never been so important to the success of a business. Plainly, it is the internal customer who is expected to deliver the new thinking and feeling around relationship marketing. Do the standard communication processes existing in most organizations motivate employees to do so?

Where do we want to be?

The future of the relationship between organizations and the people working in and around them is totally dependent on the way they communicate with each other – not as employees but as internal customers. Let's not forget that employees are, after all, other business' external customers. Just like everyone else, they have come to expect better faster and more value added products and services – why should they accept internal communication processes that are amateur, unsophisticated and downright outmoded?

The heat has now turned up in the kitchen and it is the new internal customer who is making things pretty hot! Internal communication had better rise to the challenge because failure is no longer an option when the likes of today's highly aggressive and competitive companies are prowling around the global market.

Companies are beginning to realize that they can no longer use outmoded communication processes. For example, Bruce Berger, Vice President of Corporate Affairs for Whirlpool Corporation recently spoke at a conference about the need for managers to change their view of communication and to forge new relationships with their people.

Berger said: 'Your employees are not *your* employees ... Employees may work with you and for you ... but you do not own them. They do not belong to you and you cannot force into them your beliefs, your urgency or your vision like so much sausage into casing.

'If the perceived reality in the workplace does not match your vision, then the vision will go unrealized except as a cynical dream, spawning widespread disillusionment and continuous counter-productivity. Employees choose their own dreams, commit to what they believe, readily discern truth from hollow language or gesture, seek purpose in what they do. Their two worst fears are: losing a job and having a job that goes unnoticed.'

Berger goes on to affirm the critical importance of internal communication: 'Through truth, communication and leadership you may help employees grow and open to commitment which opens your business to success far beyond your vision. But in the absence of these, employees will close into cynicism, and whisper "revolution".'

What has been his company's traditional response to these vital internal customers? Berger candidly admits: 'Our management's view of effective communication was formal, laced with company speak, largely top down and directive'.

The desire of organizations like Whirlpool is for internal customers to buy-in and build lifetime relationships with customers. Relationships like these need a commitment to deep issues like visions, missions, values, service, total quality, etc. Yet how can organizations hope to develop deep relationships with their employees if the strategy, processes, language and tools are geared towards a completely different type of relationship in a completely different era?

Where are we now?

The big question for you is, where is your organization on the timeline? This is the next part of the timeline … your part. Try plotting yourself on the timeline below. Is it easy or difficult to plot your organization? Are different parts of the organization in different places? Of course they are, but *overall* what is your organizational approach to the internal customer? In simple terms, do you tell them, get them to buy-in or do you know so much about every single one that their needs and the needs of the organization are impossible to distinguish?

Box 3.2   A big question

Where is your organization on the *internal* marketing and communication timeline? Place an X to show where you are now.

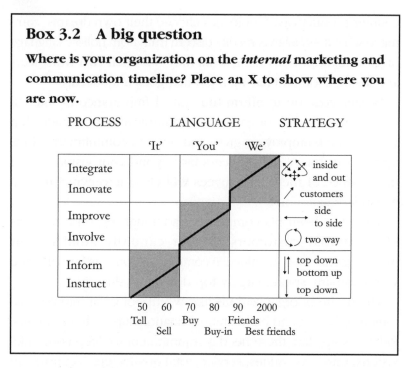

Still having difficulty plotting your organization on the timeline? One of the simplest ways of deciding where an organization sits on the internal marketing and communication timeline is to look at its methods and choice of media. The next section lists the media and approaches that characterize each different stage of the internal marketing timeline. I call these my *cynic's list of internal media,* or *how to arouse the emotions and create buy-in while really, really trying but not getting very far.*

The internal marketing timeline

1. 'Tell' mode

- **In-house newsletters and newspapers:** journalism (friendly or investigative depending on the zeal of the editor, and how much they value their job)
- **Internal or team briefings:** messages of instruction or information which require no action, cascading downwards

(from that shower at head office) also see 'sell'

- **Manuals:** training and instructions (otherwise known as book ends or door stops)
- **Policies and procedures:** safety, expenses and the like (gathering dust – see manuals)
- **Memos:** information ('need to know,' or more often 'don't need to know,' or even 'that's my back covered!')
- **Bulletin boards or notice boards:** more information (last year's company picnic and ads for secondhand cars)
- **Guides:** more training (more dust)
- **E-mail:** see memos (modern version with ability to cover your back with everyone, or blame everyone else).

All this media is basically telling or informing internal customers, with little to no opportunity for feedback or dialogue. Journalism, for example, relies on newspapers to deliver messages, usually these are the type fondly referred to in the UK as 'hatches, matches and dispatches,' or more simply births, marriages and deaths. In the US, Michael Brandon of Northern Telecom refers to these as the 'Three Bs' of birthdays, babies and ball scores.

The company newspaper represents the belief of management, and the editor, that as long as the information is imparted the job of communicating is done. So alongside the Three Bs will be articles about the senior management team and their hopes, dreams and projects.

All too often, however, the newspaper and the organization come unstuck. If journalists treat the company newspaper as a vehicle for investigative journalism, the management team is uncomfortable to say the least. When information is power, limiting information is the source of power. Besides, investigative journalism is not intended to be flattering!

'Tell' mode also requires fast methods of communication. Business TV, and often 'screen savers' are used to 'tell' people about things they need to know. Even the UK's much-used process of team briefing meetings (which begin with board meetings and end with a cascade of information through managers presenting the information to their team) was designed as a military 'tell' process.

Now don't get me wrong, the marketing and communication mix may mean that all forms of media may be necessary. None are 'wrong'. The problem is that they are used at the wrong time, for the wrong reasons, in the wrong way. 'Tell' is OK if people need and want to be told.

Such has been the case for Ernst & Young, as Nick Land, UK Managing Partner, explains: 'In the first two or three years in the life of Ernst & Young we were very top down – telling people what they had to do. This was the right strategy at that time because we had a lot of basics to get into place quickly.'

There are occasions when speed is critical, in a crisis for example. You do not debate whether to evacuate a building that is on fire. You would not be consulted if someone was making a corporate raid on your business. 'Tell' is good when 'tell' is necessary.

2. 'Sell' mode

- **Team briefing:** messages of information which require some degree of staff commitment, so the briefer's role is to 'present' the information in a way which convinces the team of its worth (see presentation skills)
- **Presentation skills:** how to convince your (gullible?) audience with the 'top ten tips of terrific talks', or even better, 'how to get your message across in 30 seconds or less'
- **Company magazines:** 'hatches, matches and dispatches' and messages from above (all too often seen as propaganda)
- **Videos:** more messages from above (in 'user friendly' 20-minute sound and vision bites)
- **Road shows and conferences:** launches, hype, with high impact but low absorption

- **Business television and other broadcast messages:** instantly over the airwaves, often loved by CEOs. See company magazines, videos, and screen savers, all rolled into one
- **Screen savers and other push technology:** more high-impact from managers trying to force their point across.

As companies move into *sell* mode, they turn to media that tends to be more complex or sophisticated. Team briefing, for example, moves up the communication ladder to *sell* by giving managers better communication tools and more sophisticated presentation skills – they are effectively being asked to sell the messages from above. Team briefing often fails to deliver, however. Neither the strategy of *tell* in a one-way cascade, nor the execution of getting managers to *sell* the messages tends to work.

A natural move up the communication and marketing time line occurs as corporate spin on stories, events, product launches and the like become commonplace. If in journalism mode, 'the answer is a newspaper, what's the question?'; in PR mode, 'the answer is a conference with dry ice, or a glossy poster and magazine, what's the question?'

Pushme –pullyou

The internal media choice of magazines, posters, conferences, roadshows, videos and cassette tapes all point to a *sell* mode. The objective is to create as much hype as possible with a view to convince people by sheer weight of promotional 'push.'

As part of the push, the more color, design and motivational bells and whistles, the better. The theory is simply that if the medium is 'sexy' enough it must work. If this were the case we would buy everything we see on TV or the supermarket shelves – not! (as they say).

Many organizations are stuck in *tell* and *sell* modes. With top-down messages being delivered through ever increasing numbers of channels of communication, the strategy is simply one of push. Yet organizations recognize a push strategy is not the way forward into the future. The study by MCA and Salford University showed in 1996 that senior managers in organizations were beginning to recognize the concept of internal marketing and the need for a different approach to employee communication in order to create a *pull* for information. This brings us to *buy* mode.

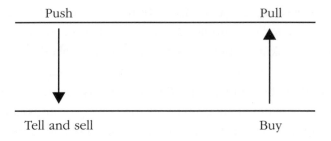

3. 'Buy' mode

- **Workshops:** interactive training sessions allowing feedback for participants 'ownership'
- **Attitude surveys:** researching employees' feelings and concerns about the organization in order to be seen as a caring employer
- **Breakout sessions:** at conferences (see workshops).

Organizations begin to make more of an effort to create processes that allow employees to voice their opinions and concerns, Unfortunately, the move into a new mode of marketing internally still overly focuses on media and the latest fashionable management methods like 'empowerment' and 'teams', not on the principles behind marketing – basically to create 'pull' from customers. The paradigm shift of getting internal customers to *buy* is still colored by a trusting belief and excessive focus on different forms of media.

4. 'Buy-in' mode

- **Project meetings:** team meetings to create awareness of issues and develop team buy in to solutions and plans
- **'Town hall meetings,' forums and 'talk backs':** meet the bosses, fire questions around the coffee table (often only covers tiny percentage of workforce, but bosses feel they are really listening)
- **Management by walking around:** one-to-one version of town halls and talk backs (advocated by Tom Peters who likes *management by haranguing about* on stage with large audiences)
- **Internal Web pages, discussion groups and databases:** enabling employees to select the information they want to receive and the feedback they want to give
- **Employee hotlines:** telephone feedback channel
- **'Skip level meetings':** boss meets his or her subordinates' staff to 'get to know you,' while subordinate worries about what will be said to the boss
- **Video conferencing:** I watch you, watching me (in the corner of the screen) while talking to each other, while being phased by the time lag.

The characteristics of *buy-in* involve far more two-way communication, combining both face-to-face interaction with technology-based communication. The fact is that buy-in comes not from media itself, but from a well-targeted message and a feeling of 'what's in it for me?' (WIIFM) in the target market. So much more important than media is to use methods of communication and marketing which generate involvement and encourage high levels of face to face meetings, which helps understanding, secures commitment and builds real relationships.

5. 'Friends' mode

- **Psychometric surveys:** tools for understanding individuals during interview, often used for executive away-day sessions (never used again). Also see 'Best Friends' for when these tools are used really well as an on-going method of developing relationships
- **Breakfast sessions:** meet the CEO over donuts
- **Team Listening®:** a process developed by my firm that combines a facilitated face-to-face team meeting with active participation and robust feedback
- **Team meetings:** any form of personal contact in any group consisting of team members who are working together over enough of a period of time to get to know each other well
- **'Didits and goforits':** Morning sessions in a team type meeting practiced by MCA, providing feedback on achievements and goals. These are a powerful way of communicating in short sharp bursts and creating knowledge of 'what's happening'. Great for building awareness as well as people feeling they are kept 'in the know'.

The characteristic of Friends – just like the TV series – is a simple one: people like and respect each other. How can you tell? They *listen*. They listen to understand; then they can act. They may not, but they *can* because they recognize the need of the others. And here is the other characteristic. Friends tend to involve a group. This is not quite yet one-to-one. What happens with friends? They move from being 'friends – for now' to becoming 'best friends – for life'. This is when the communication media really becomes very powerful, often using intimate tools for understanding and mutual discovery.

6. 'Best friends' mode

- **360-degree feedback:** if practised well, another name for research. This is the bedrock of relationship marketing. If it is done badly, it becomes more a case, 'how will I tell the boss he/she is lousy without being fired?'
- **Psychometric surveys:** this time used for deep understanding of team dynamics and individual personal types and traits, and how to maximize the relationship by developing communication styles suited to the recipient (in other words – targeting).
- **Customized electronic media:** see 'Tools of the Trade' below for a closer look at the possibilities and pitfalls of the latest uses for electronic media.
- **Regular face-to-face meetings:** the best of all forms of communication; people getting together frequently, because they want to. A win–win where added value comes from every meeting. The benefits may be tangible like plans and decisions made, or intangible like personal help. However they come, the meetings are good for the individuals and the business.

Best friends modes are a mixture of highly personal and interactive communication, coupled with far more sophisticated use of electronic tools to gather, analyze and explore the perceptions, skills and emotions of internal customers.

Tools of the trade

Imagine having a database of information about your internal markets, including a personality profile on *every* internal customer, the type of work they do, their preferred style of writing and method of delivery, and the topics they are most interested in.

If you think this sounds impossible, remember how much information has already been recorded about employees by your personnel or human resources function. Most companies would sell their souls to have that much information about the millions of customers they need to track.

Once you have this information, you can then begin to provide customized communication for each of your employees. For example, Digital asks their staff to register the types of information they want to receive – and then automatically tailors the daily on-line news bulletin for each person. Other companies ask staff to subscribe to certain types of electronic communication – and only advises subscribers when there is something new to read.

Customized communication also occurs between individual employees as they use new technologies to interact and collaborate with colleagues, partners and suppliers around the world – whenever, wherever and however they need to in order to deliver. Sounds great, doesn't it? Unfortunately, the path to customized communication is filled with pitfalls.

New tools, old problems

You may recall our discussion in Chapter 1 about the most expensive letter in the world (the letter S), and the difference between communicatioN and communicationS. That difference is at the heart of the problem.

Whilst the communicationS or tools may be technically brilliant, and getting better, the communicatioN that wins hearts and minds isn't keeping pace.

The figure of 4.1 out of 10 given in Box 3.3 hardly represents a paradigm shift. Is the reason simply that the communicationS in these organizations are well below world-class—quite the opposite! Despite having the most sophisticated tools at their

Box 3.3   The superhighway to hell?

MCA conducted a major study amongst 20 of the world's top high-tech companies, including IBM, Novell, Northern Telecom, Hewlett Packard, Dell, Intel, 3Com, Xerox, Lotus, Digital, Sun Microsystems, CompuServe and NCR. The study concluded that: 'Even with the best technology and technically literate staff, high-tech companies struggle with the same communication challenges as everyone else — proof that electronic communication is not necessarily the panacea many communicators hoped it would be.'

The survey participants saw little difference in the effectiveness of their electronic communication compared with traditional channels. Overall effectiveness of electronic communication rated 6.2 out of 10; however, the effectiveness of electronic communication in gaining staff's buy-in rated a poor 4.1 out of 10.

Source: *People, Technology and Communication: The Case for Superhighway Codes* (MCA, 1997).

hands, the expertise of these companies is in communicationS, not communicatioN. This is the root of the problem.

As companies try harder and harder to address their communication problems, they actually bury their employees in information. Box 3.4, detailing a survey of the *Fortune 1000 companies*, reveals the scale of the problem. Clearly, information overload creates its own problems in terms of stress and confusion.

The common (mistaken) assumption is that mass forms of communication generate understanding. Companies reason that since they have even more effective forms of communicationS through electronic media, then they are guaranteed greater levels of understanding and buy-in.

Box 3.4   Drowned in messages

'According to a study commissioned by Pitney Bowes, the document management group, today's office workers are overwhelmed by messages.

'Research by the Institute for the Future, Gallup and San Jose State University, found that an employee of a leading US organization deals with an average 178 messages and documents every business day.

'Meredith Fischer, vice president of communications and marketing, Pitney Bowes, says, "Because communications and traffic are increasing, user frustration over managing the volume is going up as workers send the same message several times to get through the blizzard of communications, creating even more traffic.

'"It's as if the communication demands are driving the work and the conduct of the business, instead of the other way around."

'Almost three-quarters of all the workers surveyed in the Fortune 1000 companies – from chief executives down – say they feel "overwhelmed" by the number of messages they have to deal with.'

Source: Survey of Fortune 1000 companies by Institute for the Future, from *The Financial Times*, July 1997.

E-mail = Emotional, doesn't it?

It is with e-mail that we come to the first big obstacle of electronic-based internal communication. Suddenly, people are able, through the route of mass communication, to move into mass marketing. Suddenly, everyone has the ability to target everyone else with e-mail. The problem is, that very few of these people are trained in marketing techniques, let alone the principles of marketing. Suddenly, everyone becomes a marketer without being skilled in marketing. Worse than that, people also lack the necessary communication skills.

The advent of e-mail has definitely brought in a new era. Ironically, this should be the democratization of communication, yet the new owners of communication are all too often in autocratic mode!

So, although internal customers are as sophisticated as external customers and have access to the latest electronic gadgetry, the mode of communication is often stuck in *tell* mode. The message is still being told badly. At least in external communication, *tell* mode is used by trained journalists able to write in a way that appeals to their readers.

If e-mail started the revolution by giving everyone the means to communicate to mass markets, the advent of Intranets in the mid-1990s definitely created a new breed of internal marketers – once again without giving them the necessary skills.

Think of a home page as an advertisement. Think of the reason for producing a home page in color and making it appeal to the person reading it. Think of the home page and every subsequent page as a targeted piece of communication aimed at creating a level of understanding, buy-in and, where appropriate, behavioral change. This is not simply communication, this is marketing.

Because the relationship through interactive electronic media allows two-way dialogue, they provide everyone with the capability of moving beyond simply targeting markets into relationships with customers of one. Yet we still have the same problem. The media is of the moment, ready to take us into the next millennium. Yet the mind set and skill set of users is still in the 1950s and 60s.

The medium is the message (and it shouldn't be)

Advances in electronic communications have created a situation where everyone has the ability to move up the communication

and marketing timeline, yet the principles, let alone the processes and skills of communication and marketing are not in
place. (When we go through the *Six Is of communication* in
Chapter 6, we will see how the various forms of communication
need to be used at different stages along the time line.)

There is nothing wrong with journalism. The opposite is the
case. Journalism is a critical part of the marketing and communication mix. There is nothing wrong with PR, with putting a
spin on a story. The opposite is the case. PR is a critical part of
the marketing and communication mix. There is nothing wrong
with mass marketing when a mass message needs to be delivered. The opposite is the case. Communicating to everyone, be
it through business television, intranets or mass e-mail may well
be critical. Mass marketing is a part of the mix.

It is not the use of the marketing mix that is the problem. It is
the use of the media mix in an inappropriate way that is the
problem. The vital skill is for organizations to know when and
how to use the media mix, to judge correctly whether *tell, sell,
buy, buy-in, friends or best friends* is right for their internal customers at a given time in the life of the organization.

Marshall McLuhan's famous insight that *the media is the message* can still be applied today. Intranets, for example, don't just
allow messages to be exchanged, they suddenly CHANGE the
way people work. Whole departments stop talking when individuals send off e-mails to the person sitting next to them. All of
this effort going into all these forms of media begs a question:
what good is the media if we can't get the message across?

The massive amounts that organizations are spending on electronic communications as well as other forms of communication
are to achieve two key goals: to increase intellectual capital and
to increase emotional capital. Internal communication and marketing is simply about getting people to know more and use
what they know to develop the value of the business. Yet organizations will never reap these benefits if their internal

communication remains a poor 6 out of 10 and continues to fail to deliver better business results.

This look at the marketing and communication timeline has provided us with a starting point for looking at how to improve the strategies, processes and skills involved in generating intellectual and emotional capital.

If organizations buy-in to the need for improving their businesses through their people, then improving the methods and means to capturing hearts and minds has to be a priority. The next section of this book deals with the 'how tos' (don't you just love 'how tos' – you know you should do them but you don't – yet it's comforting to know they are there when you need them!).

These are:

- how to develop a strategy for dealing with all your relationships and target markets
- how to deliver an improved P & L through a new communication and marketing strategy applied internally
- how to introduce new processes for delivering every sort of message from instruction to innovation and beyond
- how to change the language of the organization to ensure it focuses on the right things
- how to create the right language and allow people to use this as a form of cultural currency with which to trade
- how to develop an approach to creating the new forms of intellectual property and brand and corporate personality
- how to develop the new tools of intellectual capital and emotional capital.

The next two chapters will begin to address the first issue in the list, how to deal with relationships. Chapter 4 looks at how to manage internal customers to help create a new emotional contract between them and the organization, while Chapter 5 identifies which stakeholders in and around the organization need to be targeted.

2

My notes on the marketing and communication timeline

Marketing has been responsible for the customer — but this has only meant the external customer. Corporate communication has been responsible for the stakeholder — which sometimes covered the 'employee' because they were good at 'journalism'. Human resources were responsible for the staff — and sometimes they were left to write the 'touchy feely stuff' in a company magazine. The net result? 'The answer is a choice of media — now what was it you wanted to say?'

The timeline shows how a choice of media is only the answer when you have a strategy in place. It is of no use having the sexy presentation when they think it is all a bunch of lies!

Thought provokers for the future

- What do you do in each of the marketing and communication phases when it comes to media? Write down the magazines, roadshows held, corporate videos, surveys, etc. Be prepared to see that you have created a cascade — or is it a deluge?
- The message is in the media — or is it?
Tell?
Sell?
Buy?
Buy In?
Friends?
Best Friends?

Your notes

A Strategic Approach to Managing your Internal Customers

Overview

In this chapter, you'll discover:

- the emotional contract between organizations and employees
- the dynamics of top-down and bottom-up messages
- the 'top ten business and personal needs'
- communication's role in strengthening the emotional contract.

F O U R

A Strategic
Approach to
Managing your
Internal Customers

Everyone in an organization, if they are living its values and delivering its message, is a corporate communicator. Everyone can voice an opinion: to their friends in the bar, to their family at home, or even as they are interviewed on television outside the factory gate. Getting the people in and around your organization onto your side is no longer simply 'nice to have,' it is a critical aid to your long-term success.

The threat to your business, if key stakeholders in and around the business are 'against' you, can be considerable. Your business' reputation and personality will be damaged if any of your stakeholders cease to identify with its values, behaviors and practices – resulting in the nightmare spectacle of employees striking about pay, and middle-class shareholders picketing the Annual General Meeting to complain about the pay of 'fat cat' executives. The 1996 Royal Mail strikes in the UK, for example, led to politicians discussing a loss of the organization's long-held monopoly status – such a change had been unthinkable before the start of the strikes.

The previous chapter analyzed the advances in external marketing, culminating in the concept of a lifetime relationship with the customer. It stressed the importance of the employee (the internal customer), to deliver this new thinking and feeling about customers. However, despite major advances in marketing and communication tools, the internal processes of communication within the majority of businesses is woefully inadequate to help develop and support these new internal customers.

Organizations are beginning to recognize that internal marketing and communication can be a powerful tool in achieving attitudinal and behavioral change. If marketing is all about meeting needs, and relationship marketing all about meeting specialized individual needs, then the same is true of internal marketing and communication. The key goal of internal marketing and communication is understanding the needs of internal customers, satisfying those needs and ultimately gaining buy-in from the hearts and minds of employees.

Clearly, if employees know their organizations are committed to improving their relationship through communication, they in turn will look to deliver their part of the implicit 'employment contract'. But internal communication can help turn that contract into something new: an emotional contract.

The new emotional contract

Emotional contracts are defined eloquently in a journal by the Academy of Management Executive as, '… the unwritten set of expectations operating between every member and the organization. These expectations normally concern non-tangible, psychological/emotional issues, e.g. trust, security, understanding. Breaches of these contracts could result in the lowering of trust and job satisfaction and in some instances make the employee concerned leave.'

The journal goes on emphasize that emotional contracts are increasingly complex in nature. 'Traditionally, employees were expected to be loyal and committed to the organization in return for "fair" pay, career prospects and job security. This has largely disappeared and has been replaced by a new contract based on continuous learning and changing identities; employees are expected to take charge of their careers.'

Another journal, the *Administrative Science Quarterly*, also stresses that the emotional or psychological contract is highly complex because it depends on the various needs and motivations of each employee. The journal argues that this will put 'the role of communications and internal marketing center stage. They have another role to play and that is in the negotiation and renegotiation of psychological/emotional contracts (which varies slightly from employee to employee). Employers will need to find more open ways of communicating in order to minimize the level of distrust and dissatisfaction experienced by employees as a consequence of one or more of the factors affecting the emotional contract not being met.'

Plainly, marketing-based internal communication is the key to forging strong emotional contracts between individuals and the organization. Emotional and intellectual capital are created through this emotional contract, because there is an honest attempt to balance and satisfy the needs of the organization and those of internal customers.

The critical part of this contract is that internal customers know what is going on, where they fit and what they need to do. Feeling valued and appreciated and knowing that individual contributions count will increase employees' stock of emotional capital in the business. And that's where internal marketing and communication come in.

Establishing effective communication processes to internal customers is not a cheap option, however. It requires the energy, commitment, intellect and intuition of senior people. Why should it be a cheap option? Successful organizations do not view external marketing as a cost, nor do they view the task of establishing an emotional contract with customers in order to gain their loyalty as a cost. They know that this element of marketing is a vital *investment*.

The same thinking applies internally. Investing in internal customers is not a cost. It is a vital part of developing the asset base of the organization. An investment in communication provides a double benefit because of the build up of emotional capital and intellectual capital as employees become energized and committed to the goals of the business.

Many organizations, caught up in massive restructuring programs, now have the opportunity to transform their internal communication processes. Dr Carol Kinsey Gorman, an international speaker and consultant on human resources, believes the time is right for many of these organizations to give their employees a bigger picture of where they and their organizations are heading.

'Employees in a restructured workforce are waiting to be energized, to be given a framework for past change and a vision of future transformation that makes sense to them,' Kinsey Gorman argues. 'Only when transformation belongs to everyone can people shift and organize rapidly and effectively around changes in customers, competitors and environments.'

Internal communication is the key to forging new emotional contracts with internal customers. This chapter looks at the problems of existing communication approaches and then gives some guidelines for how organizations can transform their approach to employees. The basic premise is that just as external marketing develops its strategies based on sophisticated data about customer needs, so could internal communication. The next chapter will broaden this picture by looking at other vital stakeholders and the type of communication process that can be put in place to cater for every dimension of the business, inside and outside.

Top-down isn't working

The old command-and-control approach to communication is all too often one of 'top-down'. In simple terms this communication tactic is simply to move into *tell* or *sell* mode and disseminate information to employees. After all, it is thought, employees are paid to get on with the job; and if managers say this is what the job is, then that is enough. The command-and-control approach therefore delivers top-down information and is based on a communication strategy that implicitly assumes that information-giving is all that is necessary.

This approach often relies on a 'corporate megaphone' strategy of media selection to deliver information from the leaders and managers to the organization. This corporate megaphone would be something like the corporate conference or road show. Designed with a suitable backdrop and loud music, the message is blasted home – or so the message makers believe.

But how do relationships work in real life? Through connections. How do they prosper and grow? Through sharing emotional and intellectual capital. Organizations favoring top-down communication rely on their managers to be the connections between employees and the organization. Hence management structures are important in these businesses. Yet these connections should be about sharing emotions and knowledge. Too often, managers do the opposite and keep information to themselves. Rather than enhancing communication, management layers often do the opposite!

In his book *Managing for the future,* Peter Drucker cites the case of Massey Ferguson, a company that reached the stage of being virtually bankrupt. A complex business consisting of 14 layers of management, the company transformed itself by delayering. Now down to six management layers (and still reducing), the company's communication has been greatly enhanced according to Drucker, allowing it to harness the minds and emotions of its employees.

Drucker comments: 'Massey Ferguson thought about the information it needed to run its business. The moment it did so, it discovered a great truth: many levels of management in fact manage nothing. They make no decisions. In reality they are only boosters, amplifying the very faint signals that come up and down through the organization. If a company can organize itself around its information needs, these layers become redundant.'

Drucker goes on to say: 'The knowledge workers who increasingly make up the work force are not amenable to the command-and-control methods of the past.'

Massey Ferguson was dominated by the internal perception that the single most important dimension of communication was top-down, the messages from above. Try asking your employees how they perceive top-down communication. Show them the diagram below (Fig. 4.1), and ask them if the down arrow would be big or small and if it would travel very far down the organization before gaining buy-in. Time and time again, employees draw arrows that are always very wide and not going very far. Does this matter? It certainly does if you perceive the issues commonly addressed by top-down communication to be important – see Fig. 4.2 for these top-down messages.

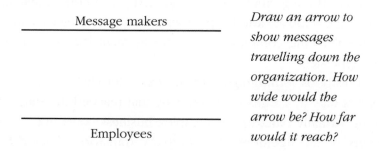

Message makers

Employees

Draw an arrow to show messages travelling down the organization. How wide would the arrow be? How far would it reach?

Fig. 4.1 A big or small arrow?

Vision
Mission
Values
Targets
Mergers
Acquisitions
Downsizing
New products
New services
Business plans
Cultural change
Customer service
Strategic alliances
Human resources plans
Business process re-engineering
Organizational change
Operational plans
Marketing plans
Restructuring
Quality
Costs
IT

Fig. 4.2   'Top-down' messages – a one-way deluge.

The list of messages is long, too long, and each one of these generates its own mass of top-down communication. If you were 'below' the arrow, firstly it would look like it was coming down on top of you and secondly, as if the arrow was 'pulling apart.' Imagine your natural reactions – duck, and remain convinced that senior managers should never be believed. In one of our client companies, discussions about the *top-down arrow* and its implications, generated the comment: 'My problem isn't worrying about a "hidden agenda" – I am more concerned that there isn't one.' In other words, the employee was worried that not even 'they' knew what they were doing!

All of the issues in the top-down arrow requires a massive increase in the intellectual capital and emotional capital held within the business if they are to succeed and generate buy-in. A new vision from a CEO, for example, could take an organization into a completely different business in completely different countries. The new vision could require a completely different way of working, with completely different customers, suppliers, stakeholders and of course employees. If any major business transformation is to work, employees need to be brought on board.

Champy at the bit – a bet on a losing horse

When Michael Hammer and James Champy estimate that 50 to 75% of business process re-engineering programs fail, and write a follow up book about the 'soft' people issues, it is not hard to see that the old 'scientific' approach to business transformation is recognized as lacking – sadly lacking. If people are the business, it is not hard to see that it is the human elements that makes them fail.

When the same sort of figures on failure are applied to total quality programs (Department of Trade and Industry figures in the UK found a 75% failure rate of quality programs) then the importance of people issues is not hard to guess. People make things succeed or fail.

Yet look at the strategic approach of top-down communication. It doesn't move past *tell* and *sell*, never mind at *buy*; and far from *buy-in*, *friends* or *best friends*. Too often, top-down communication is an arrow of enormous proportions coming down on the poor unsuspecting employee – the 'subordinate,' at 'the bottom of the ladder' who is 'paid to do a job', who 'must deliver' because he or she is 'paid to get on with it'.

Sadly, however, it is not just the front-line employee who fails to 'buy in'. During a recent board group discussion I asked: 'How many board members around this table can honestly say they have bought-in to the new vision, mission and values?' The chief executive officer looked around in vain. There were no hands raised.

All too often the arrow of top-down messages gets stuck at a very high level. And it is often not as simple as a top-down arrow going in one direction. When you ask members of the board and management team to describe where they are going, when and how, it is very common to see they are going in completely different directions, at different times, in different ways. There isn't one top-down arrow, there are many of them, and many are in conflict.

No wonder that those 'below' are confused, concerned and, all too often, downright cynical. Remember, '64% of employees often don't believe senior managers' according to the US Council of Communication Management. So, even if the messages get through because some employees are conscientious enough to read them, they would probably not believe them anyway!

Bottom-up communication isn't working

Go back to Fig. 4.1 and try asking your employees how they perceive bottom-up communication. Ask them to draw an arrow that shows how much the organization listens to people's personal needs (in its width), and how far up the organization their needs are listened to (in its height). Time and again, the arrows drawn by employees are always the same. In direct contrast to the top-down messages, the arrows are always small. However, just like the top-down arrows they too don't get very far. As Fig. 4.3 reveals, bottom-up messages are perceived as very different and very unequal to top-down messages.

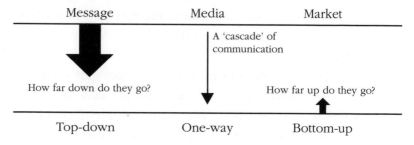

Fig. 4.3

Then add media to the equation, and think back to our discussion of commonly used communication channels from the last chapter. How many of them are two-way? Not many. How many of them give staff a direct channel to share their views and concerns with senior management? Even fewer.

The single most important force affecting marketing – either inside or out is WIIFM: 'What's in it for me?'. The illustration of the bottom-up market arrow and the one-way media arrows shows that not only do internal customers feel that their needs are being ignored, but no-one even bothers to ask what they are! If you went to a store and were ignored by the sales people, you know what would you do! Certainly, employees can complain – it's called the attitude survey. All too often, however, nothing happens and they are ignored again. The result? Employees leave, or worse, they 'quit and stay' – they stay in employment, yet behave as if they are not part of the company.

Clearly there is a major problem. How can businesses expect to gain buy-in if the messages keep getting stuck. But why are they getting stuck? There are two reasons. The first reason is the confusion, conflict and poor communication of these messages. One solution is to clarify these messages, prioritize them and plan an integrated communication campaign over a long period of time, just as an external marketing and communication pro-gram would be executed.

Simplifying these messages into a 'Top Ten List of Business Issues' enables managers and individuals to prioritize both what top-down messages need to be given and, as importantly, what employees believe needs to be communicated. (I'll explain how later in this chapter). That is the first reason for messages getting stuck, problems of clarity and priority at the top.

However, an even more important reason for messages get-ting stuck is that no-one wants to listen to them! The answer lies not with the top-down messages. The answer lies with the bot-tom-up market needs. If people don't feel listened to, is it any wonder that they in turn won't listen to others? The problem is that top-down communication is a *push* strategy. What's needed is to create a *pull* strategy.

How can companies create a *pull* strategy? By treating em-ployees as internal customers, not as employees who are told what to do. Something new starts to happen: if employees are treated as customers then organizations must find out what they want before they try to get them to want what the organization wants. This is radical stuff!

Time for another Drucker prediction. In *Managing for the future*, he describes the new approach to internal communica-tion: 'I believe therefore that we are moving toward more concentrated organizations and units of organizations, based on much clearer business *and* individual goals, on self-discipline and on systematic feedback. If this is truly the case, business will have to learn that they must build their communications systems on information up rather than information down.'

Information up (up whose?!)

What sort of upward information is required? It would be easy to say that internal customers are interested in the same things as their leaders and managers – easy to say and completely wrong. Over the last decade, MCA has been researching the needs of internal customers in many blue-chip and not-for-profit organizations. Our work stemmed from a large piece of research conducted by a major holiday group. This group was trying to identify the 'hooks' that would help retain their staff for longer periods. Poor retention had become an issue and had started to have an adverse impact on recruitment costs, induction costs, training costs and, more importantly, on customer service and satisfaction levels.

Our own research into employee 'hooks' revealed that in many cases, managers believe that they always know what their employees want. Their 'top ten' list would probably look something like this:

1   good pay
2   good working conditions
3   good holidays
4   free lunches
5   good pension
6   good hours
7   nice colleagues
8   good prospects for the future
9   good perks
10 good annual review.

Essentially, all of these are the classic ingredients of the standard job advertisement. If those managers were to talk with their employees, however, they would probably emerge with a quite different list and one that was closer to the components of the emotional contract! This might include the quality of work, the quality of leadership, or the input that the organization will give to individuals to become effective in what they can, or might be able to do.

Sadly, many organizations actually ignore the key needs of people in change situations. Ask Robyn Allan, who took charge of the Insurance Corporation of British Columbia, a loss-making organization stuck in a downward spiral. This is what she says of the importance of matching the needs of people to the organization: 'The economic order should be designed to support people's dreams and desires rather than, as is so often the case today, asking people to support the economic order at the expense of self-respect, self-determination, freedom and creative expression ... Fulfilled people will be the cause that brings about a healthy and vibrant economy.'

The top ten personal needs

So what do internal customers need and want? The list below (updated from my previous book, *Managing your internal customers*) provides a guide to the top ten personal needs of internal customers. A glance through any magazine or guide to human resources will quickly show that these are the issues commonly handled by the human resources department. However, while these top ten needs provide the golden key to the hearts and minds of internal customers, all too often human resources tackles these issues as separate parts of the jigsaw.

The good thing about the issues on this top ten list is that they are important to the business as well as to the internal customer. What has tended to happen, however, is that only the tangible benefits to the business have been emphasized. If recruitment is working, for example, then costs must be lower, right? *Yes, and* the emotional capital of the individual involved has been increased. This is as important, perhaps even more so, than any immediate cost savings for the business. It is this double whammy that makes our top ten list so powerful.

The top ten list is like the top ten of the record charts. The list changes, all the time. The record chart's list is compiled through record sales. Internally, this is the same as compiling quantitative data from an attitude survey for the whole organization. Like the charts, it is OK to play the most popular tune frequently; the majority of people want to hear it. And they will want to hear it again and again, until *they* are tired of it, not the organization (there is always the danger that bosses, the 'message makers' who deliver the tune, become bored as they have usually been 'listening' to it far longer). Yet a top ten is made up not of an amorphous mass of buyers, but of *individuals*. It is individuals who buy the records and want to hear their 'favorite tune'.

The time may come when organizations need to completely change their top ten list. Bubbling under the surface and about to explode into the charts are the tunes that 'Generation X,' a new group of 'twenty-something' employees, want to hear. These are tunes that say the organization is there simply to fund their lifestyle outside of work. This is a new group that is committed to balance in their lives, even at the expense of success in their jobs.

This will pose a huge threat to organizations. Why? The downsized organization of today relies on committed people who work long hours and give up their time and energy thinking and working for the business. They are motivated by the prospect of advancement or, in a sad number of cases, the fear of losing their job or reaching a plateau.

Times change. The next generation has been brought up without knowing hardship, and even if they have, they still have access to material possessions their parents could only dream about or read about in science fiction. In short, there are few social or even moral codes wrapped around succeeding in business or a profession for this next generation of internal customers.

We are currently investigating the implications of this 'me-ism' on whether and by how much it affects the rest of the top ten needs. As the list below shows, the ten most common needs of the 'thirty-,' 'forty-,' and 'fifty-something' generation of internal customers is very work-related and goal-oriented.

The 'top ten personal needs' for internal customers of the 1990s often consist of the following (although not always in this order):

1   recruitment
2   induction
3   leadership
4   training and development
5   future and security
6   career
7   involvement in change
8   reward and recognition
9   quality of work and environment
10   communication.

The next section will examine why this list is the basis for finding the reasons to create buy-in, and raise an individuals drive (emotional capital) to contribute (intellectual capital) to the organization. It's important!

1. Recruitment

Recruitment into a new job, or into a new internal position, is a very important personal need – but only if you haven't got a job (or you haven't got the job you want) *or* there aren't enough people in your team or department to do the work (the result of downsizing gone wrong). If this is the case then obviously recruitment goes to the top of your list of personal needs.

Many organizations focus on this area as a key plank of their internal marketing. Recruiting new staff is critical, especially in high turnover industries, or in environments hampered by skills shortages.

The quality of recruitment is becoming even more critical as knowledge management is recognized as the main driver of organizations for the future and key people are now seen as the foundation of knowledge. Attracting these key people is vital. If the way that people are recruited works, if people feel good about the organization before they start, if good people are attracted, and if recruitment costs are lower because it is successfully meeting the needs of the right potential employee, then this process must add value to the business.

The Price Waterhouse *K Factor* with its equation of new recruits joining and other people leaving will be affected by the quality of recruitment. This is especially the case for organizations with high turnovers such as professional services or more obvious ones such as catering. Here, the *K Factor* could include people who are joining and leaving in the same year. In some service industries a turnover of up to 300% is not uncommon. Reducing this figure is obviously important to businesses in this sector and to the individuals joining the business.

2. Induction

How many organizations can honestly say that they promote and package their induction programs as part of an internal marketing mix to ensure the satisfaction and delight of new internal customers, whether they are new to a job or new to the company?

The international polling organization, MORI, helps to answer this question. In 1997, it reported:

'Over one in five full-time employees have never been told formally what their job entails. This was the result of research among the UK workforce that also revealed a similar number only had a verbal description of their job content.

'Employees need to recognize a clear direction and be given performance feedback. These findings therefore reveal potential for improvements in the job description area in many companies.'

If recruiting new internal customers is as vital as recruiting new external customers, then it is obvious that the retention of customers, be they internal or external, is even more important.

A total customer experience is the goal of all organizations. Research by Ford Motor Co. for example, says that people buy their next car because of the way they are handled during the post-sale relationship such as servicing, purchasing spares, etc. The same is true internally. And nothing is more important than first impressions. Everyone is taught this in customer service training. The same principle holds true with internal customers. Induction into an organization creates first and lasting impressions.

Even those organizations with some form of induction program could do much to improve the experience for the employee. Does the new internal customer get a targeted, branded, personalized, exciting induction pack, or a boring tome? Do they get a career file with a personal development section and a guide to help them develop themselves for the future? Or do they simply get 'thrown in at the deep end'? Do they join but soon have to leave? Imagine the impact on an individual experiencing in short succession recruitment, induction and redundancy. The impact on future employment will be considerable. An example from the letters section of a management magazine shows how bad experiences only lead to more defensive and distrusting future employees (see Box 4.1).

What of the intellectual capital and emotional capital lost with this executive and others like him? What of the impact on the *K Factor*? Although this man's unfortunate experience probably had much to do with external market factors, it is significant that

---

Box 4.1   Lessons for survival

'I'd been employed quite happily as a sales manager by an international oil company for nine years when I was approached via a third party, for discussions with an established organization that wished to enter the metal working fluids market. Four months down the line [after joining] the [new] company decided to withdraw activities in this sector, making three executives redundant.

'In my own case I had given up share options and frozen my pension. I was made redundant with none of the safeguards I had previously held.

'I would suggest that anyone who is headhunted should negotiate a minimum 12 months salary payable for the first year or less of employment. This would ease some of the problems for the individual should the unthinkable happen due to poor management decisions or strategy.'

---

the 'real' cause is perceived to be poor management and leadership. This issue of leadership, number three on the *top ten list*, is of equal priority to internal customers and their organizations.

3. Leadership

Much value is placed on leadership. Once again however, it seems that the way that leadership is viewed is that it is something the organization must do *'to'* people – give strong leadership. It is seen as an organizational need; strong leadership is vital if the organization is to meet its goals. This mentality is evident in a host of businesses and while it is still very positive is illustrated by Johnson and Johnson's definition of leadership on the Internet (see Box 4.2).

Box 4.2   Leadership at Johnson & Johnson

'We recognize the responsibility of leadership – in the market-place and in the world community.

'The value system set forth in Our Credo reflects our heritage as a company committed to producing quality health care products while responding to community needs ... Our Credo has become the foundation of the company's values, and a force for binding together our world-wide organization.'

Source: home page – This is Johnson & Johnson, www.jnj.com

Paradoxically, leadership is rarely seen as a need of people. Yet MCA has found that leadership often tends to be placed near the top of the list. In plain language, leadership is all about good bosses, people who meet the needs of the individual in whatever form he or she requires. It is about time that organizations realize there is a bottom-up need for leadership, not solely a top-down organizational need.

There are no ideal leaders. In whatever way they are seen, in whatever way they behave and interact with their internal customers and other stakeholders, leaders play a critical role in meeting the needs of individuals.

People want clear leadership. Real leadership will almost always involve providing a strong vision of the future; a strong set of values by which to operate; a clear purpose and a sense of being available when asked. When organizations are asked for these, they have a remit to deliver. Suddenly visions, missions, values, goals, targets, management by wandering about (MBWA) acquire new credibility because the internal customer has *asked* for them. Suddenly, these concepts and practices do not have to be *imposed*. Meeting the needs of internal customers is so much easier than trying to *force them* to want something that the organization sees as beneficial.

The power of internal marketing to help fuse individual and organization needs can best be described in the old adage: 'let them think they thought of it in the first place'. And guess what? Most of the time, internal customers will have already come up with *whatever* the organization thinks it should do. This does not mean, however, that every issue must be debated. What is most important is that the organization is seen to be listening. Good leaders take advice – all the time. Why shouldn't they listen more to internal customers?

Strong leadership is what people *want*. Internal customers are far more likely to give their buy-in when they feel they have been consulted. An additional benefit is that listening usually adds real polish to the thought processes of leaders and supplies them with some original thinking too. By approaching leadership as a bottom-up need as well as a top-down need, leaders benefit, employees benefit and the organization benefits.

The second major benefit of strong leadership is that it has a direct impact on the emotional capital of a business. As Gary Hamel and C.K.L. Prahalad argue in *Competing for the future*, leadership is about emotion: 'It is senior management's responsibility to imbue ... work with a higher purpose than a pay check. The appeal to emotion as well as intellect must be based on more than the prospect of personal financial gain.'

This 'appeal to emotion' is the reason why charismatic leaders like Jack Welch, Lee Iacocca, Ross Perot, John Harvey Jones and Sir Colin Marshall are able to have such a powerful effect on tens of thousands of people. People want their leaders to move and inspire them. Their strength of feeling about their leaders often provides a strong indicator as to the emotional capital held in an organization.

Leadership is not just an internal issue, however. It also has a huge potential impact on the external personality and reputation of a business. Strong leaders command almost unimaginable sway over the feelings of external audiences. In the UK for example, the former head of the Royal Mail, Bill Cockburn, joined WH Smith, Britain's largest news store. Just one year later, he left. The day after, the headlines in *The Times* reported: '£99 million wiped off WH Smith's share price'. Because leadership is about emotion, one man can have the influence to affect nearly £100 million.

This is not just an isolated situation. Every leadership move is watched by analysts to assess the impact on the businesses concerned. What happens when Steve Jobs rejoins Apple? What would happen if Bill Gates were to leave Microsoft? What would happen if Anita Roddick left The Body Shop?

Does one man or woman hold the same degree of intellectual capital? No, even though he or she may have quantities of knowledge about the organization and its business sector and markets. Leaders do, however, hold in their hearts 'priceless' emotional capital. One man or woman *can* alter the destiny of a whole organization. It is not what they know – what matters is what they feel, believe, sense, intuit, desire, want, fight for and give their all for. It is these traits that drive the stock and share price externally, and also drive the organization forward (or sometimes backward).

People's need for leaders is not just for those at the top of organizations. Countless studies on leadership, including MCA's, reveal that local leaders are more important to people than corporate leaders. Internal customers are more prepared to listen to the views of local leaders. They also believe that these leaders are better at listening to them compared to senior people.

Perhaps because organizations view leadership as a top-down need, leaders often appear remote to their 'followers'. For example, during the MCA research study, one employee commented: 'I don't even know who my boss is, never mind being listened to. I haven't spoken to a manager for 18 months.' In his 'empowered' organization, everyone was too 'busy' to communicate! If you knew which organization it was, you would be shocked. The global company's external 'image' is one of a caring, sharing business. Internally their score for the effectiveness of their internal marketing and communication is 1 out of 10!

When organizations approach leadership as a bottom-up need, their practices and priorities change. For example, because the local leader is so important to internal customers, the focus changes to delivering listening and involving processes through the local manager and supervisor. Team briefing processes are based on this approach; unfortunately many fail to cater for the needs of internal customers because the manager is in *tell* and *sell* mode and is not listening in order to get *buy in*.

Let's get positive again, let's assume individual internal customers are feeling good. Their need for recruitment, induction, a good boss and strong leadership has been met. These needs slip back down the charts. What comes up the charts? Unless anything exceptional occurs, such as a huge downsizing program or a merger that will affect their future and career (which of course is happening everywhere) people's next strongest need is about being able to do a good job. How do they do that? By being trained.

4. Training and development

In the past, training and development were something the organization did to you, the employee. You were put on training courses to be trained. Why? Not for your benefit, but in order to be able to deliver what the organization sold. Once you could 'deliver' what was required, your training was finished.

Next came development. You were developed to enhance your abilities for future roles. Why? In order to move up the organizational ladder – but only because the organization needed you to fill the vacant slots made by others moving up the ladder. Like leadership, training was primarily perceived by organizations as a top-down need.

Now things are different. Individuals now take responsibility for their own training and development. Yet individuals have always known they needed training and developing. These activities have always been high on many people's top ten personal needs – if only because they enable individuals to be successful at what they do. Pride is a great emotion that drives people's needs, wants and desires. However, now that individuals are responsible for planning and organizing their own skills and knowledge, training and development is even more of a personal need than before, both at an intellectual and emotional level.

The rapid pace of change has sharpened people's need for training and development. The latest indications in the field of knowledge management suggests that the knowledge of an individual has a 'half life' of approximately three years. In other words, only half of what you know will be of use in that time. With greater job insecurity, with flatter organizations and fewer promotional opportunities, as well as the need simply to keep up, training and development are likely to stay 'high in the charts.'

The good news is that growing numbers of organizations are now recognizing that training and development is also a bottom-up need. As well as using these activities as a tool for developing the business' knowledge capabilities, these organizations also see it is a way of delivering added value to their internal customers.

Ford's UK business, for example, allows its internal customers to opt for training in areas unrelated to their jobs. This arrangement sends a clear message that the organization acknowledges the right of its employees to set their own learning agenda. Ford began this controversial program, called the *Employee Development Assistance Program* in the 1980s. The program provides a cash amount for all employees to learn new skills outside those required for their particular job. The greatest challenge faced by Ford when introducing the program was in marketing a scheme that was viewed with great cynicism. Once staff accepted the scheme, it took hold.

Rover runs a similar scheme to Ford. Unipart, the motor spares organization with a strong reputation in the UK for employee involvement goes one better. It runs the Unipart U, a 'university' where anyone can learn, train themselves and develop new skills. The organization invests heavily in training and development in order to meet the top ten personal needs of its internal customers.

Training and development is of growing importance to employees and organizations alike as a bottom-up need. The exciting part is that this profound change is being helped along by the Internet. Individuals and organizations now have access to the world's largest databank of training material, best practices, knowledge, information, experts, and a host of learning opportunities in and around every job and profession.

More and more professionals from every sector of business are taking advantage of this amazing resource. The latest research on the Internet shows that it is currently used, not by computer boffins as is often thought, but by high income earners. These users have training and development high on their list of personal needs and are a promising indication of how internal customers can increasingly meet this fourth personal need for themselves.

Dynamic companies are also recognizing the rich opportunities offered both by the Internet and its internal counterpart, the Intranet. They can now set up virtual universities, schools, training facilities, centers of excellence, knowledge centers, best practice centers, giving their employees access to incredible sources of information. Organizations like Bass Brewers, Eli Lilly and most major companies across the globe are beginning to ensure that everyone in the organization is able to access their Intranets. Many also encourage learning through the Intranet because they recognize the power, not just for the company but for its people. Levi Strauss, for example, has its own Web site, where it hails users with the call: 'This is it: www.levi.com. There's only one rule. Be original. Other than that, just be yourself. Hopefully you're both.'

Oracle is now confident of the global potential of electronic learning. In the company's annual report, Chairman and CEO Lawrence J. Ellison, boldly stated: 'Only a low-cost and convenient device like the Network Computer will enable worldwide plans to spread literacy, education, and communication through computer access. Network Computers, coupled with the Internet global network, can create a network economy and, yes, a network community.'

With all this training under their belt, people now have a big WIIFM. They can 'be themselves' and market themselves to others. They now know they have the tools to build a future, and greater security for their personal life. These are the next top ten needs.

5. Future and security

This is one of the top ten personal needs that has undergone the most change in the last decade.

Apart from the downward economic swing at the beginning and end of the 1980s, job security was not high on internal customers' top ten list of personal needs. In fact the opposite was the case in some parts of the UK. One regional area, for example, had a 2% unemployment rate. Recruiting people was impossible. It was a seller's market. Organizations needed people; they were a critical resource as job and skills shortages were endemic in the boom time. Our consultancy even ran one campaign for an international oil company which invested over $400,000 on 'getting and keeping the right people'. Things have changed!

Redundancy, downsizing, rightsizing, delayering, computer-ization, total quality programs, business process re-engineering (BPR), automation, robotics, supply chain management, and any other management strategies, processes and tools you can add, have all had a massive impact on the numbers of people now needed in organizations.

By the 1990s, people were no longer a core part of the pro-duction mix. Technology and the information age linked to computers – not people – had arrived. This dramatic change is summarized in the equation below:

The 75% Turnaround in 100 Years

1900
Farmworker + Laborers + Craft = approx. 75%

2000
Service + Clerical + Sales + Managerial + Professional = approx. 75%

Technology has taken away the production role from people. As organizations went through downsizing to become 'lean or-ganizations,' they also used technology to do the same in the information-handling roles. Job losses hit the headlines as Big People Reductions came with BPR.

Unsurprisingly, as the reduction in the percentage of people required to produce things AND manage things accelerated, the concern for jobs and security also accelerated. But not every-where. The Pacific rim was growing (and still is, although the bubble is bursting in places) and many organizations were suc-ceeding in growing too.

Future and security remains high on many people's top ten list. For a time, at the beginning of the 1990s, companies were working hard using a *push* strategy of communication to transfer responsibility for future and career to individuals. The major changes in society, and the fact that everyone seems to know someone who has lost their job, have ensured that people are beginning to recognize their responsibility.

Words like 'loyalty' have been replaced by words like 'commitment' by both individuals and organizations. But this does not mean that people don't want help from the organization when it comes to providing for the future. People would much rather choose to leave, than be told to leave. Therefore, if an organization can demonstrate that it is doing everything in its power to provide a future for an individual, giving them some degree of security in their job, then the payback will be given in commitment.

Few people now expect loyalty for 'services rendered', or even length of service. What people can expect is that if an organization is successful, if it is good at delivering its promise of rewarding people with jobs where possible, and as long as the people are capable, then commitment becomes a two-way street.

As the section on training and development emphasized, the knowledge worker of today is beginning to recognize that it is their unique knowledge that continues to provide them with a future and security. What's fascinating is that an additional dimension has now come into play. Emotional capability or emotional intelligence, as defined by Goleman *et al.* is becoming a critical differentiator. So says a US study reported in the *Financial Times* (see Box 4.3) and included in my latest book,

Passion at Work, to highlight the need for developing people's ability to communicate and relate to others.

Future and security are key concerns because people can't see into the future. Now, however, they are doing something about it by equipping themselves for life. They do not want to be at the mercy of the organization. They now look to develop themselves by planning and developing their own career, the next top ten personal need.

Box 4.3   It's your attitude that counts

'A US study finds qualifications are not a top priority for employers.

'In today's labor markets it is often assumed the main concern of employers is to recruit staff with the education needed for the increasingly skilled jobs available. But top academic qualifications are not the first consideration for companies.

'Much more important it seems, is to have "the right attitude." Not far behind in their list is that staff should have the right communication skills.

'When you consider hiring a new non-supervisory or production worker how important are the following in your decision to hire?

Applicant Characteristic	*Score – out of 5*
Applicant's attitude	4.6
Applicant's communication skills	4.2
Previous work experience	4.0
Recommendations from current employees	3.4

Source: *EQW National Employers Survey,* University of Pennsylvania. Quoted in the *Financial Times,* Spring 1997.

6. Career

Future and security are not the same as a career. Just as organizations are finding it difficult to offer a long-term future and security, offering a career to individuals is equally difficult. Flat structures diminish career opportunities. When the number of levels in an organization comes down from as many as 16 to three or four, as is the case in a petrochemical giant in the 80s, then moving up the company ladder can be a slow business.

Yet just because career opportunities are no longer as obvious or available as previously, this does not stop ambitious people from wanting a career. A career can be very high on the top ten of personal needs

Both individuals and organizations are recognizing that if the prospects look bleak up above, then there may be better prospects sideways, or indeed outwards. As more areas of business become outsourced, and more individuals become freelancers, a business can provide career opportunities, not within, but *around* the organization.

7. Involvement in change

We have come a long way since the days that involvement was low on an organization's agenda. Then, managers were paid to develop and think; workers were paid to deliver and not think, and most important of all, not to communicate. Things have changed; delayering has now gotten rid of the 'permafrost' of non-communicating managers. Now everyone is a communicator, everyone has a voice, and organizations recognize they cannot survive without everyone being involved.

Involving everyone, however, requires a degree of empowerment and autonomy. People no longer want to be told what to
do. They demand to be involved and to have their ideas and
views taken seriously. However, here is the crunch. Imagine
you have been badly recruited; your induction was lousy; you
think your boss has no idea how to manage; you feel that there
is very little training and development on offer; your career structure is unclear; your future is looking dubious and you do not
feel secure.

With all of these issues high on your list of top ten personal
needs, how likely are you to want to give your all? How much
are you likely to want to be involved in all the initiatives, programs and changes to the organization? Clearly not a lot.

The level of failure of change programs is legendary. Why?
Look to the top ten personal needs and the answer becomes
obvious. Who would want to be involved when they do not feel
as though the organization is interested in them? Where is the
'what's in it for me'?

Now imagine the opposite. Great recruitment; great induction; great boss and leadership; great training and development;
great future and security; great career opportunities in and around
the organization. People's response? 'What was it that you wanted
me to get involved in?' Try holding someone back who feels
they have a huge level of emotional commitment from an organization.

Do you have a team like this one, described by Fred Wiersama?
He recounts the outstanding success of the company's new productivity program: 'The GE Plastics performance team works
side by side with its customers to design solutions, and put
them into practice. Results? GE Plastics' productivity program
saved its customers more than $68 million in 1995 alone while
GE Plastics experienced an 11 percent increase in revenue.'

You can bet that these GE Plastics employees felt the organization was meeting their personal needs. GE Plastics' success

shows that working alongside customers and getting everyone involved in developing the business can only occur if people feel good about how they are treated by the organization.

8. Reward and recognition

Reward and recognition are two different aspects of remuneration. Reward involves financial or other tangible incentives; recognition involves emotional reward for a job well done. PepsiCo understands the importance of both, as noted in their most recent annual report (see Box 4.4).

Clearly, organizations spend a great deal of time ensuring that their reward packages are in line with their competitors and that they deliver suitable recompense for services rendered. Organizations that value the contribution of their people often demonstrate their commitment by concentrating on reward. Why? In addition to money, bonuses and the like are also a form of recognition in their own right.

Reward is plainly a critical aspect of the total return which an individual gets from a company. However, if you follow the

---

Box 4.4   The PepsiCo challenge: people

'... The people who make, move, sell and service our products have the power to make customers smile. Boosting their capability, loyalty and enthusiasm will work wonders. We need to make PepsiCo an even more attractive, humanistic place to work by offering challenging jobs and good pay, of course. But also by making sure we treat our front-line people with even more dignity and respect and by recognizing the enormous contribution they make to our success.'

Source: Pepsico Annual Report, 1996.

gospel according to Maslow, financial reward is only one of several factors that matter to individuals. Pay will, at its basic level, provide for a level of physical security. Once people's physical needs are taken care, then Maslow argues that psychological factors begin to take hold.

Frederick Hertzberg also attaches limited importance to financial reward. He simply classed reward as a 'hygiene factor.' In other words, people only notice pay when it isn't up to scratch. Both these psychology gurus help show that reward is not a positive motivator, it is mainly a lower order need on the hierarchy of needs.

Businesses should remember the theory of Maslow and Hertzberg more often. Time and again, I encounter situations where senior managers think that employee dissatisfactions revolve around pay. However, an analysis of the top ten personal needs of employees often reveals a quite different picture. It is my fundamental belief that so long as a basic reward package has been agreed, internal customers perceive recognition as more important. It is the emotional needs around recognition which help drive motivation and buy-in.

Such was the case for Midland, a UK bank. In the late 1980s, the bank was spending over £6 million on an *internal* reward scheme. However, when asked about their top ten personal needs, the majority of people said they simply wanted 'to hear my manager say "well done!"'. The real issue was not pay, but recognition (along with this, the internal customers wanted training in order to help them do their jobs).

Midland saved over £4 million by introducing a performance management program that showed managers the best practices for recognizing success. The bank's experience suggests that an investment in management skills should be a fundamental part of dealing with pay issues, i.e. too much is paid to compensate for poor leadership.

Incentives are only really needed once people are providing *extra* worth, i.e. on top of what they have agreed to do for the pay they earn. This occurs when they help deliver significant business improvements or innovations (unless they are in R&D). For example, if people improve quality or innovation and help deliver better business results, they naturally expect to earn more if it is above and beyond the call of duty. Reward should matter only when people really are delivering above expectations.

All too often, the opposite is true. Incentives are used to motivate average performers when their other needs are not being met and the organization is effectively failing them. Too often incentive schemes are introduced to replace poor management motivation. They don't. They also create major problems for those who don't receive the incentives. On top of this, the levels of expectation for reward rise higher and higher. As Dickens' orphan boy, Oliver Twist, said, 'please sir, can I have some more'!

9. Quality of work and environment

There was a time reminiscent of the Charlie Chaplin movie, *Modern Times*, when routine work throughout an organization was the norm. Even management jobs were routine and simply involved looking after large numbers of people. Although the quality of work and the environment in which people worked was important, this issue rarely reached the top ten of personal needs. Workers knew they just had to 'get on with it', while managers concerned themselves with 'pleasing the boss' and moving up the company ladder.

Now we are in a situation where technology has removed much of the routine from all levels of jobs. And technology has removed many of the managers too! Computers now carry out routine administration and management functions. Robotics now perform mundane and repetitive physical work. Just think of the difference between a line of workers producing cars in the past and a line of robots producing cars today.

Today the largest percentage of workers can now be classed as knowledge workers. Technology has not only reduced mundane work and routine, but has also offered these knowledge workers new opportunities. As Jim Shaffer, Principal of Towers Perrin, comments: 'Technology replaced layers of middle management that frequently blocked communication. Now, technology allows anyone with e-mail to move information throughout the organization, posing questions or suggesting new product ideas and getting a direct response.'

Knowing that computers can take the drudge out of work and allow them to be more creative and challenging means that people are no longer willing to accept boring jobs. We move to a situation where people want to feel excited, motivated and passionate about what they do. They want to have fun, enjoy themselves and get a kick out of working.

The process and principles required to ensure that people feel motivated about what they do, why they do it and who they do it for are those of communication and marketing. Getting people excited about the challenges, the opportunities, the problems, the targets, the improvements, the new ideas, the relationships in and around the organization, is a marketing and communication task.

Professional communicators are rising to the challenge. So are many more businesses taking steps to ensure their people enjoy their jobs and are motivated by the quality of communication throughout the organization.

For example, people are leaping at the challenge of producing exciting home pages and material for the Intranet for example. More and more departments, functions and teams are holding events of one kind or another. Greater team working, team learning, more and more empowerment, greater opportunities for feedback – these are all signs of wanting to give everyone in an organization the opportunity to be involved and therefore create a greater sense of enjoyment of their work.

Great, but what if the other needs of individuals are not met? Will people be ready and willing to buy-in to these commendable processes? Perhaps not. Enriching people's work and environment, especially through communication, is the correct solution, but the timing has to be right. Organizations with the right timing will get the right results.

Peter Senge emphasizes the readiness of people over processes. In *The Fifth Discipline Fieldbook,* he declares: 'Ultimately, the most compelling reason for building a learning organization is because we want to work in one. Or because there is nothing we would rather be doing with our lives right now than building a learning organization.'

And now we are almost there! Communication may be last on the list but when it comes, look out! When people say they *want* better communication, they do not want better communication *per se*; they want to know what is going on, and they want to take part in it – whatever it is.

Look out when people say the problem is poor communication. The real problem is almost certainly that they do not feel part of what is happening. Their real need goes beyond involvement and is really a yearning for a sense of ownership and membership in their organization.

10. Communication

From little issues to big issues, communication is the hub that gets the wheel of business moving. Business leaders around the world now recognize the importance of internal communication as a critical success factor. Everyone wants it to deliver better business results, and deliver better personal results. Communication is seen by Anita Roddick, Founder and Chief Executive of The Body Shop, as the lifeblood of her business. 'No matter how passionately you might care or believe in something – if you don't communicate it, you might as well not be there,' argues Roddick.

Growing numbers of business leaders also recognize the destructive power of poor communication. Mary Lewis, Manager at EDS' Corporate Communication division in Dallas, makes the following admission. 'If you don't ever follow through on any of the things that employees say to you in this two-way communication, and then communicate that back out to the workforce, it almost can become a deterrent rather than a help in the communication process.'

Business reasons aside, there are further compelling reasons for effective communication. A recent survey in Management Today highlights communication as the most significant factor in creating stress within managers in organizations; and stress creates issues over health, motivation, morale and the ability to do the job. Improving communication can be a vital means of allowing the individual and the organization to be in harmony.

Communication is a major issue to both individuals and organizations, yet time and again, qualitative and quantitative research into organizations across the globe shows that communication is still considered to be poor (see Box 4.5).

Studies by MORI (Market and Opinion Research International) and ISR (International Research Surveys) reveal that communication in the last twenty years has not only failed to improve, it has actually got worse. This is something of an indictment of the communication industry itself, of some of the communication 'experts' who have failed to deliver, and of organizations who have failed to invest in this area.

Perhaps the reason for this failure is that the internal customer's need for communication is growing stronger, yet this need is complex and intrinsically bound up with the other nine personal needs. The truth is that if organizations did a better job of delivering the other nine personal needs, communication would be much less of a problem!

Box 4.5   Building credibility through communication

Tom Moore wrote the following article summarizing a discussion between leading communication specialists.

'"Two-way communication, always critical for credible internal communication, will become ever more so in the 1990s' company. In the 90s, if an organization is going to succeed, it can't do it without making strategy work through people. How is that going to happen unless there is two-way dialogue?" [says] Paul Sanchez – global communication practice director for Watson Wyatt Worldwide, San Diego.

'Nonetheless, Paul Sanchez says that research done by his company showed that many companies are failing to foster two-way communication between management and employees: Eighty percent of employees say the organization is doing a better job of communicating downward; only three out of 10 employees· say the organization is doing a good job of promoting upward communication. All of the indicators of the best organizations point to the fact that when an organization succeeds you will find good communication; usually, an ingredient of that is good upward communication ...

'"Employees today need communication that will allow them to have some influence over their jobs, and communication that recognizes their contributions" said [Roger] D'Aprix. "Employees are looking for two things today", he said. "One, the ability to influence decisions, and two, some sort of appreciation. Unfortunately, many employee surveys show that employees feel they are not appreciated and nobody acts on their suggestions."'

Source: *Communication World*, September 1996.

Communication needs a message in order for it to be required by organizations. If all the other nine areas of personal need are being communicated and delivered, then the proper processes and tools of communication will have been used. Let me say it again; communication per se is not the problem.

But communication in the other nine areas is not happening. All too often, communication in organizations is simply in *tell* or *sell* mode, delivered in a top-down way through inappropriate media channels.

The top ten and its role in emotional contracts

The top ten personal needs list came from a decade of studying what internal customers say they want, *not* from what organizations say they should give internal customers. Many organizations have used the list to *match* these needs to the messages the organization wants to give. Using a researched list of top ten personal needs to help target communication has helped organizations prevent a number of national strikes and to help deliver huge programs of change; it works. The top ten list is made up of the most powerful tool for the marketer, the WIIFM factor, and is therefore essential in any internal marketing and communication program.

The top ten personal needs provide a powerful measure about the success of an organization in delivering better business results, increased intellectual capital and higher levels of emotional capital.

What is almost as important as the list of top ten personal needs is how each and every one of these is monitored and measured. If these needs really are the key to internal customers wishing to deliver better business results; if they are the key to creating increased intellectual capital and emotional capital then they must form part of the measures of success in delivering the organization's goals.

It is when 'the deal' is put to individuals that the significance of the *top ten needs* comes into play. Here is 'the deal':

> *'We, the organization, will listen to your needs; we will do everything to meet your needs as this will benefit us both. The deal is that as we are listening to your needs – so you listen to our needs.*
>
> *'The deal is that we will MATCH your needs to our needs whenever, and wherever we can. This is a win-win situation.'*

Just think through the implications. Organizations with satisfied internal customers, with high levels of satisfaction on their *top ten personal needs,* will not only deliver better business results, they are likely to do so on lower levels of financial reward. Why? Because nonfinancial reward is its own reward. If this were not the case, everyone would simply move to the highest pay jobs.

If it is to be successful, the living company needs individuals who want to help it grow. The way that the organization creates this buy-in is to help vital stakeholders to grow as well. This is just what individuals want too. By adopting a communication strategy, based on the top ten needs, businesses can show their internal customers that they are willing to meet their needs wherever possible.

Here we have another win–win where people begin to feel good about themselves and the organization. The stocks and value of emotional capital are going up; and people are buying both. What are they going to do with all this knowledge and emotion? They want to be involved with what is going on. They want to contribute to the organization and make a difference. They want to help change things for the better.

The next chapter looks at how organizations can widen this community of switched-on and involved people by addressing the needs of other vital stakeholders around the organization.

Internal marketing becomes a force that works outwards to transform every dimension of a business.

My notes: managing your internal customers

If you define customers as someone having a choice, then employees fit into the category. The trouble was that the scientific management approach, or to put it more crudely the 'top down' approach sees the employee as someone who is there to 'do as they are told'. Why? Because they are paid to 'get on with it'. But they do have a choice; they always did. No amount of pay will 'make' someone do something they don't want to — at least not with the levels of motivation, passion and obsession needed in today's competitive environment. So they have a choice — whether or not to give you their 'hearts and minds'. The secret is to find out how to appeal to the 'what's in it for me' — the WIIFMs.

Thought provokers for the future

This chapter has revealed the top ten personal WIIFMs. You can do these on whole organizations — what are yours?

Place your current personal top ten needs in order — say why.

- *Recruitment*
- *Induction*
- *Leadership*
- *Training and development*
- *Future and security*
- *Career*
- *Involvement in change*
- *Reward and recognition*
- *Quality of work and environment*
- *Communication.*

Your notes

C H A P T E R 5

The Six Dimensions of Marketing-Driven Relationships

Overview

This chapter explains:

- the importance of face-to-face communication and the 'Concern Scale'
- the three internal dimensions and the three external dimensions at work
- the different types of models involved in stakeholder relationships
- the new customer–supplier chain.

F I V E

The Six Dimensions of Marketing-Driven Relationships

Imagine an athlete. Imagine that he or she is looking to take on the world. Before doing so, it's pretty obvious that s/he needs to be fit, well and healthy, not just physically but also mentally and emotionally. But additionally, s/he has to have a sense of inner strength and belief in the ability to deliver – the golden key to success.

Now compare this to organizations that you know. Do they demonstrate the same healthiness, confidence and inner strength? In too many cases, morale and motivation is probably less than world-class standard. Employees have little faith in their ability to deliver and they are constantly obstructed by the inability of one part of the organization to talk to another part. The final drawback is that employees often feel there is no external goal to achieve, that all that matters is what is going on inside the organization.

This type of organizational introspection leads to one conclusion: if the inside isn't working, then the chances of delivering a promise on the outside, in the organization's key markets, remain lower than they could be. Obvious, really.

Healthy, inside and out

If organizations on the marketing and communication time line are at the point of one-to-one lifetime relationships with their external customers, yet they are still telling their internal customers what to do, then we have a mismatch of gigantic proportions! At the simplest level, if senior people are failing to apply relationship marketing to their internal customers, how will this approach ever take root in the organization?

Unless they experience relationship marketing themselves, internal customers are never likely to understand or be motivated enough to use the approach to drive all their dealings with external customers or with other vital stakeholders within and around the organization.

In short, if 'inside in' (the organization talking to itself) isn't working, 'inside out' (the organization talking to customers and others) is even less likely to work. Of course, the business will still achieve certain goals, but at what cost, both to the organization and the people?

These hard won achievements are frequently delivered by using a 'control' approach which relies on various 'sticks and carrots'. Vital services like customer service, complaint handling, technical backup, and after sales and call centers can be made to work through sheer determination and the imposition of processes and policing methods. These are the 'sticks' of the controlling approach. Conversely, incentives and rewards act as 'carrots'. Both approaches are a 'push' strategy – even the carrot tries to push the internal customers into going where they may not want to go.

Wouldn't it be so much easier if instead of having to use a push strategy for cultural change, a pull strategy was the goal? Just like the pull strategy that companies use now with customers, organizations could use internal marketing to embark on a journey where everyone is sharing everything along the way.

This is not fantasy. This is the opportunity that relationship marketing holds out to organizations.

Take the concept of the 'mystery shopper' as an example of how this can be transformed from a 'stick' exercise into a process that encourages people to engage with and learn from the customer. The current stick of the mystery shopper is that if you 'fail' to deliver the required service to the mystery shopper, you will get a bad report – naughty you. If you impress the mystery shopper, you get a carrot in the shape of a prize or plaque, etc.

Why not turn this process into one involving *real* customers? Why not get *everyone* to ask their customers, face to face, in the open with no mystery: 'What's good about the service that I and my organization give?' These are one-to-one relationships. Imagine the impact on your people when they receive a positive or negative response. This approach would create real pull. Internal customers would be motivated to look for ways to improve things if the response was critical, or they would want to share the good news if they and their team/department was praised. Now the organization can recognize success, and help with negative feedback (I did not say the *f word*, failure).

If *inside in* communication can be made to work (and it can by meeting the needs of internal customers*) inside out* communication *will* follow. If employees become internal customers who are treated with the degree of respect that is an integral part of relationship marketing, then the next logical step is to use the power of the organization's internal culture, personality, values and skill to transform its relationships with customers. Internal marketing is the starting point for a program of relationship marketing and lifetime customer relationship management.

How do businesses become marketing-driven and ensure that *inside in* communication begins to work? By recognizing that there are potentially six dimensions of marketing relationships, three within the organization and three around the organization.

These are, internally:

- top-down
- bottom-up
- side-to-side

and externally:

- customers
- stakeholders
- suppliers/strategic alliances.

By focusing on these six dimensions, organizations can move from an introspective, internal focus to an external focus. In the past, the responsibility for marketing and corporate communication stayed with the 'experts'. Now everyone who has contact with a customer or a stakeholder becomes the expert. Every piece of information in relationship marketing is vital. Your people are now your marketing, corporate communications and customer service departments.

The following section examines the six dimensions of marketing relationships.

First and second dimensions: two-way communication

Fig. 5.1   Top-down and bottom-up working together.

In the previous chapter, we discussed the first two dimensions of marketing relationships: top-down and bottom-up communication are two sides of the same coin and need to be treated as an integrated process. As we look at this process in greater detail, this section simply emphasizes the importance of implementing top-down and bottom-up processes that dovetail each other. Organizations need both to define their own needs and those of their internal customers. They need to match these needs, and to express and deliver them in an appropriate style and language.

The pace of change facing businesses has meant that the need for two-way communication has never been so strong. Senior managers need to communicate the ever-evolving goals and strategies of the organization; internal customers need to give feedback about these high-level issues and how best to deliver against them, as well as communicate their own needs and wishes.

But in addition, there is a more basic reason for effective two-way communication. People need other people; people are driven by emotions. If organizations are to develop their intellectual and emotional capital through people, then the strategy for attaining this goal must be to allow people to work in the way they were designed for – by getting together!

Organizations are beginning to recognize that information distributed electronically, by telephone, or by print is no substitute for face-to-face communication.

The famous study by Mohrabian shows the importance of tone of voice and body language compared to the words used in face-to-face communication. He put only 7% importance on the words being said; 38% percent of the effectiveness of the communication came from the tone, speed and pitch of the voice, and a massive 55% came from body language.

Neither body language, nor verbal intonation are delivered in an e-mail, memo, magazine, newspaper, or a home page.

Obviously, video, business television, conferences and road shows attempt to deliver the human element. However, as Chapter 3 highlighted, these forms of communication are all too often used as a corporate *sell*, or even a *tell*.

Face-to-face communication is a crucial component of communication, especially in a situation of change. Elizabeth Kubler-Ross' famous upside-down bell curve shows how people typically respond to change. Their emotions tend to dip down the curve, going from anger, to denial, to rejection and coming back up again to acceptance and integration. Face-to-face communication plays a critical role in this journey. Without 'real' talk, especially between managers and their teams, how can organizations expect their people to move through this emotional curve? Face-to-face communication is even more critical, given that many employees are now faced with not just one change, but many, each happening one after another.

Communicating major change is often a difficult, perhaps unpleasant task for many managers, yet it must be done openly and in person. Unfortunately, many managers are using technology to shirk this responsibility.

'Firms implement e-mail to improve communication and productivity,' says networking giant Novell. 'But 36 percent of people use e-mail to avoid face-to-face contact. Managers hide behind e-mail and use it for people management.'

Novell estimates that the ensuing morale and performance problems could cost a medium size enterprise an average £182,000 per year, totaling an estimated cost of £106 billion to the UK economy.

Without face-to-face communication, people inside organizations get stuck in anger, denial and rejection. No matter how painful a proposed change, people are far more likely to accept it when they have an opportunity to question their bosses, voice their feelings, especially their fears and concerns, and discuss the options available to them. The importance of face-to-face contact in important top-down/ bottom-up communication is surely commonsense!

Tackling the concerns of internal customers head on through face-to-face communication can be a rewarding strategy. Below is an example of how the UK's Inland Revenue communicated change through implementing one of the largest change programs ever to be seen in the country (Box 5.1).

Box 5.1   Communicating change in the UK's tax authority

The Inland Revenue was in the midst of an internal revolution. Faced with severe cuts in public spending, the Inland Revenue has taken the lead in improving its efficiency through a change program that the *Financial Times* had said would 'rival the most ambitious private sector corporate re-engineering projects'.

Part of this change involved a fundamental shift in the way tax in the UK was assessed. Historically, UK taxpayers had their taxes assessed for them by the Inland Revenue. In the early 1990s, the Revenue began moving to a more 'do-it-yourself' model much like the US system where a large number of tax payers conduct their own self assessment.

The myriad of complex changes facing the Inland Revenue were enormous and would affect all employees. The changes included outsourcing the IT department to the computer company EDS, relocating offices, dramatically reducing staff numbers, reducing management layers and changing the nature of jobs – all of this affecting more than 68,000 employees in over 1,100 locations.

Vital to the success of these changes was the ability of staff to understand the change and adopt new team-based and 'empowered' roles. This required a substantial cultural shift, which could not be achieved without radical changes to the internal communication strategy, processes and style.

As in many organizations, the Revenue's culture did not encourage the free flow of information. Managers and supervisors had tended to use knowledge as power; something not to be given away. However, a more open style of communication was essential if Revenue employees were to buy-in to all the proposed changes. The challenge for the Revenue was to develop more open communication in a sceptical, tough environment that had a history of very traditional top-down, autocratic communication.

MCA worked with the Revenue to develop its new communication strategy, which then helped drive a major training program. The first task was an extensive program of internal market research to identify the areas where the Revenue needed different forms of communication, to explore the need for involvement and to determine the appropriate communication vehicles.

Tackling the WIIFM

One of the most important objectives of this work was to win over managers to the need for different types of communication. They also needed to understand that these different types of communication depended on how worried or concerned staff were about what was going to happen. Employees especially needed to know how the changes would affect them personally the WIIFM factor or more correctly 'what *isn t* in it for me!'.

Building on one of the Revenue's own models of communication, we introduced the *Concern Scale*. This model, seen below, hinges on the tremendous importance of face-to-face communication, either within a group or between the individual and his or her line manager, as a means of helping people buy-in to change.

The Concern Scale, as shown opposite, formed part of the Revenue's program of introducing the new communication strategy and tactics and was used in management workshops with

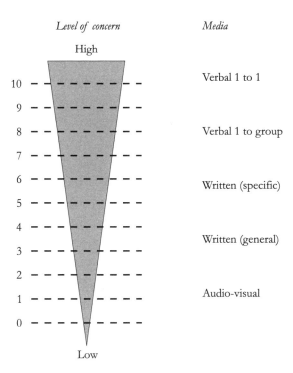

Level of concern	*Media*
High	
10	Verbal 1 to 1
9	
8	Verbal 1 to group
7	
6	Written (specific)
5	
4	
3	Written (general)
2	
1	Audio-visual
0	
Low	

The Concern Scale

over 9000 managers. It showed managers the need for face-to-face, two-way communication and heralded the introduction of MCA's involvement process called Team Listening®. (This process will be described in detail under the heading of involvement in Chapter 6.)

Understandably, before agreeing to a roll-out to all 68,000 staff, the Revenue's senior management needed evidence that such a major change of approach would succeed. One particular concern was that middle managers were unlikely to buy-in when they themselves were under great pressure and stress. They therefore conducted a pilot program, which quickly revealed that the process could and did work; in just three months, 67% of people in the pilot areas believed communication had improved.

The following excerpt is from an article that appeared in *Insight*, the Revenue's business journal for staff, and shows the level of commitment from the Board to two-way communication: 'The communication pilot has shown that *Insight* (the business journal driving the two-way communication process) and Team Listening improve the overall effectiveness of management communication. In response to your views, the Board has decided to extend the project gradually to allow for the improvements you've suggested. These include more openness, faster responses to questions and a reduction in paper from Head Office.'

Thanks to two-way, face-to-face communication processes, meetings between Revenue line managers and their teams are no longer briefings. Briefings do not work because they are stuck in either *tell* or *sell* mode. Listening does work – it's psychological commonsense really!

The Revenue's change program is a continuing success and is often used as a communication benchmark.

(Team Listening is a registered trademark of The Marketing & Communication Agency Limited.)

The Inland Revenue example (Box 5.1) helps show that face-to-face communication processes, whether they are Team Listening, workshops, focus groups, lunch with the boss, or skip-level meetings, help get people together and ultimately, have considerably more effect than distributed media.

Bringing people together is a strategy of success. Bringing people together to work on the most important top-down issues and priorities requires them to add their own value. When people are involved in a two-way debate or discussion, they want to deliver the products and services which meet the needs of the organization and its customers.

Once people understand and buy-in to the top-down goals and once the organization has understood people's bottom-up needs, then getting on with the business becomes the next strategic imperative. For this a new form of communication and internal marketing is required: side-to-side.

Third dimension: side-to-side communication

Individuals, teams, departments, divisions, companies – people sitting next to each other or across the globe working together to give added value

Side-to-side communication comes through creating the processes, tools, and skills of communication and internal marketing that allow everyone in the organization to engage with everyone else. Effective side-to-side communication ensures, in short, that everyone sings from the *same* hymn/song sheet.

An exciting book, *Internal Markets*, expresses the essence of the new philosophy entering the workplace. This book, which gives many case-studies and benchmark examples drawn from the private and public sector of the US, is written by Professor William Halal, Dr Ali Geranmeyeh and John Pourdehnad. They comment: 'Internal markets carry today's evolution of management thought to its logical conclusion by providing a broader conceptual foundation based on the principles of free enterprise; complete internal-market economies that bring all the advantages of free markets *inside* large organizations, just like external economies.'

What does this mean, 'free markets inside large organizations?' This is in fact the crux of side-to-side communication within organizations. In simple terms, everyone is a supplier. Everyone has customers. Everyone is responsible for their own internal marketing. As *Internal markets* shows, the same is true on a larger scale – from teams, to departments, to divisions, to separate companies – all are marketing to each other.

Side-to-side communication involves communication between peers. It therefore requires individuals to get their peers on board, rather than to use a *tell* or *sell* mode. When *buy-in* becomes a key factor, it plainly makes sense to base side-to-side communication on marketing principles.

The concept of internal markets, of internal customers, of everyone being responsible for helping deliver a quality product, is the new strategy for side-to-side communication. And if a quality product or service is not delivered by you, the supplier, someone else will. Such is the new internal market philosophy that is currently driving the trend towards outsourcing.

Side-to-side internal marketing and communication needs to occur at every level in an organization, with:

- individuals taking responsibility for marketing themselves, their products and services to their teams and other departments
- teams taking responsibility for marketing themselves to other teams and other departments
- departments taking responsibility for marketing themselves to their division and other divisions
- divisions taking responsibility for marketing themselves to other divisions and other key players along the customer-supplier chain.

As a *Marketing Week* article, quoted in Box 5.2, makes clear, a key benefit of side-to-side communication is cross-functional integration. This form of integration is increasingly being sought

Box 5.2   High-tech companies lead the way in internal marketing

'There was a time when internal communication might, at best, have been a corporate newsletter or, at worst the company grapevine. Marketing was regarded as something you did externally, and it was often the case that sophisticated external activities appeared to co-exist happily with internal marketing efforts that were stuck in a sixties time-warp.

'Recently established hi-tech organizations are cited by many as models for effective internal marketing: their leaner, flatter structure helps to keep lines of communication clear.

'According to Dr Gil McWilliam of the London Business School, another factor comes into play: cross-functional integration. "Companies such as the newer, smaller IT firms intuitively market internally because they are smaller and staffed by like minded people, making communication that much easier. When these companies start to grow and become filled with financial or marketing bureaucrats, they might have to change," says McWilliam. "Companies then inevitably go through a period of specialization, resulting in a loss of functional silos. Then you can have turf wars," she adds.

'For larger, role-based organizations with defined functional specialisms, the challenge of internal marketing is a tough one and it is to these companies' credit that they are now starting to adapt. While they cannot always get rid of functional specialization simply because of their size, they are now realizing that making internal communications more of a two-way street can only help them to compete.

Source: *Marketing Week*, 9 April 1997.

as companies recognize that narrow functional thinking is diminishing their creativity and ability to innovate. *Marketing Week* shows how young, entrepreneurial IT firms are pointing the way ahead through one-to-one communication and marketing – and need to beware of slipping into functional thinking as they expand and recruit more specialized staff.

A 'two-way street' is another definition of a customer-supplier chain, and where you have customers you have marketing. Side-to-side internal marketing is the key to everyone creating the desires, passion and other emotions of emotional capital; and using them to drive the knowledge and intellectual assets of an organization.

For a view on how you can deliver buy-in and create greater levels of emotion, like passion, in a one-to-one situation, please read the sister book to this one, *Passion At Work*. It is a 'how to' develop the personal skills and tools to improve on what I call 'interrelationship marketing' with everyone at work, and it is a lot of fun.

Quality is a two-way street (that runs side-to-side)

When everyone is engaged in delivering the goods and services together, not separately or despite each other, the outcome is better business results. Customers truly get what they want, when they want it, and most importantly – how they want it. They are dealing with an organization that is singing off the same song sheet.

Does this sound like the beginnings of a definition about quality? It is. Side-to-side communication is the vehicle that allows an organization to deliver what it promised. Side-to-side communication is all about people getting together, talking together, working together, to make, buy, distribute and sell the products and services an organization produces.

Side-to-side communication and the quality movement are intimately linked. When side-to-side communication fails to allow organizations to talk to themselves, quality measures also fail to deliver the expected benefits. Without side-to-side communication working, how can any quality program succeed? Yet we've already determined that employee communication as it stands today isn't working.

Ironically, one of the founding fathers of the quality movement hints at the communication problems that are so clearly limiting the success of quality programs. Philip Crosby inherently talks about the importance and problem of side-to-side communication – in the very first paragraph of his book *Quality Is Free* written in 1979. He asks:

> 'What does "making quality certain" mean? "Getting people [through communication] to do better all the worthwhile things they ought to be doing anyway" is not a bad definition.'

It is not hard to diagnose the reasons why quality initiatives all too often fail to deliver their promise in organizations. Communication is the problem, both top-down, bottom-up and side-to-side. When top-down isn't working, when bottom-up isn't working, when functional silos and a specialist focus dominate, when there are low-levels of emotional capital, the results are destructive. An organization suffering from these symptoms will be hampered by a 'not invented here', mentality and an overall failure of communication processes and tools.

How can any quality initiative hope to succeed in this scenario? In simple terms, quality cannot work if side-to-side communication is not working. Side-to-side communication cannot work if the other two dimensions of communication and internal marketing are not working.

No doubt there are many quality fans who will at this very moment protest by pointing out that quality has been able to deliver substantial improvements in most world-class organizations, with many of today's products delivering 'zero defects'. My answer is a question – at what cost?

Quality has required incredible investment from organizations in terms of time, energy, commitment, and various other organizational resources. Business process re-engineering, and knowledge management, both extensions of the quality principles, still continue the search for ways of delivering goods that are better, faster, cheaper and more reliable. These processes all require communication, good communication.

The quality model underpinning all these approaches is the Japanese model, originally based on the work of Deming, and the method was to create processes and systems to mimic this model. Yet the Japanese culture starts from a different base. Quality principles are easier to introduce on an island of so many people where 'getting along with each other' is a social, cultural and economic imperative.

The West does not have a similar culture of communication; quality principles do not necessarily square with cultural values. Indeed, the increasingly individualistic, egocentric, diverse, antagonistic and highly self-centered culture of some Western countries actually works against a team-based, supportive and communicative environment.

Does this mean that organizations should abandon the quality philosophy forever? Quite the opposite. Quality can work – internal communication is both the problem and the solution. Quality will work when organizations realize that internal marketing has a new role to play – to help meet the needs of the customer by the suppliers in the chain.

Communication has to be seen as responsible for improving the ability of organizations to talk to themselves, top-down, bottom-up and side-to-side. This is not talk just for the sake of it, nor talk that celebrates 'births and ball scores' to help improve morale. It is communication that can and does deliver better business results.

Technology – anarchy's best friend

The best place for organizations to start is with a *strategy* for side-to-side communication. Sadly, most organizations have failed to do this and instead have opted instead to focus on the *tools* of technology. Yet without a strategy that gets the three internal dimensions of communication working – top-down, bottom-up and then, and only *then,* side-to-side communication – investment in technology-based communication is simply putting the horse before the cart.

Technology-based communication tools are a means to an end, not the end themselves. In many instances, technology actually hinders side-to-side communication. The Intranet, talked about as a vehicle that promotes the 'democratization of communication' often delivers something far more dangerous – anarchy.

Don't get me wrong, I like technology. It's part of my everyday life, from checking up on my e-mail, to giving presentations from my laptop, to surfing the Internet. And I recognize its potential benefits to organizational communication in terms of speed, accessibility and interactivity. What bothers me is that organizations invest money in the technology without first investing time and energy in a strategy.

Here's an analogy: you want to be fitter, so you invest in a home gym. You buy all the gear, the latest treadmills and weight machines, the works. You set it up and then you go right back to living your life the way you always had … and wonder why your fitness hasn't improved!

Companies make this same mistake every day. They buy the equipment without considering how to change their day-to-day lives. And things will have to change for the technology to do any good. If people in organizations don't trust or believe their senior managers, if they don't feel listened to, if 'not invented here' and functional silos are a way of life, then putting in a technological marvel that allows communication *from* anyone *to* anyone is likely to produce the wrong kind of results.

An excerpt from research into the 'weaknesses' of electronic communication, conducted by MCA, reveals the type of problems that technology generates when organizations lack an effective side-to-side communication strategy (see Box 5.3).

Box 5.3   Weaknesses reflect overdone strengths

The benefits of technology are speed and accessibility; yet these very strengths also limit the effectiveness of electronic communication according to the research participants.

Common complaints included: 'too many sources of data are leading to an overload of information' and 'there is a degree of conflict between widely shared communication and confidential communication'.

Information overload becomes a feature of e-mail systems and Intranets, as use is encouraged and few controls are established. This same accessibility also means that every department and service function can make use of electronic communications to market itself. The result is a proliferation of home pages and e-mails – massive quantities of information presented in a variety of styles, with limited feedback mechanisms.

With the intensive capabilities of the technology itself, some participants are concerned about the ability of their company and staff to keep pace. This concern is reflected in the weaknesses of electronic communication identified by the participants:

1 Lack of standards:
- 'we have no central strategy for the use of electronic media'
- 'we need to ensure employees are informed before they read about it through external sources'
- 'sheer volume of e-mails is off-putting'.

2 Technical issues:

- 'not everyone is conversant; information gets lost'
- 'bringing together 100 Intranet sites is complex'
- 'there is a danger of becoming too reliant on technology, which creates problems when systems go down'.

3 Communication versus Information:

- 'people don't understand this as a channel of communication'
- 'there are no checks to ensure that information is received or understood'
- 'there is a lack of commitment from some senior managers who see this as a "fluffy" issue'

Source: *People, Technology and Communication: The Case for Superhighway Codes*, MCA, 1997.

If this research is the view of seasoned professionals in the information technology industry, then what chance do people outside this industry have of gaining rather than losing from technology? Clearly, even if people feel good about top-down and bottom-up communication, the actual practice of side-to-side communication is in all probability still seriously flawed in many organizations.

Organizations need urgently a strategy for side-to-side communication. They also need to put in place the necessary processes, tools and skills, based on proper standards and controls. While we are now beginning to see better communicationS (the media for getting messages from A to B), this is *not* the same as the ability to get understanding or even less for getting buy-in. No amount of 'colorful' Home Pages will do that trick, probably the reverse!

The organizational 'feel good' factor

Our experience shows that good side-to-side communication can only occur when people feel good about the organization and the part they play.

What if they don't? Well, we know that motivation and morale are pretty low with many people, thanks to all the downsizing and consequent 'upstressing' (I have just coined that expression!). So, what happens when people have low levels of emotional capital? What happens when their belief and trust and respect for an organization is low? What happens when talking to others is tough; when the whole organizations has failed in its ability to communicate with itself? People become frustrated, angry and have a tendency to lash out.

A survey conducted by Novell on e-mail shows that better communicationS can lead to worse communicatioN (see Box 5.4). Given the symbiotic link between communication and in-

---

Box 5.4   Novell Survey – Flaming, Blaming, Shaming

'Electronic mail has become a major source of workplace bullying, according to a survey by Novell. Over half the respondents admitted they had received "flamemails," and 54% said the bullying came from their superiors …

'The consequences of flaming are serious – one in 70 of the employees said they had left a job as a result of abusive e-mail. Nearly a third said they had wanted to stop communicating with the colleagues in question; 14% said their relationship had deteriorated as a result, while 6% stopped communicating altogether. Feelings range from "upset" (42%) to "unable to continue working."'

Source: *Management Consultancy*, June 1997.

tellectual and emotional capital as demonstrated throughout this book, the problems revealed in this survey must have an adverse effect on the performance and value of the business.

This research paints a picture of emotional capital painfully lost as a result of lack of communication strategy, processes and tools. At worst, people are leaving their jobs; the *K Factor* of Price Waterhouse goes UP. What chance of building an asset of intellectual capital through electronic communication if people are concerned, and even prepared to leave a job, because of the communiqués they receive?

The survey also found that: 'Despite the abuse, e-mail was still rated a popular medium, largely because of the convenience it offered the sender'. Good news? Not in the slightest – the benefits are all to the 'sender'. This sounds like more *tell* and *sell* coming our way. What about the benefit to the internal customer? A strategy of everyone recognizing they are suppliers, not dictators, autocrats, parents or superiors, in an internal market is a part of the whole internal marketing philosophy.

Fourth dimension: customer communication

The
New
Role
For
All
At
Work
Is To
Meet
Customers
Needs
One-to-one

In this next dimension of communication, being close to the customer requires something new to happen. *Everyone* is in customer service and marketing.

In his book, *Customer Intimacy*, Fred Wiersema points out that customer intimacy does not mean merely 'customer satisfaction'. In his view, it means giving customers 'complete solutions' to their needs. This is the beginning of an integrated model, where everyone in the organization is dedicated to delivering results for the customer. Wiersema says suppliers 'become indispensable partners, often merging their operations with those of their customers'.

Whether it is customer intimacy or one-to-one relationships, when everyone in an organization is dedicated to providing unique solutions for every individual, the implications are clear. Everyone in an organization becomes responsible for delivering results for customers rather than simply delivering their specialist skills to whatever internal department they join. Many accountants, for example, join to practice accountancy – but they don't, they join to help deliver customer results. IT specialists join to practice their skills in information technology – they don't, they join to help deliver customer results.

This focus on customers is a cultural issue, a strategic issue, a process-driven issue. It becomes a fundamental approach that says everyone in an organization is a brand ambassador. Everyone is responsible for delivering, not just the product or service, but everything around the brand that customers are looking for.

If everyone is a brand ambassador, then I believe the next logical extension of this principle will be that everyone must become a brand manager. This is where customer intimacy starts and ends, with everyone being 'intimate' but not randomly so, or in any way they choose – imagine the results!

A brand manager's job is to manage the customer's needs, requirements, expectations and perceptions and to align these with the products and services the organization offers. The issue is not customer service, which is only a small part of the delivery mechanism (customer service can simply be a smile, answering the phone in three rings or saying 'have a nice day'). Brand managers may deliver all of this customer service and more, but they also have an additional dimension to their job, that of marketing.

Brand managers need marketing skills and tools to find out who the customers are, what they like, what they want, how the organization can deliver and how customers' needs can be for a lifetime. Relationships with customers in our strategy of creating six dimensions of relationships mean marketing-driven relationships.

If everyone in the organization understands they are part of the marketing department, and that they are dealing with customers who have individual requirements and who together produce a market, customer intimacy and mass customization become part of the culture, strategy, processes and skills.

If your people are your brand managers, responsible for managing the reputation of your products and services to your customers, then the next stage must surely be they are also the managers of your corporate reputation. Everyone is in marketing; everyone is in corporate communication. This brings us to the next dimension.

Fifth dimension: communication with stakeholders

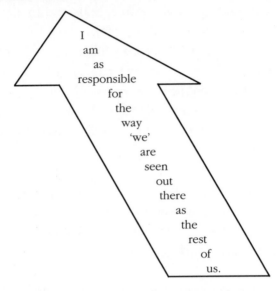

I am as responsible for the way 'we' are seen out there as the rest of us.

If everyone inside your organization had made it as far as being committed to the first four dimensions of marketing-based communication, applying the stakeholder part of the model would be simple. Why? Because just as everyone inside the organization is a customer, so too are they all stakeholders. Everyone knows how they feel about a variety of issues surrounding business in the community. It is just a step away to say 'YOU' are responsible for 'US', the business.

Here is what this conversation might look like in an organization where this is NOT the case, between the Corporate Communication Director and Joe on the shop floor (why are they always called Joe?).

> **Director:** *'You are as responsible for our corporate and brand reputation and personality as the company is – you are the company, you are our reputation, you are our personality.'*

Joe: 'Who me? Nah. You're kidding. I just work here. Do my job, that's all. Leave work, go home, moan about work to the wife and kids, tell my friends in the bar what a lousy place it is to work. In fact I put off a guy the other day from applying for a job, I said the pay was as lousy as the bosses. Oh, I sold my last few shares from the employee share program the other day too – good program that, I'd forgotten how good, oh well. Anyway, I told my stock broker what a lousy place it was. While I was at it, I said that we were likely to be taken to court over that environmental issue. Funny, he must have told someone in the press what I knew about that manager who was taking a kickback to get rid of that toxic waste I'd heard about – was it true by the way? Anyway, I said to the union boss that we should go for a big pay increase in case the lawsuit causes the company to fold in a couple of years. He said he was going to speak to a couple of people in politics, and a couple of the TV and press people he knew, about how the company is looking to take advantage of people, with all this talk of closures ... now what were you saying about me being responsible for our corporate reputation – what is that anyway?'

This may be an exaggeration, but the point is that your staff has a tremendous power to influence all kinds of different stakeholders. In the past it was easy to handle almost all aspects of corporate communication; directors simply said: *'No comment'*. Now it is different. Television crews are quite likely to arrive outside the factory gate to talk to anyone who cares to speak up; the Internet is a great aid to gossip, and newspapers are hungry for stories about the 'big bad employer'. All this means that global communication is in the hands of every single one of the people in an organization.

It is employees who not only deliver the brand, they deliver the reputation of the brand. They are the brand. And the trouble with the brand having a brain, or lots of brains is that it is a walking advertisement, talk show, news broadcast, advertising agency, PR agency, corporate spokesperson and spin doctor... WOW. Is this frightening? Yes. And powerful too. You just want to make sure that the power is tapped, channeled and fed into the right socket!

If not, look what happens. In the US currently, Intel is fighting an ugly and highly damaging battle with its own employees – I won't dare describe them as internal customers in the light of what is happening. The company is actually being sued by its own employees for defamation, discrimination on the grounds of age, race and physical handicaps and other US labor code violations.

It gets worse. These employees have joined with nearly 200 sacked employees and have formed a pressure group called, 'Former and Current Employees of Intel (FACEIntel)'. The wonders of technology now make Intel's nightmare that much worse – FACEIntel is publicizing its grievances on the Internet. How is Intel responding? By blocking employees' access to the site and preventing any e-mail correspondence with the group.

How would you assess the health of Intel's emotional assets if you read the following comments, published in *People Management* (June 97):

> *'Intel has been targeting the weakest performers for so long now that there are no weak performers left – only good, solid workers, many of whom have been employees of the company for many years. These are the people who are now being given unattainable goals and therefore being terminated.*
>
> *'It is our opinion that the stressful work environment that this system creates is detrimental to the health and welfare of the employees ... Intel needs to wake up and see what it's doing to its people.'*

Intel Outside

So 200 people can now communicate with the world. Just one can, actually. However, the implications of everyone becoming a global communicator do not stop at the emotional end of the spectrum. One Wall Street analyst who has visited the FaceIntel Web site has recognized the huge implications for the Intel managers, its staff, and the likelihood of it struggling to recruit high-caliber people. The analyst pointed out that, like her, customers will be unhappy about purchasing a product with negative connotations and go to competitors in preference. If things like this get out of hand the results can be lower sales and this means lower profits. Lower profits means lower dividends. Lower dividends mean lower share price. The value of the company is down graded.

In Box 5.5 is a selection of quotes from a very large Web site, in which a lot of very angry people are looking to attack Intel's bank of emotional capital. And now this site is in this book and so the story spreads like wildfire ... doesn't it? Will you visit the site, will it still be open? Is it truth or lies? Time will tell.

Box 5.5   FACEIntel: Former and Current Employees of Intel

Who we are
'The price of justice is eternal publicity.'

Arnold Bennet

Our primary goal is to expose and help put an end to Intel's discriminatory and predatory employment practices

Our messages are simple and to the point. We want Intel to stop discriminatory practices and get back to making it a great place to work as it once was.

'True development puts first those that society puts last.'

Mahatma Gandhi

At Intel's annual stockholders meeting, Craig Barrett, Chief Operating Officer replied to question: 'How is downsizing increasing profitability?' He replied by pointing out: 'the half-life of an engineer, software, hardware engineer is only a few years...'

Fact – over 90% of members [of FACEIntel] are over 40.

Intel has screens at cc:Mail gateways to block our messages. This is why we need to encode our messages. We are not secretive, we are just looking for creative ways to get the message to Intel employees.

Our intention is not to hurt Intel, but to help Intel by pointing our their wrong doings.

'Employees are our greatest asset' – is one of Intel's values. This sounds wonderful, but, first to show some integrity, Intel must align their policies, practices, decisions and actions to be in line with this claim.

We hope and pray that the executives at Intel will allow their human spirit to thrive again, because money can't buy it, and technology cannot create it.

Quotes from staff and site users

- 'I wonder if the people who started the company realize just how terrible the employees at the bottom are treated sometimes? Maybe they don't care.'
- 'I had intended to apply to Intel in a few months, but your web site makes me pause.'
- 'Intel seems to have grown cancerous with age, and is now cannibalizing its own.'

Perception is all – especially if you are out of work and angry. I have no doubt that 'there are two sides to every story'; but if it is true that 'perception is all' then reality does not matter. I am not trying to relate the facts here, just the story. In fact an Intel staff member in their PR department recently told me: 'this has not damaged our reputation, in fact our share price has never been higher'. No doubt the 'real' story will come out.

Some organizations may be saying: 'There but for the grace of God go I'. If your staff are doing anything to affect the emotional capital of those inside or outside the organization – beware! The three letters, WWW, will allow anyone to set up FaceXYZ. So everyone on the inside can communicate with everyone on the outside, across the globe, at the touch of a button. Suddenly, all relationships become open to view and the reverberations go far and wide.

If the FACEIntel issue becomes even more serious, how would you feel if you were an Intel supplier? How is your stock price? Do you have a 'special relationship' with them? Are you linked as a strategic alliance? If you are, perhaps you want to make a quick exit, or perhaps you will decide to come to Intel's aid during this time of need and (hopefully) learning. Whatever you choose to do, you would have some serious questions and issues to resolve.

Stakeholders outside the organization

Thanks to examples like Intel, business leaders are taking on board the fact that their internal customers play a critical role as stakeholders in the business. Yet there are other critical stakeholders: shareholders, customers, the media, members of the local community, in fact anyone and everyone with a particular interest in the business and the ability to air their opinions. As Roger Hayes argues in Box 5.6, it is the responsibility of corpo-

Box 5.6   Corporate communication comes into its own

'Where there is a corporate brand, it can be valued, total reputation matters, and what happens in one part of the business affects the rest. In that sense the corporation is a system, and corporate communication a general management function embracing both external and internal staff and line functions, and requiring access to the top management, especially the chairman and chief executive. It is therefore strategic, not only a message distribution relationship between the corporation and stakeholders, but anticipating their expectations, as well as reacting to events.

'But corporate communication is only just coming into its own, firstly because of its importance to global communication strategies and programs, but also given the changing environment out there and the corporation's changing role within it.

The way forward

'Corporate communication therefore means that internal cultural matters should be integrated with external dialogue on the company's strategy and position on issues; that the PR people feed back attitudes and expectations early enough so they can be fed into the strategic planning process; so that issue management replaces crisis and anticipation replaces reaction.

'We live in a new era where people and communication are center stage.... Corporate communication has to be consistent, co-ordinated and coherent to be credible. If so, it impacts the bottom line – operational ability and sustainable success.'

Source: Roger Hayes, President, International Public Relations Association, *CBI Corporate Communications Handbook*, Kogan Page, 1997.

rate communication to manage the relationship with stakeholders and to also help break down the false distinction between internal and external organizational issues.

It has to be said that shareholders are sometimes neglected members of a company's group of stakeholders. If an organization asked its people to do the exercise (see below), most would find that their people don't view the anonymous shareholder as being more important than them, probably not even as important, and usually less! To them, it is what takes place in and around the organization that seems most important.

Reality check

Ask people in your organization to say whether an 'owner', i.e. the shareholder, is:
❏ less important
❏ as important
❏ more important
than what is 'owned'?

Organizations cannot afford to subscribe to this parochial view. Today, as never before, the life of an organization is most important to those who are looking to 'stick with it'; and in the brave new world of lifetime customer relationships it is then when long-term customers and community relationships become the key to survival. Long term relationships are the basis of both short-term and long-term success. If the customer kicks you out you, have a problem. But it does not stop there. If the community kicks you out, you are in trouble. You can have all the short-term troubleshooting measures in place to please the analysts, but you will still probably lose sales, customers and a business.

But they did spill it

The effects of Exxon Valdez in the US and around the globe are well documented, and still being talked about. More recently, Shell, the international oil company, has had to come to terms with the damage done to its reputation because of its highly public sparring with the environmental group Greenpeace over towing the Brent Spar into the Atlantic. These events have undoubtedly damaged both Shell and Exxon's relationship with their key stakeholders.

The power of a positive corporate reputation with stakeholders is less visible but nevertheless affects business values, revenues and profitability. In the UK as well as the US, the concept of stakeholders is taking hold, as the results of MORI research shows (see Box 5.7).

Business leaders are rapidly recognizing the power of corporate communication, not just PR, and how this is tied to stakeholders relationships.

And so to the last of our strategic dimensions of communication and relationships, that of suppliers and strategic alliances. This is another relationship that has once again been in traditional *tell* mode – 'you are a supplier, do this', or *sell* – 'you are a business customer, buy it, it's great!' Even here, a new culture of caring and sharing has taken place, with a fair amount of *friendships* being created and sustained. The era of having 'suppliers' is changing to having 'strategic alliances'.

Sixth dimension: communication with suppliers and strategic allies

If there are radical changes going on in the world of stakeholder relations, then the world of supplier arrangements has turned on its head over the last decade.

Box 5.7   Stakeholding wins out in tomorrow's company

'Business leaders have radically changed their attitudes towards stakeholders, according to "Captains Of Industry" survey by MORI for the Center for Tomorrow's Company.

'Today 72% of business leaders agree that in order to become successful you must focus on the needs of its customers, employees, suppliers and the wider community.

'"Five years ago two out of three business leaders would have agreed that shareholders are the focus of their attention, today shareholders are down in the low percentages," said Mark Goyder, director of the Center for Tomorrow's Company. "In their statements this year over 70% focus on all the needs, which is what Tomorrow's Company is about."

'The survey found that stakeholders areas, which five years ago were not high on captains of industry's agendas, had also risen: 44% said that businesses could not succeed without recognizing that they are accountable to other stakeholders as well as shareholders; and 31% said that successful businesses needed to be responsible towards society and the community, as well as to shareholders.

'"For over 40% to say that business is accountable to these other groups is a significant change for business leaders," said Goyder. "I believe there has been a significant shift and it has a lot to do with BP, Shell and pressure groups. If you get the community relations wrong the damage that this can do to shareholder value is frightening."'

Source: *Management Consultancy*, May 1997.

This is the last dimension of communication and marketing. This is a dimension where, with such fragmented and confusing structural relationships forming between organizations, the people relationships are critical. High stocks of emotional capital and relationship management are an asset that has to replace the now out-of-date customer/supplier ordering system.

Today's and tomorrow's customer-supplier chain is now seamless, as is shown by two corporate examples taken from *The Quality Revolution*. Ford and Lipton move away from making distinctions between outside and inside the organization. For example, 'Ford, who had a reputation as one of the toughest managers of suppliers, reversed their policy in the mid-eighties from "divide and conquer" to partnership relations'. Partnering in Lipton has reached such a high profile that the whole Quality process is entitled *Partners in Quality*.

The author, Steve Smith, goes on to say: 'For many, however, partnering plays the strongest role at the interfaces – supplier to customer, customer to supplier, both inside and outside the organization'.

Quality and marketing turn customers and suppliers into friends

What is fascinating about so many customer-supplier relationships is that the driver of the relationship process inside and around the organization is once again quality. However, a better driver would be marketing. If suppliers are attempting to get organizations to buy their goods then surely their role is a marketing role? And just as marketing to consumers has moved along the communication and marketing timeline, so too has the relationship between suppliers and customers in business to business markets.

Supplier arrangements are now turning into 'strategic alliances'. Isn't this the same as *tell* and *sell* arrangements moving into marketing and relationship marketing arrangements of *best friends* for life?

If this view of the new relationships with suppliers is correct, then something new needs to happen with communication too. Now is the time to improve customer-supplier communication and relationships by adding the strategies, processes and tools of marketing.

Let's compare some of the traditional models with the paradigm shifts taking place. The conventional approach for a relationship between a purchaser and supplier has been confrontational. The relationship has been described as a bow-tie by 3M (and adapted by Stewart in *Intellectual capital*). I prefer to describe it as a see-saw.

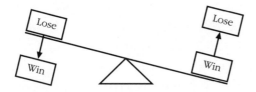

The relationship rests on a limited point of contact between the two organizations, typically between the sales and purchasing departments. Other relationships that do build up, for example between drivers and people signing 'goods in' are all too often incidental. As you can see from the diagram, the relationship between the two organizations is also very finely balanced. Purchasing departments let suppliers compete for the 'contract' on a 'win/lose' basis. The attitude of the purchaser is 'keep them on their toes'. Agreeing the sale between manufacturer and supplier usually depends on price and other factors around the product such as speed of delivery. Relationships, such as they are, center on an 'us and them' mode, rather confrontational and places no focus on working together on behalf of the consumer.

The opposite of the traditional see-saw model is the maypole. In this model, *everyone* gets involved. Every department in each organization is looking to work in a 'dance around a customer'. The goal? To wrap customers so tightly in a soft warm set of brightly colored ribbons that they don't want to leave – and guess what? They can't!

In this relationship the real customers (instead of the purchasing department) are telling the suppliers what they want and need. This relationship also tends to be win-win since it helps create lifetime relationships between customers and the entire supplier chain. All in all, maypole relationships hold the key to the future and help to make the relationship between customer and business more enduring, compatible and fulfilling.

3M contrasts their bow-tie model with two triangles joined at the base, where every part of the two organizations is touching and working together to create a perfect whole. The resulting relationship is similar to a diamond, transparent to everyone looking in from the outside, yet enduring and ever lasting

An example of a *maypole* relationship occurs in organizations like Wal-Mart. Both Wal-Mart and their suppliers are dedicated to the final sale of the product to the customer. In this symbiotic relationship, manufacturers like Procter and Gamble work with Wal-Mart to ensure they are both successful. If the supplier doesn't get paid until the till rings, then this is a strong incentive for a strong customer-supplier chain. And wherever there are customers and suppliers, then there must be marketing.

In his book, *Customer Intimacy*, Fred Wiersema talks about giving customers 'complete solutions' to their needs. This is a critical benefit of the maypole model, where everyone in the customer-supplier chain is dedicated to delivering results for the customer. Wiersema says suppliers 'become indispensable partners, often merging their operations with those of their customers'.

If marketing in the customer-supplier chain can create 'indispensable partners' and deliver increases in intellectual and emotional capital, then applying marketing philosophies will surely add to the quality mix and create a quality *and* marketing mix. This will allow marketing and quality, hitherto traveling on parallel lines, to at last be brought together in a new and infinitely more powerful combination.

Quality has been viewed as the traditional driver of customer-supplier relationships. Yet has quality truly been able to meet the needs of a partnering relationship? Quality is not using the right tools for this part of the job because marketing (apart from the tell and sell variety of business-to-business marketing) has been notably absent from the whole quality movement.

As other chapters in this book point out, a notable exception is the way quality has met some of the needs of the external customer. Here quality and marketing may well have been working together. But what about the rest of the customers in the chain? Who is using all the marketing tools and techniques to assess and meet their requirements?

In his book on relationship marketing, Adrian Payne uses the three concepts of marketing, customer service and quality as the 'three critical areas' that need to be brought 'into closer alignment', He put it another way when he talks of quality being the missing link for marketing: 'Quality has become an integrating concept between production orientation and marketing orientation. Marketing has always lacked a method of making operational the connections between what the customer wants on the one side and the activities of a firm, on the other. Quality management is the missing link ... Relationship marketing guides us to the activity captains called the customer value chain.'

If marketing is the answer to improving the customer and supplier relationships throughout the quality chain, then introducing the principles, processes, tools and skills of marketing to everyone in the chain must be the next logical move. In my last book, *Managing your internal customers*, I suggested that linking quality and marketing should in fact be easy. Why? Because quality and marketing are essentially about the same thing; delivering customer satisfaction, improving customer retention and providing a strong lifetime relationship. The links between quality and marketing are so strong that I compared the definitions of quality to those of marketing. They still apply today. In the list below, I quote definitions of quality from Kaizen, *The Key To Japan's Competitive Success'* by Imai, and add my own comments in italics.

- **Analytical approach** (to management improvement): an approach based on learning from the evaluation of past experience. *The marketing approach to this is called research.*
- **Check points and control points (Jidohka):** a word to describe a feature of Toyota production system whereby a machine is designed to stop automatically whenever a defective part is produced. *This is the time when a powerful customer complaints system provide constant feedback.*
- **Cross-functional management:** the inter-departmental coordination required to realize the policy goals of a KAIZEN and a Total Quality Control (TQC) program. After corporate strategy and planning are determined, top management sets objectives for cross-functional efforts that cut laterally through the organization. *This can only happen with an efficient, targeted communication system.*
- **Improvement:** improvement as a part of a successful KAIZEN strategy goes beyond the dictionary definition of the word. Improvement is a mindset linked to maintaining and improving standards. *Customers continually demand improvement.*

Every marketing strategy and tactical execution to respond to customers' demands will be constantly changing. A successful KAIZEN strategy clearly delineates responsibility for maintaining standards to the worker, with management's role being the improvement of standards. *A successful marketing strategy recognizes that it is the responsibility of the supplier to constantly check the standards demanded by the customer.*

- **Just in Time:** a production and inventory control technique that is part of the Toyota production system. *The customer expectation is not 'just in time'; every marketer now recognizes that the customer wants things 'yesterday'!*
- **KAIZEN:** KAIZEN means improvement. Moreover it means continuing improvement in personal life, home life, social life, and working life. When applied to the workplace KAIZEN means continuing improvement involving everyone – managers and workers. *Marketing through the customer-supplier chain is based on exactly the same premise.*
- **Quality Control:** When Quality Control (QC) was first introduced to Japan by Deming in 1950, the main emphasis was on improving product quality by applying statistical tools in the production process. *When marketing was first introduced in the 1950s, the main aim was selling products by applying broad-brush advertising techniques.* In 1954 J.M. Duran brought the concept of QC as a vital management tool for improving manual performance. Today QC is used as a tool to build a system of continuing interaction among all elements responsible for the conduct of a company's business so as to achieve the improved quality that satisfies the customer's demand. *Today marketing, relationship marketing, and one-to-one marketing are tools to build a system of continuing interaction throughout the customer–supplier chain.*

Source: *Managing Your Internal Customers*, Financial Times/ Pitman.

If marketing is good at developing emotional capital and creating lifetime relationships, and communication improves intellectual capital by sharing information and knowledge, surely they need to be added to the quality discipline, right throughout the customer-supplier chain.

Such has been the experience of Xerox, pointed out in Payne *et al.*'s *Relationship Marketing*. The authors comment: 'The survival strategy Xerox chose was quality improvement, both as a marketing role and as a process for internal change. Quality as a competitive strategy has since revitalized Xerox's approach to marketing, human resource management, and operations, right across the world.'

Here is how Xerox sees the link between quality and internal customers. (My thanks to Debbie Yeomans for allowing me to use Xerox material. She is proud of it, and rightly so.) Called *Xerox – A study in internal customer marketing* (yes their words!) the following definition is taken from one of a number of prominently displayed posters around the UK Headquarters: 'The Xerox Quality Policy: Xerox is a quality company. Quality is the basic business principal for Xerox. Quality means providing our external and internal customers with innovative products and services that fully satisfy their requirements. Quality improvement is the job of every Xerox employee.'

Inside, outside – everyone communicating

Box 5.8 is an excerpt from an article prepared for a special issue of *Human Resources* magazine for the 1997 Annual International Conference of the Institute of Personnel and Development. This is the largest management conference event of its kind in Europe. The article tackles the topic of outsourcing, which has become a critical issue in HR today because of the new composition of organizations.

Box 5.8   In-laws or outlaws?

The success of outsourcing relationships depends on communication, say Kevin Thomson and Adrian Lenard.

Large or small, public or private sector, most organizations today are outsourcing some of their activities – not just to cut costs, but to buy in specialized knowledge and expertise that can deliver real competitive advantage.

The business results gained from outsourcing depend very much on communication and its ability to draw on this expertise and build successful relationships throughout a new customer/supplier chain.

Strong as the weakest link

Using an outside supplier or provider to produce a product or service on your behalf is nothing new. What has changed is the complexity of activities being outsourced, from simple tasks to highly complex services, and the communication stakes that are raised as a result.

Outsourcing traditionally involved only the supplier side of operations such as facilities management or distribution. Today entire functions, many of them customer-facing, are being outsourced. For example, the Body Shop has in effect outsourced its retailing through its franchising. Quintiles has built a multi-million dollar business by contracting everything from sales and marketing services to product development to the healthcare industry.

These types of outsourcing arrangements are adding new dimensions to the customer/supplier chain, creating relationships in which individuals and groups share a common customer while serving different 'masters'. And there is no central communicator – everyone in the supplier chain is now a communicator.

The nature of outsourcing relationships vary dramatically – from individual contractors who serve as virtual employees for a defined period of time, to whole departments or functions who are outsourced along with their responsibilities to a specialist organization.

Communication is both the glue that holds these complex relationships together and the structure that used to come from clear, vertical reporting lines lost in re-engineering exercises. Communication is also the tool that can strengthen weak links in this more complicated customer/supplier chain by ensuring everyone in the organization, whether 'insourced' or outsourced, is focused on common goals and delivering real shareholder value.

According to Dave Pendleton, Outsourcing Human Resources Manager for IBM UK, it is important to manage the communication as a process rather than an event. 'Making the initial announcement about outsourcing to the staff is only the first step', says Pendleton. 'Once the relationship is announced, we then like to "lay out our wares" to the staff who will be transferring to IBM, explaining the business rationale and what will happen in the transfer. We give people as much information as we can, and also let them talk with individuals in IBM who've been through similar experiences. This phase of communication is important opportunity to make a positive impression, and it needs be handled well.'

'The hardest bit is overcoming the honeymoon period', Pendleton concludes. 'You need a good plan of communication activities to sustain the momentum. A good communication program will have plenty of follow-on after the transfer.'

Managing independent contractors

For many organizations, outsourcing is managed one job at a time. 'The critical issues for us revolve around the outsourcing we do with independent contractors', says Richard Baker, UK Human Resources Director for Hoechst Marion Roussel (HMR), a global pharmaceuticals company.

For Baker, the key question is 'whether you regard your staff to be everyone working for you in the building, or whether you have a different philosophy for those on your payroll?' Baker opts for a consistent approach with everyone working for HMR: 'Yes, there are legal and factual differentials with outsourced staff, whether they are contracted from an agency or self-employed. But once they are in the door they become part of the team.'

In HMR, being part of the team includes having broad access to business information and attending HMR's team meetings. 'There is a perception by some HR professionals that contractors can't be as committed as employees', says Baker. 'That's rubbish in my view. If you involve contractors in the business, they'll be every bit as committed – and in some cases, even more so.'

Source: article prepared for *Human Resources*, November 1997.

This section on supplier communication and marketing has turned the concept of the customer-supplier chain into one where both marketing and quality work together to increase the intellectual and emotional capital inside and around every organization. The success of this focus on quality, people, relationships and marketing across the customer and supplier chain is demonstrated in the report and accounts of virtually every organization today.

This now gives us the last of the six dimensions of relationships that are involved in a strategy of building intellectual and emotional capital through communication and marketing principles. The six dimensions, three internally, top-down, bottom-up, and side-to-side, plus three externally, customers, stakeholders, and suppliers give us a big picture of a strategy that says everyone in an organization is responsible for communication and marketing to everyone else.

The six dimensions model is a powerful tool for discussing these concepts. We will go on in more depth to discuss the processes and language of marketing applied internally to create emotional capital. For now here is a graphic representation of a strategy everyone can, and does understand.

A summary – the six dimensions of communication and marketing in and around every organization.

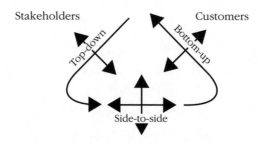

Stakeholders   Customers

Top-down   Bottom-up

Side-to-side

Suppliers/strategic alliances

My notes on the six dimensions

It sounds simple — a strategy of communicating to six dimensions so that everyone is included; the six Ds. It is simple — deliberately so. Everyone in an organization needs to understand the strategy — otherwise it isn't a strategy. If people do not understand that they are part of an overall approach to matching their needs, as well as customers, and other stakeholders to the needs of the organization then you might as well not have a strategy. You might as well go back to those complicated communication strategy documents that talked of 'open, honest, timely, appropriate, relevant' and depicted a host of media to deliver all this stuff like visions and missions, change, etc. A complicated strategy with simple tactics — corporate megaphone! This chapter suggests a different strategy — easy to understand but really hard to deliver; listening is much tougher than talking!

Thought provokers for the future

Now that we know what the strategy involves, it's your turn to assess what you are communicating (or not) and why.

- Top down messages — What are they? How integrated? How well understood? How well bought in to? What are your top ten business issues? Are your top people aligned with them?
- Bottom up messages — Who has a handle on the top ten personal needs at corporate, team or individual level? Who really knows the needs of internal customers on a one to one level?
- Side to side — Does best practice, knowledge management, total quality, benchmarking, business processes re-engineering, ISO 9000, etc., have buy in? Why not? Do you have functional silos? Do people talk to each other? Does your organization think 'technology = techknowledgy'?
- Customers — Is marketing the only one talking to them in a meaningful way? Is everyone in your organization in marketing? Are all your people seen as 'brand ambassadors' for your products and services?

- *Stakeholders* — Is corporate communication the ones who say 'no comment'? Or does everyone have a right to 'represent' your organization (albeit on what they are responsible for)

- *Suppliers / Strategic Alliances* — Do you have a seamless 'customer supplier chain'? Do your suppliers or alliances talk with the same voice, and act in the same way as you when they are involved in your organization?

- *Overall* — you can rate the emotional capital level across each of the six dimensions on the following (very sophisticated) scale!

Your notes

Processes for Business Success: the Six *Is*

Overview

In this chapter, you'll discover:

- the six stages of marketing and communication processes, called the six *Is*
- how these processes have been implemented in many blue-chip organizations
- the link between the six *Is* and emotional capital
- what these processes can mean for your organization's business performance.

SIX

Processes for Business Success: the Six *I*s

The intention of this book is to build a big picture of communication and marketing that shows how everything an organization does and says, both externally and internally, can become be a seamless whole. Earlier chapters on the marketing and communication timeline explored how organizations have responded to customer demand and moved from a focus on production towards sales, then on to quality and customer service until finally arriving at the concept of database, then relationship marketing. This transition has required a new approach to communication that enables businesses to understand and gain the emotional buy-in of six key groups of stakeholders within and outside the organization.

We arrive at a point where organizations realize the tremendous value of their stakeholders' emotional and intellectual capital and recognize that marketing and communication hold the key to releasing this hidden resource. How are companies to do this? What processes do they need to implement successfully an integrated, six-dimensional internal marketing and communication strategy as described in the previous chapter?

This chapter discusses the communication processes that give life and power to the new marketing and communication strategy. It introduces the 'Six *I*s' – six communication processes, which when aligned with business processes enable organizations to move up the ladder of buy-in towards complete integration. This is when relationship marketing becomes a reality.

The six *I*s are a simple and extremely powerful way of demonstrating how different processes of communication and marketing need to happen at different times in organizations. This model enables communication processes to be seen as separate, yet interlocking, parts of a business. They help complete a total marketing mix inside and out. They provide a flexible toolkit of communication strategies, processes and skills that ensure everyone hears what they need to hear in the language and style most suited to them.

The blueprint model, which we are building up throughout this book, helps to show how business focus, communication strategy and processes are all interlocking parts of a total business picture. It shows how soft and hard issues combine. Of course they do! They always have. The problem has been to demonstrate it and prove it. Each part of the model has a direct link to the all the other parts, the soft and the hard. For example, if you look across from the six processes of *Instruction, Information, Involvement, Improvement, Innovation and Integration,* you will see the six arrows of communication. As Chapter 5 detailed, these arrows are the directions needed to ensure the organization is looking, talking, listening, learning and responding to all its stakeholders. Each of the six communication processes links to the six strategies of communication opposite. Instruction, for example is clearly 'top-down.' This model therefore shows a neat and accurate link between strategy and process.

Six Is and ROI too – that makes seven

In previous chapters, we've explored the business benefits of effective marketing and communication, and looked at the time, energy and money spent on them as an investment. So, if an *investment* is being made, then there must be some kind of financial *return* that ultimately comes from these strategies and processes. Why else are they doing it? To make employees feel better? To achieve a good score on employee attitude surveys? To get a high attendance at team meetings? To get good feedback after a conference? To make CEOs feel they gave a good performance on the staff video?

All too often in the past these 'soft' benefits were the *only* reasons why organizations did all the things they did under the title 'employee communications' (yes, with an S on the end). 'Employee communications' was often done for its own sake, for a 'feel good' factor, rather like giving candy to the children. No longer!

The new six-dimensional strategy delivers a set of six new communication processes for one reason only – to deliver better business results. In this integrated approach to communication, the soft issues become the features which ultimately deliver hard benefits. For example, keeping staff informed (feature) increases their knowledge, which enables them to make better decisions on the job (benefit). Making people feel appreciated for their contributions (feature), strengthens their commitment and desire to stay with the organization and helps reduce staff turnover (benefit).

The reason for doing all this soft stuff is to get a huge measure of the hard stuff in return. The reason for introducing the new processes and language (language and culture are covered in Chapter 7) is to affect the old profit and loss statement (P&L). If we affect the P&L, we affect the balance sheet. It all starts to make sense, doesn't it?

So let's get tough, talk tough, act tough and deliver. Let's get into John Wayne mode! Let's bring communication and internal marketing into the *business* arena – where it belongs.

Now is the time for internal marketing and communication to take their place at the top table. They can justify their new place because at last they have the ability to deliver hard business results through strategies, processes, skills and a language of marketing and customers that works. This chapter is about the communication processes, the six *I*s that create intellectual and emotional capital.

The six *I*s of communication

The six *I*s link directly with the six dimensions of communication covered in the previous chapter. So not only do we have a strategy to follow, but we now have the 'how to' deliver the strategy as well.

1. Instructions – delivering 'top-down' messages

top-down

These are the 'must dos', for example fire regulations, expenses procedures, cooking instructions, etc. Instructions are mandatory and are not there for discussion.

In many cases, 'tell' mode is appropriate for instructions. The most appropriate way of telling people what to do may simply be through a manual, wall chart or even a video. In some cases, however, other modes of communication may be more appropriate; for example a 'sell' or 'buy-in' mode may be required in situations where people perceive the instructions to be irrelevant or unimportant. The process for communicating and marketing instructions, especially life-preserving instructions, is therefore as critical as the content of the instruction.

2. Information – delivering 'top-down' messages and receiving bottom-up information and feedback

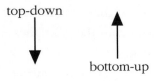

top-down

bottom-up

This process focuses on the facts, figures, data and intellectual property of an organization. This information may be tacit (unspoken and not written down) or it may be explicit (formally recognized, spoken about and written down). This information, tacit or explicit, will need communicating because it is often the bedrock of the organization. It may well include vital information about the following:

• the organization's vision and mission
• the requirements of the business
• the needs, wants and concerns of internal customers.

Matching the information needs of the business and the individuals who use the information is a fundamental part of the communication processes, which is why you need bottom-up feedback. You also need to determine the most effective communication channels to match the level of concern about the information with the media you choose (remember the Concern Scale?).

3. Involvement – delivering two-way discussion (listening and response)

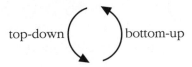

top-down   bottom-up

This is the core communication process that puts people together with people, and people together with information in order to develop every aspect of the business. It involves both listening and response so that *the information received is acted upon.* This can either mean that the 'messagemaker' responds to the feedback from staff or vice versa.

The key difference between information process and involvement processes is that involvement is an ongoing dialogue or interaction that requires everyone taking part to listen and take action – regardless of whether the communication is face-to-face, written on paper or delivered electronically.

4. Improvement – delivering side-to-side exchanges inside the organization

side-to-side

Often labeled as 'continuous improvement' in a total quality program, where the goal is to achieve perfection (or in quality language, zero defects) or operational efficiencies to deliver cost savings, etc. The goal is better business results. However, improvement is a communication process as well as a total quality process that involves the sharing of knowledge and the exchange of best practices across functions, teams, locations and any other invisible barrier you can think of!

Thanks to technology, the logistics of side-to-side communication across geographic boundaries and time zones are far easier. Unfortunately, many organizations put in the technology without bothering to give people the skills or the motivation to use them to genuinely improve the way things are done. And, as described in Chapter 5, side-to-side communication on its own can create anarchy without effective top-down and bottom-up communication in place. If people don't feel informed and in-volved, why on earth would they care about making improvements or sharing best practices?!

5. Innovation – delivering side-to-side collaboration inside and outside the organization, for the customers' benefit

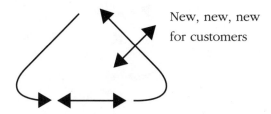

New, new, new
for customers

Innovation is about seeking the new, not the improved, to ex-cite the customer of tomorrow. If you think of improvement as the *exchange* of good ideas and best practices between people, then innovation is when those people *collaborate* to build on each others' ideas and best practices and create a new usable, profitable product or service.

Of course, successful companies don't just come up with a new product and then hope that customers will want it (that's a method of innovation suitable for the manufacturing mindset of the 1950s – remember our timeline?). Given the investment that has to be made to bring a new product or service to the market, companies want to innovate based on the needs and wants of customers.

Creativity and innovation are totally reliant on communica-tion processes. People cannot create or innovate without either talking to themselves or others! And they certainly can't inno-vate with the customers' needs in mind if they communicate badly, or not at all with the customer on a one to one basis. In today's ever changing environment (and ever changing needs of customers), businesses die if they cannot innovate.

6. Integration – linking all six dimensions of marketing-driven relationships

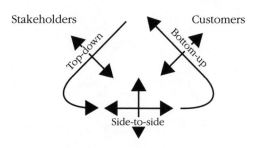

The will to deliver whatever the business or customer needs today and in the future requires an inspired, dedicated, passionate and even obsessive work force. As people become-driven by a passion about the company, the brand and the customer, they act as brand ambassadors in all their relationships in and around the organization. This is the essence of one-to-one relationship marketing.

Six simple steps – one at a time

Each of the Six *I*s need to be understood and implemented in turn. Why? Because each is a different part of the house we are building *and* because we can't start from the roof and work down. Each part of the communication processes builds on the one before.

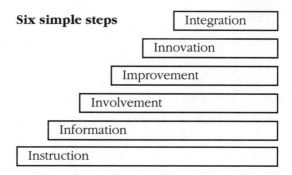

Six simple steps

| Integration |
| Innovation |
| Improvement |
| Involvement |
| Information |
| Instruction |

This is an important part of the concept of the six *I*s. To move up this communication and marketing process model, each one is best handled *in order*. For example, take a function like Research and Development. R&D is high up the model since its main role is to innovate and integrate data, information and knowledge (plus a huge slug of emotions) from anywhere and everywhere. Could R&D staff innovate if they didn't know *what* they were supposed to be innovating? How do they know? They get top-down instructions or information about where the organization is going. Would they innovate if they did not feel listened to themselves (their bottom-up needs) or if they did not get cooperation from colleagues or other departments (side-to-side exchanges of best practice)? Could they innovate when the basic quality of existing products and services was so lousy that the chances of producing something new which worked was unlikely? What use innovation and integration if nothing else was working?

Plainly, an area like R&D can only succeed when all the preceding processes of instruction, information, involvement and improvement have been put in, step by step.

The six *I*s are simple, but they are not simplistic. They become blindingly obvious when organizations look at them for the first time, but despite this, few have ever tried to take a marketing approach to their communication processes. The majority of organizations try to communicate everything at the same time. Suggestion schemes vie with instructions; information competes with the process of generating new ideas.

If they stop to think about it, organizations will of course recognize the processes of instructing, informing, involving, improving, innovating and integrating that take place every day. However, they have failed to realize that these *business processes* require *communication processes* to make them succeed.

Not only are the six *I*s communication processes, they are processes that need to occur in the right way, at the right time, to the right people about the right things with the right messages. In other words these are also marketing processes.

Even an instruction about fire, if not 'targeted' properly, will fail. Does the standard set of instructions ('In the event of fire …') definitely work? Is the intended audience literate? Can they read English? Were the instructions clear, explicit, short, graphic, bold, powerful, memorable, and compelling, or boring, dull, stupid, obvious and forgettable?

The following section explores the six *I*s in greater detail and provides case studies and examples to illustrate how they work in organizations to build and grow intellectual and emotional capital.

Instructions – just do it!

This is an important yet often overlooked process of communication. Most individuals and organizations view instructions as tedious and mundane statements that tend to appear in lists and adorn walls and official documents. However, if organizations adopt a marketing-based approach to their instruction processes, they soon come to realize that it is their responsibility to take a far more creative approach to giving instructions.

Typically, organizations issue instructions and then leave it to luck whether or not anyone takes the slightest notice of them. Many instructions tend to concern important issues however.

Instructions are not just about fire or safety. Top-down instructions can be about any number of business issues. All too often, organizations believe these instructions 'have' to be done and so fail to ask themselves whether they may also need buy-in. Even if the instructions are life-preserving, like safety instructions, people can still choose to ignore them. If people cannot see the WIIFM – the *What's In It For Me* – they will do whatever they think is best.

Think of the health warning 'smoking kills,' on cigarette packages in many countries. Many smokers acknowledge this to be true but … 'I just want another one, and anyway my father smoked and he lived to a ripe old age.' People may well feel it is their right to decide whether to follow certain instructions, but this can pose serious problems for businesses. If their people ignore instructions and are hurt or even killed, the business is also hurt in all sort of ways – people are distressed, morale suffers, customers may hear about it and eventually the company's reputation suffers.

Can businesses afford to leave their people to decide whether to comply with certain essential instructions? Can they just shrug off the problem and say it is the employee's responsibility? In one global organization, the goal on safety is obviously zero deaths. In one year they had six. Whose responsibility was this? Was it the victims – after all they ignored the many, many instructions given in the training sessions, video and the countless posters dotted round the company? Was it the responsibility of the company for ensuring that the training, videos and posters were saying the right things in the right way to the right people?

The answer is that responsibility lies with both organizations and individuals. If businesses accept that the process of instruction is also a marketing process, they have to accept that they must do something to ensure their instructions are complied with. Thankfully the organization mentioned above takes this stance. It believes with all its heart and head in its responsibility to achieve a 'zero' on accidents, however minor.

MCA worked with a large merchant bank to internally market a program about computer security. Endless manuals, screensavers and the like had been used to instruct people to follow basic procedures for passwords, e-mail encryption and other security measures. Because a financial institution's integrity and reputation depends on protecting information, and because so much information is now stored and transmitted electronically, we had to move from 'tell' mode into 'buy-in.' This required a very different approach that involved far more face-to-face communication and a clear use of WIIFM for staff and for the banks' future.

All information, even simple instructions, needs targeting. If a customer is switched off by a series of messages, then it is the targeting which is at fault. (For a much longer explanation of 'how to' target a message to every individual read *Passion at work*. It covers the many psychographic and demographic profiles of people and how this affects the way they receive and process information.)

On target

Should every message be targeted to every individual in an organization? Ideally yes. The goal of relationship marketing is mass customization through one-to-one targeting. If this can happen with external customers then why not with internal customers? In practical terms, the tools now exists to enable such targeting. Organizations now have access to software which could customize every piece of instruction or information.

Clearly, mass customization is not necessary where a fire instruction poster on the side of an oil tanker is concerned, but why shouldn't a training program be customized? CBT or computer-based training has taken this approach to a certain extent since it allows users to move at their own pace. But CBT rarely goes the whole way. How many packages cater for the user's psychometric profile and favorite style of learning? How many are cloaked in the user's preferred style of language – not a foreign language but a psychometrically adjusted language? CBT often does a great job at targeting individuals, yet its design is still catering for mass markets or at best, niche markets.

All messages can be targeted to *you*. This is the vision of Don Peppers and Martha Rogers for external marketing and it is my vision for internal marketing. Consider what Don Peppers and Martha Rogers say about external products in the *Harvard Business Review* (1995). The words in parenthesis are mine and refer to internal messages.

The title of the article is *From Mass Production* (of untargeted 'top-down' instructions) *to Mass Customization* (of targeted individually designed messages). Peppers and Rogers argue: 'Mass customization (*of instructions – or any other type of messages*) calls for a customer-centered orientation in production (*of the messages*) and delivery processes (*the media channels*), requiring the company to collaborate with individual customers to design each one's desired product or service.'

Apply Peppers and Rogers' logic to messages that the company wants to give. Aren't they a service? Doesn't the organization want to 'push' them at the internal customer? Yes, but if they want their people to 'buy,' then a 'pull" strategy is much more likely to succeed.

Am I saying a company should have to tell every single employee what to do in a completely different way? *Yes*. Take safety (it's worth repeating a message if lives are at stake). If an organization's toll of deaths is dependent on targeted communication then *target* it. If its future as a business is at stake because the staff levels *have* to be cut, then *target* the message.

Let us take a tip from what some would call that 'flaky' West Coast psychology, Neuro Linguistic Programming (I think of it as marketing in another guise). NLP advocates believe that the skill of communication is in the *sending*, not the receiving. If you do not understand me, the communicator, it is my mistake. You did not 'mishear' or 'get it wrong,' I did. The same principle is true in marketing. If the customer misunderstood the advert, copy, design, intention, humor, etc. it is not his or her fault. The same principle is true for internal marketing. It is the responsibility of the communicator to target any and all types of information.

So whether it is instructions, or any message, the move to targeting messages is critical. But apart from a very few 'must do' imperatives, the world is not run on instruction, it is run on information. It is here that mass customization really 'kicks in.'

Information – from 'useless overload' to 'loads of use'

Is there much to say about information? I suspect that many managers would be tempted to assume that an effective way of communicating information is simply to 'tell' groups of employees whatever they need to know in simple, unambiguous language. The more enlightened might also add that the information should be couched in language suited to the culture of the organization or – if we are lucky – even to the group of employees concerned.

A marketing-based approach to communicating information reveals the inadequacy of simply 'informing' people through top-down communication. The whole informing process becomes transformed when employees become internal customers.

At the moment, companies treat their internal customers like a mass market – and the resulting communication failure is very similar to some of those seen in external mass marketing!

Take, for example, the task of communicating mission and goals. Consider for a moment that employees are internal customers and that the corporate information is a product or a service that you are trying to sell. Consider a mission statement as a piece of consulting advice that will help internal customers perform their job better. Consider a business goal as a product that you want your internal customers to buy-in to, so that their input enables you to meet your targets. What do you do?

In all likelihood (especially in the 80s), you take a mass marketing approach and target all your customers in a single blanket approach. For example, you put your business goals in a list on a notice board or in the company magazine or maybe now the Intranet. You put your mission statement on a credit card or a screen saver and distribute this to every member of the organization.

Organizations are effectively adopting a mass marketing strategy when they try to communicate various forms of corporate information. This strategy is top-down and heavy handed – it targets 'everyone' and hits no one.

Here is my own early view (if 1989 is early) of mass customization *inside* an organization, taken from *The Employee Revolution*, the first book of its kind about corporate internal marketing:

> *'We have a term (employees) used to describe all the amazingly complex and varied internal target markets, which creates a perception something akin to the term "peasant" (as in the French Revolution). Unfortunately, perception is all. If this is to change with 'the employee revolution,' then the easiest way to do it is for the term to change. The word 'employee' must disappear and be replaced by a term which creates different perceptions, placing the importance on the individuality of the people in the organization and those who will be attracted to join it. It must also reflect the need to apply internal marketing techniques, when attempting to market or sell products and services, and*

attempting to match the needs of the individual to that of the organization. The term should be "internal target market".

'Having accepted that people can no longer be seen as "employees" then the next move would simply be to see them as "individuals." Everyone in the organization would then be seen as having a unique set of characteristics that need to be taken into account whenever they are on the receiving end of corporate internal marketing. The picture can be built up from there as necessary.

'Once the organization buys into the new language and philosophy that individuals actually are different from employees, and that they cannot be told what to do, the questions will be asked, "What skills do I need to be able to deal with individuals? How can I as a manager, and they as people with their own needs and desires, get what we both want?"

'To answer the first question, it is necessary to define the needs and desires of the individual. In other words, before a marketer decides, for example, what shape the advertising campaign might take, he needs to find out what people want and therefore what they might buy.'

This is where the strategy of matching the *top ten personal and business needs* comes into play. This is as much the domain of HR as of internal marketing. If the organization wants the internal customer to buy in to a business need and it knows that this individual has training as a *top ten personal need* then the two parties have an obvious base from which to start.

Apply the logic of one-to-one relationship marketing again. I use the same HBR article by Peppers and Rogers (with my italics inserted again). 'A company that aspires to give customers exactly what they want (*top ten personal needs*) must look at the world through new lenses. It must use technology to become two things: a mass customizer that efficiently provides individually customized goods and services, and one-to-one marketer that elicits information from each customer about his or her specific needs or preferences *(in order, in the case of a company, to ensure that they want to deliver its business needs).*'

Consider what's happening in Unisys; 'Unisys provides employees with the opportunity to improve their behavioral skills within six specific programs: presentation, communication, personal effectiveness, negotiating, leadership and consideration skills. Christine Carroll, director of external marketing for Unisys Services Group, says:

'"These courses may make Unisys employees more marketable elsewhere but, this is of little concern to the organization. If an organization gives employees the opportunity to learn, they are more likely to develop loyalty to the company, feel better about themselves and be more interested in the work they are doing."'

Once again, the focus here is on matching the *top ten personal needs* with those of individuals.

Forward-looking organizations recognize they have to look after the personal needs of their individual members in order to achieve key business goals. We begin to see what marketing-driven information processes are all about – not just top-down information about business needs, but also bottom-up information about individuals' *top ten personal needs*. We can also see from the Unisys example how the two can work together and be marketed together.

The following case study (Box 6.1) shows how British Nuclear Fuels plc (BNFL) is ensuring it has effective information processes in place in preparation for a move up to involvement.

Box 6.1   Internal customer research drives success

BNFL is the most experienced nuclear fuel company in the world, with some 12,000 staff worldwide. Facing a period of immense change, BNFL is striving to transform the company into a commercially minded organization succeeding within an international and competitive environment. The company asked MCA to help it develop a communication strategy, which was seen as vital in order to obtain the 'buy in' of staff to the new business strategies and develop a commercial focus in the workplace.

The Board recognized that achieving staff ownership of the reasons for change through effective two-way communication would be vital to BNFL's future business success. The first step, and the focus of this case study, was to understand the current state of communication through a communication research, and determine improvements to enable effective delivery of key business messages.

Our approach

We knew that to undertake purely quantitative research would not achieve our objectives. We needed to find out *why* messages were not getting through effectively and *why* staff weren't buying in to them. Therefore, we undertook extensive qualitative research in the following areas:

- *The messages* – To ensure that the business needs of BNFL were met, we first needed to identify the nature and scope of the messages that needed communicating. This was done via interviews with key message makers. We interviewed senior managers and communication practitioners within BNFL to explore the critical messages, the channels used and their perceptions of communication.

- *The media* – Concurrent with the interviews, we analyzed all existing media channels, formal and informal, to evaluate:
  - the content of the media to compare findings with the messages described in the interviews and note any inconsistent or incomplete messages.
  - the purpose or role to assess the role of each medium, using a variety of criteria.
- *The market* – Our ability to match crucial business messages to the needs and concerns of the target markets or audiences was key to the success of the communication research. To identify these needs we took a two-stage approach:
  - one-to-one interviews with staff to discuss the messages staff receive and begin to explore the consistency, clarity and relevance of these in preparation for the Issues Groups™.
  - Issues Groups™ – We used the core data from staff interviews as a starting point of discussions in Issues Groups, MCA's unique approach to the traditional focus group. The Groups identified the key 'bottom up' needs or 'hooks' used to match with the key messages of the business. Each of the six one-day groups involved around 12 randomly selected individuals.

Results

The research was very successful in meeting its objectives of identifying ways to overcome the barriers to communicating the business objectives and developing an appropriate two-way communication strategy for BNFL.

The following paragraphs provide insight into the deep understanding we now have of staff needs and drivers.

The message

- People throughout the organization did see the need for change but feared their futures.

'There'll be no feel good factor until the changes are settled.'
'We're living in the dark ages.'

- Not feeling united as one team, staff worked within their own sites or Divisions, often without consulting the rest of the organization. This culture mirrored the infrastructure.
  'We just work in individual pockets with our own agendas.'
- People saw change to be 'for the sake of it' with no final destination, not understanding the potential for BNFL in the global market.
  'I don't really know what the company stands for anymore.'

The media

- There was no clear source of information about the organization's 'big picture', i.e. its function, goals and progress towards those goals. Instead there were numerous sources of information, each containing pieces of the picture. This prevented people from understanding the wider perspective and from linking their local activities to the wider corporate goals.
- This was reinforced by the majority of media being one way – top down – again preventing feedback from staff about the message. We found no guarantee that corporate messages were delivered consistently across the organization, if at all.
  'We only get the bare facts, we don't get the chance to discuss things.'
  'I'd like to get a translation of the big issues into local ones.'

The market

- Morale was very low. Previously offering very secure employment, BNFL had to make efficiencies to become more internationally competitive. Staff fear losing their jobs and, in such a specialist industry, saw little or no chance of being able to find similar employment outside the organization. Staff would not buy into change messages without an understanding of the implications for jobs.

- There was a deep seated lack of trust in all senior management and the Board. People felt that they had no control over their own future. They felt that if change was implemented with consultation and involvement, the result would be far more effective.

  '*We need to create a culture where people can speak up without fear of recrimination.*'

- The majority of managers were not confident that they possessed the necessary skills to communicate effectively and avoided rather than welcomed opportunities to talk with and encourage their people.

These findings gave us invaluable insights into the best way forward for driving the desired cultural change. We are now in the process of implementing 'Talking Business' a two-way communication process, designed to address the needs of the organization and the people and move from information- to involvement-based processes.

Discovering the internal customer

How can organizations gather rich enough information about their internal customers to match their personal needs with those of the business?

The solution is to revolutionize the data base on every internal customer and to keep this permanent and up-to-date. This can be achieved without creating massive workloads for an internal research department. Internal customers can develop their own data base themselves or they can get their managers, peers and suppliers to develop it for them.

One method is 360-degree appraisal. This is based on the strategy that everyone is responsible for gathering feedback from everyone – hence 360-degree appraisal. Great strategy, yet often the 360-degree appraisal is only used as an HR tool for annual appraisal, not as a marketing tool for constant customer feedback. However, the beginnings of an all-embracing information tool are just beginning to be put in place as part of MCA Innovation process, I call it 360-degree marketing.

Consider how Peppers and Rogers' concept of 'learning relationships' between external stakeholders and customers can be applied to individuals inside the organization. The parenthesis are mine. In the *HBR*, the two marketers argue: 'Another option for a manufacturer or a service company *(the organization)* is to form tighter partnerships with retailers *(internal individuals)* so that together *(top-down and bottom-up), they* control the learning relationships *(side-to-side)* with individual end customers *(and other external stakeholders, suppliers and strategic alliances).'*

This is the secret of any organization – becoming successful in communicating data, information and knowledge. Information flows must be two way. Information must also be understood as well as being exchanged if it is to become useful information – otherwise it is just data. Data needs sifting, sorting, adding, subtracting, massaging and generally being worked on for it to become information which is useful. To do this, even data needs to be adequately communicated.

Once organizations have the basic data and the information that ensures individuals know what they are doing and why, a different form of information can begin to take hold. Everyone begins to recognize that if the business is to deliver quality and drive innovation, they need to communicate information that allows people to improve, innovate and integrate.

Overload ... danger ... overload ... danger ... boom

As well as the positive effects of being able to access information and to use this to develop the organization and its products and services, there can also be a negative effect. Organizations can go from massive *data* overload, produced by electronic technology, to *information* overload produced by the ability to communicate through information technology. Yet ironically, they can also suffer from a scarcity of information at the same time when internal customers cannot or will not release vital knowledge to others.

What is the real problem? Not information overload or knowledge blockages. The real problem is emotional overload and an unwillingness to *do* anything with vital information. This now brings us to the next process; involving.

Involvement – knowing me, knowing you

As organizations begin to implement more marketing-driven processes of instruction and information, they reach a point where they must ask the following question: do their people want to do something with the data, information or knowledge? The answer is that they will only do something with all three if they are involved. Involvement, the third *I*, includes being involved with others, involved in a dialogue, involved face-to-face, involved in producing the solution, involved in implementing the answer, involved in receiving recognition of success.

Human resources has offered a host of skills which involve involving; coaching, counseling, listening, empathizing. The field of psychology offers methods like transactional analysis, neuro linguistic programming, gender communication, Myers Briggs and a host of other psychometric instruments. They are perceived to allow communication because they help people 'understand' each other. (I cover many of these concepts in *Passion at work.*)

Marketing has not added very much to the topic of 'employee' involvement. While there are acres of print, countless courses and many professional and academic specialists on how external marketing engages customers, internal marketing has sadly lagged behind. Yet internal communications have not developed either if our 6 out of 10 score is to be believed.

The 'best' example of an involving process so far has been the failed process of 'team briefing' cascades, or 'trickle downs' as they are known in some places. Yet in many organizations across the world even a cascade (or trickle) of 'tell' is not used. The mushroom theory reigns supreme – keep them in the dark and feed them …!

The opposite to the mushroom theory is explosive – involve everyone. Yes, everyone. As we have seen, there is a wealth of training for individual manager and team leaders in subjects like coaching, counseling, listening and learning. But what we are talking about here is much bigger. It is involvement through what I call 'organizational listening'. What happens when you get this?

One of MCA's associate researchers, Louise Berkye, has looked into how involvement can become a 'deep learning process' for individuals and organizations. In the course of her research, she discovered that 'deep learning' at the organizational level can only occur when people are able to reflect on experiences and feelings. The important factor is mutual self-disclosure, which symbolizes feelings of safety and trust (remember the dynamic emotions). It is at this point that collective learning occurs and groups and/or organization(s) will begin to move forward and become unstuck.

In other words, face-to-face encounters between individuals build trust and create an environment or 'space' where learning occur. Open, honest talking *and* listening enable people to reach new levels of trust and to move forward together.

We also uncovered other benefits of participative meetings or encounters. Creating situations in which managers are *not* in control (like a truly interactive team meeting) strengthens team-building and gives rise to self-governance.

In marketing terms, involvement is created by processes which move organizations on from 'talking at' employees in 'tell' and 'sell' mode to 'listening to' internal customers in 'buy' and 'buy-in' mode. When organizations achieve this transition, they are moving towards becoming the type of learning organizations described above in the academic literature.

One of the most powerful and effective involving tools developed by MCA is Team Listening®. This is a face-to-face process for *involving* people, not talking at them in presentations, cascades or 'team briefings'. This process of involvement is illustrated by the following case study (Box 6.2).

Box 6.2   Involving staff in achieving tough business goals

Royal Mail Streamline is the letters and electronic services group of the UK's national postal service. The organization had set itself an ambitious plan for growth – to double in size in four years. It was apparent that the only way it could achieve this goal was to change its ways of working. Communication had to play a key part in delivering the objectives for Royal Mail Streamline, by involving people in its business objectives:

- to move from a £1bn to a £4bn organization by the year 2001
- to move (direct mail) from a 17% to a 25% share of the advertising market
- to be involved in the development of new products and services to achieve these goals
- to become more systematic, ensuring consistency of policy, process and deployment
- to become more creative, innovative and entrepreneurial
- to maximize internal resources and develop people to meet the challenges.

To achieve these goals, the communication process had to encourage ownership, involvement and understanding of the goals.
It had to avert cynicism and manage people's expectations. It
had to be sustained over an 18-month period and also provide
measurement criteria and techniques to monitor and evaluate
success.

Overview of approach

MCA's approach was based on the principles of marketing – that
success is assured if people 'buy-in' to change and the hard
business messages, rather than 'selling' it to them. Keeping these
principles in mind, we focused on moving Royal Mail Streamline's
communication strategy from one of information-giving to involvement.

The change program – and the communication associated
with it – was branded under the heading 'Building on Success'.
We implemented Team Listening®, an effective involvement
communication process, by:

- using initial qualitative research to understand the 'hooks'
  and concerns of staff and to match them to business messages in order to achieve 'buy in'
- launching a bi-monthly business journal that would deliver
  the business messages in a consistent, readable manner
- implementing two-way team meetings to discuss the messages in the journal, put them into a local context, give people
  the opportunity to feed back their views and then agree local
  and individual actions
- monitoring the understanding and buy-in to the communication program and its messages through targeted questions at
  the meetings, followed by individual and team feedback forms
- developing a comprehensive program of skills development
  for managers/team leaders so that they could take the process forward

- helping review and develop the process as it matured, maintaining the involvement of people in culture developing, whilst increasing the communication of key business issues.

Results

Team Listening has fundamentally changed the way in which the business communicated from an ad hoc approach to one that was focused, consistent and involving.

The response from the market to Issue 1 (June 1995) was:

- 94% of all respondents were very happy with the process
- 66% found the journals useful
- 100% thought it was useful to receive the journal in advance.

The response to Issue 10 (December 1996) was:

- 100% found the journal useful
- 100% agreed participation in Team Listening was good
- 80% said the topics raised were of interest to them
- 60% said the articles were clear and readable (although they could be better targeted)
- 100% were satisfied with the Team Listening process.

The process has been running in Royal Mail Streamline for well over a year. It has been used successfully as a forum to gain input and involvement on several efforts including flexible working arrangements, finance training and a new induction program. At Streamline's Business Excellence Review in September 1996, Team Listening was identified as a Best Practice within the whole Royal Mail business.

What do organizations need to do to ensure that an involvement process like Team Listening works, when just about all other face-to-face processes fail? A lot.

Here are just some of the steps:

- set a strategy for communication and internal marketing
- communicate that strategy – through targeted sessions of training and development
- gather data on the *top ten business and personal needs*
- launch the process and the issues involved
- target information
- promote the messages with support material
- produce the right media
- produce the right designs
- use the right language
- develop the skills and any support package to encourage listening and debate
- capture any feedback
- plan the rest of the campaign.

All of these strategies, processes, tools and skills are based on marketing principles and practices applied internally – with a lot of human resource and psychology thrown in. The core philosophy we have discussed is the strategy of matching the needs of the organization to the people then allowing them to develop the answers about how to implement the solutions. Remember that this does not necessarily entail involving people in deciding the business strategy – remember the need for strong leadership is often one of the *top ten personal needs*. What it does require is getting them involved in areas where they can best contribute.

Starve a company, feed a grapevine

Organizational listening generates strong involvement, and it also helps unify an organization. When there is poor communication, everyone tends to gossip about everything. The informal grapevine works overtime – just imagine what is happening in

Intel while FACEIntel is active; everything from the future of the company to the future of every individual is probably up for debate. Yet our research shows that in a company where face-to-face involvement is positively encouraged, the informal grapevine withers – to be replaced by a powerful, united formal grapevine.

What's the catch? There is one, a BIG one.

Involvement through organizational listening is a simple format but it is *hard work*. The opposite process of mass communication is complicated but easy. Mass communication may require many channels and massive message dissemination but ultimately, the media can be created by one person with desktop publishing software. Listening and involving include everyone. The payback? Involvement is the first move into the paradigm shift of treating employees as customers. It is the first step to internal marketing.

Once people feel 'listened to'; once 'top-down and bottom-up' are working; once people feel involved then the next step of the six *I*s begins. When the people in an organization have bought the top-down 'big picture' and they feel their *top ten personal needs* (in a bottom-up list!) have been met what happens next? Next, the people in the organization will want to 'do better all the worthwhile things they ought to be doing anyway' the quality message from Philip Crosby! But this time, instead of being 'told' to 'think quality' and to 'exchange best practice,' they *want* to.

Improvement: getting better all the time

'Tell me what you want, what you really, really want' goes the global smash hit by the hot pop group of the moment, the Spice Girls. And what do businesses want? How about your whole workforce working together to go beyond quality into delivering improvements to everything from the production line, to safety, to your sales and marketing? What you really, really want – is everyone:

- Delivering unbeatable and constantly improving **quality,** and wanting to play their part in it
- Giving outstanding **customer service**
- Helping build **sales volume**
- Providing the right level of service throughout the **customer chain**
- Getting close to customers to keep **'up to the minute'** with market, and individual needs.
- Adding to the **'knowledge bank'** in the organization
- Exchanging **'best practice'**
- Working to stay ahead of the **competition**
- **Researching and listening** to customers to find their needs – inside and out
- Designing and delivering **improved products**
- Upgrading **production processes**
- Working effectively with other **internal departments**, teams, companies, international operations
- Encouraging customers to buy through delivering the **brand value**
- Cutting customer **complaints**
- Working on **problem solving**
- Using **customer comments** to improve the quality of products and services
- Reducing **faults,** errors and damages and saving time
- Getting together to drive motivation and increase **sales**
- Cutting **accidents**
- Sharing findings throughout all **shifts**
- Working better with **partnerships**
- **Learning** in the business

- Creating a knowledge base about the company to improve understanding of the **'big picture'** as well as the pieces
- Creating an improved **spirit of competition**
- Improving the overall **brand positioning**
- Sharing business information to involve everyone in the results and the **future goals** of the business
- Improving the **safety results**, admitting there is a need for improvement, looking for everyone to assist
- Becoming **'employer of choice'**
- Help in opening a **new market sector**
- Increasing the **intellectual capital** by sharing knowledge of what is going on around the business as well as in it
- Adding to the **emotional capital** like 'pride' in the organization
- **Overall** – Beating the competition with better product, lower costs, better service, better knowledge and showing what individuals can do *to help improve on what the company has done* and what the major competitors are doing and may do in the future.

Can you say that everyone in your organization is focused on delivering against a list of improvements like this?

'Improvement' is another simple word, to describe what Michael Porter would deem as 'operational effectiveness.' It won't, he says, give you a strategic edge, but it sure gives you a tactical edge when everyone else is looking to cut costs, improve efficiency and effectiveness in just about everything.

'Improvement' is a simple word to describe all those initiatives in business we have looked at along the communication time line. It is as word which sums up much of management focus for the last 100 years – from the early scientific management approaches to deliver manufacturing and production improvements around volume, volume, volume, to the recent value added initiatives of Total Quality Management (TQM),

Business Process Re-engineering (BPR) and any of the other TWA (Three Word Acronyms) so popular in the 80s and early 90s.

Creating the type of culture and mindset needed to achieve this tactical edge takes robust improvement *processes*. The following case study illustrates such a process in action. It is a speech by Emma Westcott, Manager of Organization and Management Development for Walkers Snack Foods, part of PepsiCo, presented at a recent conference about using internal communication for commercial success. Our thanks to Walkers Snack Foods for allowing us to share what is obviously valuable commercial information. They do it to help the business community.

Box 6.3   Tapping into the power of best practices

'When you talk about communication strategies for commercial success, continuous improvement is a big part. At Walkers, we've worked for the last 12 months on a program about three-way communication: top-down and bottom-up as well as side-to-side communication across locations and functions. It's a program that is enabling Walkers not only to inform our staff, but also to involve them in the business' success and to provide them with a forum for sharing good ideas and best practices in order to improve our business.

About Walkers

'To put the program in a business context I must give you an overview of our organization, our culture and the business challenges we face. Walkers is part of PepsiCo and the no. 1 producer of salty snacks in the UK.

'Clearly, maintaining our success and leadership position is vital for us. Our aim is to double our business every five years. To achieve that, Walkers' vision is to be the UK's best consumer products company. Our success and ambitious goals also present some unique challenges: People can easily become complacent, or lose sight of the role they need to play in our growth and see it as someone else's problem – which is why we decided to look at ways to use our internal communication as a tool to respond to these challenges.

Our approach

'We hadn't been ignoring communication all this time. In fact, we had put a lot into internal communication in the past.

'Unfortunately, the gap between intent and effect had been quite big in the past … we had invested a lot of time and money, and unfortunately had a low return in terms of effect on employees or on business performance.

'To avoid repeating our past experiences, we decided to work with MCA in order to take a more results-oriented approach to communication. Our approach involved a number of steps:

- using qualitative research to understand people's issues and our past experiences, and to identify opportunities
- setting communication goals that support Walkers' day-to-day focus
- testing the program to ensure effectiveness
- using staff feedback and surveys to track our progress.

'We spoke with individuals and groups of staff from a cross-section of functions and levels and deliberately used qualitative research to get under the skin of what people really needed and wanted from communication. We then designed our program with these views in mind, tested it again with groups of staff and fine-tuned it before going forward.

'What we learned was that past communication had been too "top down" – in other words, we hadn't addressed the "what's in it for me" factor. Communication was also seen as being low on managers' agenda, in part because it wasn't measured. And cascades were causing messages to be reinterpreted (and misinterpreted).

'It also become clear that people were hungry for more information about how our business was performing as a whole. They are regularly told about local targets, but didn't see how they fit within the larger picture. And our operations staff really wanted to know more about the business from a marketing perspective – new business, competitor activity, marketing plans – to really feel involved.

'We also found that best practices – as a way to improve by working smarter instead of harder – was a strong hook for people already giving 100%. Plus, we discovered some areas with excellent communication practices in place – regular team meetings, good listening, an involving management style. We had an opportunity to build a consistent process around these good habits so that all areas could perform to the same standard.

Our communication process

'We introduced a communication process based on MCA's Team Listening model that, in the simplest terms, involves a bi-monthly business journal that goes out to every member of staff. It combines best practices from around Walkers with business news and updates.

'Teams meet bi-monthly to talk about the journal and any other issues of interest and to agree local action. They can combine this with existing meeting structures if they like. At the end of the meeting, the team leader fills out a feedback form with actions and best practices. It also includes a scoring tool so we can track our effectiveness. They use this form as a reference in their next meeting, and send copies to the HR department to help shape the next journal.

'A typical journal will contain 3–4 best practices from around the company, as well as new product launches and marketing programs, fast facts about our industry, new business wins and performance against five key company goals. We also provide notes to team leaders with suggestions for incorporating topics in the journal into their discussion.

'We've branded this process and the journal under the banner of one of our day-to-day focuses, "Finding a Better Way". The good thing about this approach is that it enables the exchange of best practice, it covers how we work and how we're doing, it links communication to day-to-day business, and it encourages individual involvement

Best practice champions

'One of our aims was to ensure a more consistent standard of communication. To achieve this, we needed to develop managers to the same level as communicators through training and then continue to provide them with support.

'We felt we'd have more buy-in if this training was delivered by someone within their own organization instead of an outside consultant. So we developed a train-the-trainer program and set a window of time for all of the champions to deliver their training. The champions also serve as a 'network' for us to test ideas, generate input, and identify areas for improvement.

Creating a best practice culture

'One of the real benefits of having an established process for best practice is that it truly begins to build a culture of continuous improvement. The process alone wouldn't be enough though. Just as important is the way we've "wrapped and packaged" the process – the most important feature being our non-gloss approach.

'We've had to tackle a lot of business issues in a hard-hitting, honest way, because if we're not prepared to acknowledge what's not working then how can we possibly improve it?! Yet there is often a temptation to want to put a positive spin on things out of concern that bad news demotivates, when in fact being candid builds trust and involvement.

'We've also been very deliberate in supporting team leaders who run the meetings, giving them training in facilitation skills and providing them with Team Leaders' Notes with each journal to help them gain the most from their meetings. What's interesting is that some teams are using their team meetings not only to discuss which best practices in the journal they might apply, but also to brainstorm other problems and issues right there on the spot.

'Having designated champions has also been valuable, both to deliver the training and to maintain momentum by being right there at the front line.

Benefits and results

'We've certainly benefited by achieving our goal for a consistently high quality communication that is both involving and results-oriented. We've also benefited by having managers that are trained as facilitators and a process that works for a variety of situations. Since its launch, we've been able to use the process as part of an internal crisis communication, and it provided us with a responsive and effective channel.

'On a business note, we're seeing teams finding ways to improve quality, simplify work processes and satisfy their customers more effectively. Of course, not everything is perfect. We have a lot of work still to do in order to achieve the level of improvement we want. A benchmarking survey we undertook one year into the program showed us where to focus our attention, and we are acting on those gaps now.

'On a personal note, it's very rewarding to have finally found a focus for communication that can make a difference for our people and for the business. We are striving to make Walkers the UK's employer of choice, and this is another step in that direction.

Source: excerpts from a speech by Emma Westcott, Walkers Snack Foods, at a conference hosted in London by the International Quality and Productivity Center (IQPC) in August 1997.

How can organizations build the intellectual and emotional capital to be able to deliver internal marketing programs like 'Finding A Better Way?' The way to do it is through building the stocks of emotional capital. Once again 'hearts and minds' are inextricably linked. Getting people to want to 'make it better' is the starting point for quality and constant improvement. Here's the catch. Most 'improvements' look to making things better, faster, cheaper, which has presented a few problems for people:

- What's in it for me, the individual, when 'improvement' means I am probably doing myself out of a job? It's like turkeys voting for Christmas!
- Most of the research points to a 50–75% failure rate for initiatives delivering the promises they offered (hint: nos 1 and 2 are linked)
- Even if you become more operationally effective, everyone else is doing the same thing.
- Improvement is *not* Innovation – the two are completely different. Creating something *new* and *different* is *not* the same as being better. That is the reason that 'Improvement' is only two-thirds of the way up the process model, shown at the beginning of this chapter. It will only get you part way to the top of customer buy-in, especially if it is 'new' not 'better' that customers want.

The bottom line is that 'better' will keep you *in* the game; 'new' is what you need to get *ahead* of the game. Quality is no longer the name of the game. Customers have played that game. We have moved along the marketing and communication time line; now we are now looking after the customer of the 90s. Quality is a 'given' now; they expect it; it is a 'hygiene factor.' What do customers want, what do they really, really want? New, new, new.

And new, new, new is not improved, improved, improved. Meeting the customers needs of tomorrow is a process for today called Innovation.

Innovation – new, not improved

To really appreciate the speed of change in every organization, including yours, think about everything that occurs as a result of one simple act occurs: a new product is launched. Can your people in your organization cope with every one of the issues raised in this list?

> *New product launch, new advert goes out, new pro-motion follows, new PR, new customers, new demands, new markets, new factories, new staff, new sales force, new distributors, new franchisees, new agencies, new campaigns, new countries, new alliances, new suppli-ers, new laws, new governments, new crisis, new take-over, new culture, new bosses, new vision, new mission, new values, new discovery, new investors, new plant, new manufacturing process, new production methods, new quality processes, new communication strategy, new internal marketing processes, new tar-gets to meet, new product to launch, new advert goes out, new promotion follows, new PR, new customers, new demands, new markets, new factories, new staff, new sales force, new distributors, new franchisees, new agencies, new campaigns, new countries, new alli-ances, new suppliers, new laws, new governments, new crisis, new take-over, new culture, new bosses, new vision, new mission, new values, new discovery, new investors, new plant, new manufacturing process, new production methods, new quality processes, new com-*

munication strategy, new internal marketing processes, new targets to meet, follows, new PR, new customers, new demands, new markets, new factories, new staff, new sales force, new distributors, new franchisees, new agencies, new campaigns, new countries, new alliances, new suppliers, new laws, new governments, new crisis, new take-over, new culture, new bosses, new vision, new mission, new values, new discovery, new investors, new plant, new manufacturing process, new production methods, new quality processes, new communication strategy, new internal marketing processes, new targets to meet ...

Confusion he say ...
may you live in innovative times

If only we had the time to stop still for long enough to have something tried and tested, we could go back to the good old days and focus on improvements like best practice and benchmarking. But you can't benchmark something where there is no bench and no mark!

Innovation requires two formidable reserves: the intellectual capital to navigate through the unknown and the emotional capital to overcome the fear and arrogance that can often block innovation.

Why is communication involved again? Well, as the saying goes 'You don't know what you don't know.' Getting to know what you don't know is a basic component of innovation. Knowledge management requires that people are aware of what needs to be innovated – from customer requirements to whether it already exists (the chances are that it does).

The trouble with innovation is that it has been confused with creativity. Creativity is the process and language for inventing something new that does not exist. Processes like brainstorming have given innovation an image of happy days spent scribbling wacky ideas on a flip chart.

Although creativity is a vital component of innovation it is but one small part. Many of the workshops we run on innovation produce comments from participants saying that their problem is not lack of creativity (a lack of ideas), the real issue is innovation. *Turning ideas into deliverable business results* is now mission critical.

Why do many organizations struggle to transform ideas into tangible results and assets? Their problem lies with their communication processes. If these processes and the organizational language and culture stuck are stuck in 1950s, who would want to, be able to, or know how to express themselves in such a way as to be able to innovate?

A large spanner in the works

Innovation doesn't just happen. Those organizations who rely on innovation have put strong processes in place and they also have strong languages wrapped around these processes.

However, much of the work of creativity and innovation is still done by trained experts in research and development. If organizations are to survive they need everyone involved in innovation. Think back to the profound changes that resulted from one new product launch, described at the start of this section. Even if an organization does not actually invent a new product or service but merely decides to use or sell someone else's ideas, the effects of this will usually require many people to do many new things to make using the product or service a success. If these individuals do not have the process or language which creates the climate for innovation then someone, somewhere, will put a large spanner in the works.

The guru of innovation, Edward de Bono, created processes like 'lateral thinking' and he also created a language for thinking in his book, *Teach Yourself to Think*.

Dr Min Basadur of the Center for Research in Applied Creativity has written, *The Power of Innovation* (1995). This book centers around a process for 'making innovation a way of life.' Basadur does not specifically talk of a language of innovation yet he produces one, for example he uses catchphrases like 'How might I' and 'Why – what's stopping me?'

MCA has developed an approach, centered on a process and language which we are in the process of launching as part of our innovation program of new concepts. However, our experience has shown that it is extremely difficult for whole organizations to get to this stage of the six *I*s. Innovation and creativity require an amazing shift in just about everything people think, feel and believe before they can say or do anything different. Yet if organizations do not change the culture and climate for innovation, they will simply find themselves swept aside by more innovative competitors.

Here is an excerpt from Ernst & Young's journal on innovation in organizations. 'Managing creativity really requires a new managerial mindset,' writes John Kao. 'If you think what traditional management is all about – how it is taught in business schools and practiced in organizations – the skills that are rewarded have a lot to do with analyzing options, decreasing uncertainty, and paying a lot of attention to detail. But those kind of skills (and the language around them) may actually be highly dysfunctional in an environment where the mission is to generate new insights, ideas, and processes that lead to the realization of value.'

If managing creativity and innovation is difficult, with the need for a completely different set of processes and words to create a language within the organization, imagine now the next step in the continuum. In order to move towards true relationship marketing, organizations need to ask their people to adopt a new set of processes and language to deal with all the dimensions of communication to customers, stakeholders, strategic alliances and suppliers.

These processes and language are of communication and marketing itself. The processes and language are those developed and used by the marketing specialists in the organization. Now that everyone is responsible for the product, service, brand, corporate reputation and personality, they have to be able to play a part in this integrated approach.

Integration – the challenge for the next millennium

There is a rich debate going on in the worlds of corporate communication and marketing about an integrated approach to dealing with customers and stakeholders. This was the central theme of the 1996 'One Voice' International Conference of the Chartered Institute of Marketing, and the 1997 IABC International Conference in Los Angeles on 'New World Strategies'.

CNN ... outside your offices ... reporting live

So the issues of integration are recognized. Yet how to make it happen? If everyone in your organization *is* your brand; are they capable of being your brand managers? Do they have the marketing and communication processes and tools to deal with that one-to-one customer? The same is true if they are your Corporate Communication Director. Are they capable of responding to CNN outside the office door if there is a crisis of confidence in your business? The same is true if they are part of your advertising agency. How are they creating the design, language, hooks, copy for their new home pages. Is your staff able to act as part of your editorial team when creating news for the Intranet?

Integration involves everyone. This has been the key message of this book; a message that says the emotional capital reserves are there to use in *every* aspect of business and for *every* dimension of communication and marketing, both inside and out. I talked at the beginning of this book about not reinventing the wheel. So I am including an excerpt (Box 6.4) from the article I wrote for the Financial Times Handbook of Management (May 1995).

This excerpt covers the issue of integration from an internal marketing point of view. This article was written for the leaders and managers of business to challenge the conventional wisdom that only the experts are responsible for talking with the world at large. It shows how the marketing processes, as well as the marketing philosophy, can be used by everyone to create buy in inside and outside the organization. Clearly we have touched on many of these issues, for integration is all about pulling everything together we have discussed. However, this is perhaps the most difficult issue of them all.

Box 6.4   Integration through internal marketing

Customers and markets, once considered as existing only outside the organization, are now seen as existing within it as well. What is true of the external market – that best satisfying its needs is what drives the organization – is true also of the internal market. Both need to be served if companies are to continue to meet corporate goals.

Where there are markets, marketing activity follows. As a result, a new discipline, internal marketing, is emerging, not as a pale shadow of external marketing, but as a powerful new force with a strong link to revenue generation.

Internal marketing is a process which recognizes that people within the company have a big influence on customers. How people get on with their employers, managers, and with others inside the company, has a direct bearing on the quality of their own relationship with people outside the company – the customers of the organization.

Organizations set on introducing internal marketing practices first need to take a new view of the people within the organization and the way in which they are managed. If people are seen as customers (internal customers) then it follows that each has a supplier (their colleagues).

The organization can then be thought of as comprising a series of internal markets, each of which needs to 'market' to the other in the common cause of best meeting external consumer requirements. The next step is to get the people in the organization to take the same marketing-based view.

As with external marketing, the company should start by understanding its new customers. What do they want? What motivates them? What do they think of the 'service' they currently receive? What will persuade them to buy-in to the proposition that they themselves are customers, and, indeed, suppliers to their colleagues? It is by listening and understanding the needs of its own people that the company can convincingly respond to the big question to follow, 'What's in it for me?'

The director-general of the Institute of Personnel and Development, Geoff Armstrong, says: 'You have to know the people, to recognize cultural differences, to analyze their capabilities and to relate all that to the business environment to creates sustainable business advantage. Without that, important ideas such as total quality management and business process re-engineering become no more than flavors of the month.'

The phases of an integrated internal marketing process are shown in Fig. 6.1.

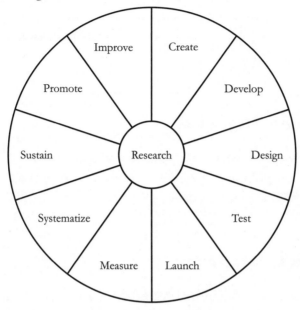

Fig. 6.1   The process wheel for integrated internal marketing.

Internal marketing is appropriate to most types of organization, not just to those who have actually established internal markets – that is to say autonomous profit centers that compete in an internal market. Here, it might be expected that internal marketing would be most visible.

In their book *Internal Markets*, Halal, Geranmayeh and Pourdehnad made the point that where internal markets were established, managers should actively strive to make the idea work by marketing their services to clients, working with them closely to solve problems, and developing methods to evaluate their satisfaction.

Source: chapter from *The Financial Times Handbook of Management* on internal marketing, written by Kevin Thomson and published by Pitman Publishing.

The six dimensions of integration

If we agree that integration makes sense, what will it look like when we have it? Here is a simple check list based on the six dimensions that gives a glimpse of a time when, as they say 'the planets are aligned.'

Top-down integration

The message makers are integrated and their 'arrow' of communication is pointing in one direction toward everyone in the organization. Which leads to....

Bottom-up integration

Everyone in the organization understand the 'Big Picture' and the pieces *and* where they fit *and* they want to deliver because their needs have been listened to. Which leads to...

Side-to-side integration

Individual, teams, departments, functions treat each other as internal customers and internal markets where there is a continuous customer supplier chain delivering a quality product or service in order to meet the needs of the external customer. Which leads to...

Customer integration

One-to-one customer service, and marketing-based relationships occur with *everyone* in the organization; to ensure that the customers' basic needs for a quality product and service are met *and* they are delivered in a way that is consistent with the brand and corporate personality. Which leads to …

Stakeholder integration

The brand and corporate personality are seen as the creator of its reputation; a reputation that if integrated with the community in which it operates, extends beyond the shareholder into all its stakeholders. Which leads to …

Supplier/strategic alliance integration

The business community in which the organization operates is all communicating in an integrated way. They use each of the six dimensions to interact with all those involved, starting with 'top down' with their internal customers. Which leads to …

And so the cycle of integration goes around, just as the process wheel of marketing goes around in trying to research and de-fine and create and produce and stimulate customer needs – both inside and outside the organization.

> *'What! Us talk to them? You have to be joking!'*

Integration is a subject until very recently would have been met with a mixture of incredulity or derision.

> *'What! Merge marketing and HR? Unthinkable!'*

Yes, why not? It is happening now. I call it the new PR – People Relations (managing relationships with all of the people).

'What! Let workers help decide our fate?'

Yes, in Europe the 'Works Council' is a directive which does just that.

'What? Listen to these crazy conservationists?'

Yes, more and more companies have trained environmentalists affecting board-level decisions.

'What? Let the trade unions' communication on job losses go out with ours? You cannot be serious!'

We were serious, and our clients have done just that.

And as our role in communication and internal marketing covers all the dimensions we are seeing this big picture of integration growing geometrically.

We looked back so that we could move forward

We have now traveled along an exciting timeline of the past and looked into the present and future using the Six *I*s. The only problem is that the external customer has been carried on the journey and is now heading for the next millennium; however, the internal customer is still back in the journey planning stages in the 50s and 60s.

How do we move forward 50 years? This sounds like a cultural shift of truly awesome proportions. The next section on the new business cultures puts forward the proposition that to change culture the last thing you do is try to change culture. The first thing we look to achieve is something very different – a change in climate.

Building the blueprint: the six *Is*

Six Is
Six internal marketing and communication processes – each of which corresponds to the six *D*s, so you are able to implement them to maximum effect if you want to deliver your business strategy.

Six Ds
Six dimensions of a strategy that includes all the relationships in and around an organization.

BUSINESS FOCUS

Product→Customer→Relationship

LANGUAGE

PROCESS	'It'	'You'	'We'	STRATEGY	
Integrate					inside and out
Innovate					customers
Improve					side to side
Involve					two way
Inform					top down bottom up
Instruct					top down

50	60	70	80	90	2000
Tell		Buy		Friends	
	Sell		Buy-in	Best friends	

CUSTOMERS
inside and out

Physical Capital→Intellectual Capital→Emotional Capital

ASSETS (BALANCE SHEET)

CULTURE

Paternal→Empowered→Passionate

REVENUE & COSTS (P&L)

Vision→Value→Volume

Revenue and costs
The top and bottom line are affected by the impact of the communication and marketing strategy on the business strategy.

Culture
The six *Is* create one of the two core parts of a climate in an organization (language is the other) – and climate is the way to create and sustain culture change

My notes on the six *I*s

Here were you thinking that communication was all about 'sending something out'! 'And who' you may also be thinking 'is this guy to come along and spoil it all? Now we need to look again at something we just used to leave up to someone in the communication or HR department.' Or are you saying 'Yes! Now I see it. A blinding flash of the obvious really. (Do these people really earn a living doing this sort of thing — ah well.)'

The six Is are a simple — yet hard way of taking whole organization up the Timeline. Listening, involving, innovating and especially integrating are infinitely more difficult than instructing and informing — and look what a pretty lousy job some organization have made of that!

The six Is are described in linear fashion because that is exactly how they operate. So if you want to climb to the top of the mountain you can't take short cuts. You could try to helicopter to the top — well you can try but you will only take a few people with you at a time!

Thought provokers for the future

What are you doing in your organization with each of the six Is to systematize these core elements of business processes?

- *Instructions — How well targeted? How often are they ignored, or just forgotten?*
- *Information — How well integrated are your top-down business messages? How well understood are your internal customers top ten personal needs?*
- *Involvement — How good are you are you at getting people to contribute? How good are your feedback loops?*
- *Improvement — How successful are your change programs or initiatives? How successful are your mergers and acquisitions at delivering the apparent 'savings'?*
- *Innovation — Is your organization innovating a very high % of new products and services — if not why not? And if not how are you doing in the market?!*
- *Integration — How flat (vertically) is your structure? Now, how well integrated (horizontally) is it? How well integrated is everyone inside with your external relationships?*

Your notes

C H A P T E R 7

Climate, Language and Culture

Overview

In this chapter, you'll discover:

- how the culture of a business is created and sustained by process *and* language
- how the language of the organization – what people talk about and what they say – is a result of the business focus
- the effect of language on communication processes and operating styles.

SEVEN

Climate, Language
and Culture

We've been travelling smoothly along the marketing and communication timeline, and now we encounter a problem. While
externally marketing and communication have made great
progress and are heading for the next millennium, *internally*
they are still locked in the *tell* and *sell* modes of the 50s and 60s.
The problem is, these traditional communication processes engender cultural norms that are no longer appropriate. This leaves
organizations with cultures akin to the paternalistic or autocratic
styles, i.e. 'top down'.

As many organizations now believe, corporate culture is very
difficult to change – or is it? This chapter demonstrates that to
change culture, the *last* thing you do is try to change culture.
The *first* thing you do is to change the business' processes and
languages. In other words, focus on what people say and do
rather than what they think and believe.

Behavioral and attitudinal changes can only be brought about
by working on the drivers of change; the 'hub' of process and
language in our model of change.- It is only when a business
changes its language and the way it operates that the changes in
culture will occur. Culture is a *result* of changing the way you
do things, *not a catalyst* for change. It is a result of changing the
climate that brings us back to the everyday things you do and
say, and the way you say them and do them.

This point has been proven time and again by organizations
that have tried to achieve a genuine and long-lasting shift in

their people's beliefs, behaviors and perceptions about the business through culture change initiatives. Have they succeeded? Experience, and most surveys on attitudes, behaviors and beliefs in organizations, suggest not.

Changing the culture of an organization by tackling it head on as a single facet of organizational life is really, really tough. To go 'deep' into cultural change you have to be talking about beliefs and values, and these go to the very soul of the organization and its people. It is much easier to change the climate and language of the business. (We'll look at the difference between culture and climate shortly.) When businesses change their processes (the six *Is* we discussed in Chapter 6) and their language (from information-giving and telling to involving and listening) with all their key stakeholders inside and outside the organization, culture change *will* follow.

Now we come to the critical question. If we are to change the language what do we change it from, and to? To a large extent, the language of an organization – what people talk about and what they say – occurs as a result of the business focus. Does the business focus on the product, or on customers and relationships?

Business focus is key because it creates the imperatives that shape the way an organization talks to itself and its customers. For example, a focus on customers in the 70s created a whole new language of marketing. Suddenly everyone talked about 'targeting', 'qualitative research', 'branding', and more. The language of total quality in the 80s sprang up from a focus on delivering a product that fulfilled the customers' expectations. Expressions like 'zero defects' and 'right first time' became commonplace.

Now comes the tricky part. Organizations can only change their language when the other pieces of the puzzle are in place. For example, people won't think about 'right first time' if no one thinks about them. How would you feel if someone from 'above' tells you the customer is the most important person, when you *know* you are! Organizations have to understand the needs of their internal customers and implement an appropriate communication strategy before they can expect their internal customers to buy-in to any initiative from the organization.

As we have discovered, there is no point in organizations delivering a 'top-down' message that employees must deliver a quality product, if the 'bottom-up' needs of these internal customers are not being fulfilled. Who wants to listen to messages from above – let along talk with other departments, 'side-to-side' – when no-one is listening 'my' messages from below? Who is likely to come up with new, new, new if no one is interested in me, me, me?

If these elements of the jigsaw are not in place, the language of the business can become:

- confused, particularly when there are so many initiatives (it's like having a multilingual society with no interpreters)
- confrontational, when departments vie for supremacy of 'their' issues (which others may find totally incomprehensible)
- anarchic, when everyone 'does their own thing' and creates their own language and style (the Internet is a very visible example of this, with a profusion and confusion of 'home pages').

It may even become destructive, when war between people, teams, functions, and departments break out (when the bellicose language of patriotism can run rife, and 'us and them' is redolent). How can this happen? Remember that two-thirds of employees do not believe their managers. When employees hear, for example, a message from above that says 'lean production', what many hear is 'redundancy'. The numerous top-down messages over the last 20 years have all too often had a similar effect. In one of the organizations we worked with, for example, people said that BPR (Business Process Reengineering) actually stood for Big People Reductions! Getting people to change what they say and do, against such a cynical background, is far from easy. Too often they retrench into their own areas of comfort and put up barriers – and language is one of those barriers. Add to this the real problem of international cultures and languages hitting people hard in a multilingual and cultural world, and we have a recipe for potential conflict, with little hope of real and lasting cultural change. Yet it can be done – just not in the way organizations try to do it today.

Change the climate and the culture changes

More and more work by psychologists suggests that in order to change culture, you first have to change climate. Often, the notions of climate and culture are poorly understood, with the two terms seen as synonymous. In reality, the two concepts are very different, with climate being a driver of organizational culture. Here's a helpful definition:

• climate is what organizational members **experience**
• culture is what the organization **values**.

The analogy of a real climate can best serve to highlight the difference between the two concepts. This analogy shows clearly that climate is the day-to-day experience: the temperature, the wind, rain, thunder and the whole ecosystem. As people experience this climate, they construct appropriate languages and processes – from there flows their distinct regional, ethnic or national culture.

Imagine then you are an Eskimo of old. You are working in half light much of the time, darkness a lot of the time and sometimes even complete darkness for days on end. (Does this sound like people in your organization?) There isn't much to see, do, touch, feel or smell. There are few people to talk to. You stay in your igloo and communicate with your immediate family in the middle of the polar night. Now imagine the culture that comes about as a result of the climate. This culture must base its values on heat, protection, long periods of close contact with few people, a supportive environment in the search for food, etc. It is based on danger, extreme conditions, short 'good' spells, followed by long bleak periods.

Now place these Eskimos in the Amazon. The climate changes – so does everything else. The process for gathering food, the way of interacting with others, the mores, beliefs, the gods, the values – everything changes. The people are still people but the day-to-day living environment creates a total change in their processes, language and culture. Now the focus is not inward. It is outward, on the dangers from other tribes, on the threat from what else is out there in the jungle and on the looming danger of people from 'outside' destroying everything (does this sound like the culture that senior managers feel they are in?) So now we see two completely different climates. You cannot tell an Eskimo to worship a 'sun god' (the customer?) and dance in homage. The jungle dweller cannot understand the protective and insular nature of the Eskimo (people hiding away in their own environment keeping the cold and danger at bay). I don't want to stretch the analogy too far; however, I think the point is clear. In the world around us, the day-to-day actions and words that develop around 'the way we do things around here' all flow from what people experience – the climate. In the same way, the organizational climate determines the culture of the business. What we do and say based on the things around us begins to create the things we believe and value.

If businesses want to change their cultures towards one for example that is more passionate, involving and customer driven, they first need to change their climate. Such is the assertion of business psychologists Schneider, Brief and Guzzo. They argue: 'We propose that culture can be changed through a focus on climate. Climate reflects the tangibles that produce a culture, the kinds of things that happen around employees that people can describe.'

Marketers know the power of 'tangibles' and their potential to alter the lifestyles of customers. Externally, consumers are persuaded to 'buy-in' to whatever an organization produces and from there, the product starts to affect the way they live on a day-to-day basis. These reactions can be described in terms of cultural change – you can see, for example, how products like Nintendo and more recently Sony Playstation have changed a passive TV-watching culture to an active CD-ROM games culture. The car changed Western culture, so did the telephone, the television, the computer and the Internet.

Every advertisement, direct mail letter or meeting with a salesperson creates a process and language between the customer and the organization. New ads create a new language. If the customer buys in, s/he will start talking the same language and do things differently with the product. This is the job of external marketing to change what people say and do.

Products and services change actions and words, which change cultures. The same is true internally. Change *what* you do and you can change *how* you do things. To take a simple example: getting people involved by listening to them creates (guess what) a listening culture. Giving people problem-solving tools and the authority to execute the answers creates an empowered culture. The six *I*s of communication *can* change culture.

According to Schneider, Brief and Guzzo, climate has the following elements:

• hierarchy
• interpersonal relationships
• work
• support and rewards.

These four elements are an ideal way of understanding climate so that we can see how to change culture. I have used these headings to demonstrate how to move along our timeline and to understand the 'why' and 'how' it is done.

1. The nature of hierarchy

Whether a hierarchy is top-down can be determined by such factors as how business decisions are made. Are they made by top management alone, or through participation from those affected by the decision?

Clearly, if a hierarchy is top-down, then the resulting communication processes are likely to be top-down also. This in turn will mean that the culture will be created in the image of the processes. The *tell* climate promotes a 'patriarchal' culture. This is the typical culture found in the old style owner/manager business reminiscent of the 'factory owner' of the past. The patriarchal culture came about through the boss being either a benevolent, or sometime malevolent 'father figure'. The employees would look up to the owner for everything. The culture would be deferential with a language of 'yes, sir' and processes based around business controls like time and motion, with a 'work harder and faster' ethic based on volume.

For over a century, many owners acted like father figures, looking after their workers in either a benign patriarchy or, at the other end of the spectrum, a dictatorship. The hierarchy of a family unit created this patriarchal approach to business. Indeed the same approach is reflected in a broader way within society, when governments are in charge of the 'welfare' of the state.

Gradually, however, with new forms of ownership coming through with the publicly, not privately, owned company taking over, patriarchy declined in most major businesses. As managers took over from business owners, harder approaches to business were developed. A new approach to communication emerged, one based on *sell*. The resulting culture was an all too often dominating, autocratic culture. Powerful business leaders and mangers used pressure techniques to get the employee on board. Think of the style of many of the sales directors of the 60s. They were autocrats, albeit benevolent ones.

Driving the numbers, or production processes, or even fleets of trucks, requires a strong focus on business needs. Changing cultures requires a strong focus on people needs and ways to get people to change. The two were incompatible. Any attempts at finding out what people thought, through breakout sessions in roadshows, telephone hot lines, attitude surveys and the like were a token attempt at two-way communication. These leaders were still driven by the goal of ensuring their employees 'got the message'. Many a 'campaign' was devised around the numerous change initiatives, with a failure rate legendary for its inability to get the 'buy in' that the business leaders demanded. Yet how could they succeed when they were trying to put in new languages, which in themselves no-one really wanted, and just as importantly they were 'imposed' with top down processes of communication that fell on deaf ears.

As companies move up the timeline, the hierarchy becomes less distinct and more fluid. Leading thinkers begin to argue that the way to engage employees is by changing the operating environment. From a top-down approach began to emerge the recognition of the need for two-way communication. This usually means changing the communication and marketing processes (like researching your internal customers needs), and it also means changing the language within which people operate. 'Tell me what *you* think' is very different to 'Let *me* tell you what to do'.

2. The nature of interpersonal relationships

Interpersonal relationships, the second dimension of climate, also help form an organization's culture. This is the side-to-side part of the strategy. How do people act on a day-to-day basis with each other? Is there mutual sharing and trust or conflict and mistrust? Is there a focus on teamwork or on an individual responsibility to act? Do people say 'We worked on this together' or do they say 'We gave them the answers but they just didn't seem interested'? Does 'not invented here' rule the organization?

It is the way of acting, the nature of relationships, that create the culture. If people do not have the skills, processes or language to be able to work in, for example, a team-based or empowered organization, then a team-based or empowered culture cannot follow. Saying 'you are empowered' can only result in confusion if there is no recognition of the top-down needs or a process and language to allow empowerment to happen.

In *Organizational Cultures*, Andrew Brown asserts, 'Since the 80s there has been a growing realization that the fundamental task facing leaders and managers rests in creating appropriate systems of *shared meaning* that can mobilize the efforts of people in pursuit of desired aims and objectives.' He goes on to say that these systems of shared meaning, what I would call the organizational culture, cannot be changed simply by '… looking at just the technologies, structures, the abilities and motivations of employees … the emphasis must be placed on *understanding the processes that produce systems of shared meanings …'*

How do organizations create shared meaning? By using a shared language. These 'shared frames of reference/meaning' are found in stories, myths, legends, ideologies, symbols, ritual and especially jokes and humor, as well as the organizational systems and processes. So how do you create shared meaning? How about letting the organization talk about the things it finds funny, annoying, exciting, and depressing instead of the constant discussion on 'business, business, business' or 'initiative after initiative'. But this can only be done *very* carefully. It takes a lot of precise targeting when looking to changing language. The marketing process for changing the customer from being 'aware' of a product to becoming an 'advocate' requires very different types of copy and creative approaches to create the right language, stories and imagery for the customer. The same is true of the internal customer.

3. The nature of work

Is the work challenging or boring? Can people adapt their jobs to the way they work or are they rigidly defined so that everyone must do them the same way?

Do the people in your organization say: 'Same old thing day after day, nothing new around here ever happens', or do they say 'Wow! 50% of our product and service range are new this year – and I came up with one humdinger of a new concept?'

Listen to the language of your organization and see how this is affected by work roles. Are they driven by customer needs or because they need a pay cheque? Take the example of the technology industries, where companies see a product life-cycle in terms of months, not years. Operating at this rate of change requires some amazing processes and language to be developed. Who, for example, can listen to a 'techie' for more than two sentences! But if they didn't talk in code, their own language, their product development cycles might be twice as long. Innovation requires an innovative language and innovative processes to make it work.

When the day-to-day language and processes are in place, culture will follow. You cannot have an innovative culture in a monotonous climate. What organizations need to create is richly textured *positive* language, through the use of words (like 'yes ... and'; not 'no ... but'), metaphors, stories, quotes, examples and humor. Did you know humor and laughter generates endorphins in the body, which improve the immune system and create healthier people. So if organizations are living organisms, and they clearly contain living organisms (people!) then why are they using languages which create stress and ill health? Is it not time for a change of language?

4. The focus of support and rewards

Are the goals of work and the standards of excellence widely known and shared?

Are the feedback mechanisms in your business part of the 'praise' that generates pride, drive and the desire to do better? Is 'well done' or 'you did it!' heard often? Does 'satisfying the customer' produce rewards that ensure your organization and the individual get some form of pay back? Do they get feedback as a form of recognition? Is society winning too? Do the shareholders get their rewards? If they do, who knows about it and how often is it talked about? Does your organization talk to itself about its success?

If the answers are yes, then the processes and language of support and rewards will create the basis for a climate which favors integrated cultures. A 'customer focused' culture cannot operate in an environmental climate where the language is all about 'get the product off the shelves', or where 'mystery shoppers' engender fear of reprisals among employees. Passionate cultures require their very own language – of passion, and the 'red hot' climate that operates where people just love what they do.

So, if you want to change your culture, start first with your climate. Climate is formed by appropriate communication processes and organizational language. When these two components are working together, then a sustained change in culture takes place.

The language of business success

Let's now explore the words that create the language that captures the spirit that drives the culture of organizations. As Charles Handy says in *Gods of Management:* 'You can detect an organization's heart by looking at its language'.

Language is often overlooked because of the mistaken assumption that it is something that happens by chance. Organizational language is so much more important than that – any individual privileged enough to work with various organizations will see the variations in language in an obvious and unmistakable way. The differences in language among organizations are *stunning*.

Some organizations have begun to recognize the power of what is said and how it is said. The real problem for them is how to use the right words to help their people think and behave differently. Compare day-to-day exhortations of 'live the values', or 'fulfill our mission' or 'deliver the vision' or even 'achieve our objectives' with the resulting actions!

These same organizations often ask their managers to 'walk the talk'. The 'talk' is blatant, clear, obvious and top-down. The 'walk' is the actions – the leader is 'out there showing commitment'. Tom Peters immortalized this practice in MBWA – Management By Walking Around.

These concepts are fine in theory, but managers often do not want to 'walk' or do not know how to 'talk' when on the walk. To make matters worse, the unwritten management rule in the traditional hierarchical culture is that 'knowledge is power'. In climates of fear, mistrust, politics and a mindset of every man for himself, – many managers decide to follow the rule of 'keep it to yourself'. So, not only can organizations have the 'wrong' language, they can have *no language at all*. This is hardly creating the climate in which an open and honest culture can develop!

Language is important, not just to help shape the culture for the future, but also to express what the climate is like today.

The frequency of a single word; 'It', 'You' or 'We' can indicate where an organization is on the marketing and communication timeline – whether in tell, sell, buy, buy-in or friends and best friends. We can actually use these words to show how language creates the culture in organizations. By necessity, the words and catch-phrases used in this section oversimplify the situation. While it may be 'simple' to describe what has happened using short words, it just makes it easier to see how the processes, language, culture and focus of organizations impact on each other. For each of the three phases of 'it', 'you' and 'we', we'll look at three areas that business focuses on. These are:

- internal focus (what goes on inside)
- customer interface (what happens between)
- external focus (what goes on outside).

Each of these three areas of business focus would produce its own language. For example, an internal focus in the 50s and 60s would create a language based on manufacturing looking at creating more volume. Why is this important? Because the language creates the climate that creates the culture that helps or hinders the organization to pursue the processes (like improvement or innovation) that affect the revenue, costs, profit, that deliver the assets that add to the balance sheet. (These systemic knock on effects are always fun to explain – or are they?)

'It' – a focus on the product

In the 1950s, the product (whatever 'it' was; the thing organizations made, distributed, and sold) was of paramount importance. Employees were paid to do as they were told, and when organizations said 'make it' and 'sell it', they meant it. So 'it' was what they talked about – a lot. The business goals were to increase volumes and maximize the means of mass production to satisfy the insatiable demand of consumers. The consumer didn't know much about quality – like Dickens' *Oliver*, all they wanted was more. The *internal focus* was on mass production. The language was of 'time and motion' and 'piece rates' used by people who 'knew their place' and did their job.

People could be 'told' what to do. Instructions could be given. Information could be handed out. The language internally was top-down. Organizations simply said what they wanted and the workforce did it. The 50s and 60s were therefore dominated by a language of macho, male management with little room in this climate for 'touchy-feely' cultures to thrive. The exhortations of the humanistic school of management fell on the deaf ears of the scientific management.

Bryan Gladstone of Sheffield University Business School describes this focus as 'Fordism; a period encompassing the whole business philosophy of mass production from about 1900 to the mid 1970s'. According to Gladstone, the key characteristics of this period included:

- mass or crudely segmented markets
- ever increasing speed of production
- physical overloading of workforce
- loss of meaning in work
- increased specialization
- inflexibility.

With so much emphasis on manufacturing, the *customer interface* involved little more than distribution, and later a huge emphasis on having the physical outlets through a retail presence, or alternatively mail order. The language of the time was of retail – 'location', 'sales per square foot', 'footfall' and of 'instore display'. Because the focus was on making and moving 'it' the product, the approach at the interface was to do things 'to' the customer. The *external focus* was on hard selling. Too often, the approach was 'Do what you have to do to make sure you hit this week's target'. The sales training courses were full of 'Close that sale' techniques and anything else that would help them manipulate the customer. The 'pushy' sales people always got their order. Techniques like 'tie-downs' and 'objection handling' were the sale person's stock in trade. Get the order, at any cost.

As with production staff, organizations relied on an order-and-obey mode with their sales managers acting in a chain of top-down command. The paternal culture changed, however, as professional managers took over. They still operated in a traditional command-and-control structure that allowed a top-down approach to flourish. While the culture became autocratic, the method of communication changed as the old order and obey of the owner–manager no longer worked.

The new regime began to appreciate that for example the increasingly professional and educated sales force could be motivated by hype and money, the mode changed internally to one of *sell*. Instead of just telling people what to do, the next trick was to try to sell them on doing it – in the 1960s came the hype, the flashy conferences and roadshows. The language used matched the promotional language of the spin doctors. The *external focus* of sell, sell, sell was via high-profile PR approaches moved internally.

Manipulation was implicit in the methods used for motivation. The tactics of communication were simple, it was just get the messages out. Internally, the processes used were almost exclusively the first two *Is* – Instruction and Information. The organizational hierarchy, with its layer upon layer of managers, was the route to controlling information. But something was changing … everything!

Customer demands and marketplace trends forced organizations to change their external communication, so they moved up the timeline. Internally, organizations began wanting empowerment, team working, continuous improvement, innovation, and customer focus. But, too often, the autocratic language of 'must' proved hard to change internally. So hard that the language of tell and sell are still having an affect on internal communication today (see Box 7.1).

Not only do tell/sell processes and top-down language still dominate communication, but they are perpetuating climates in which people feel undervalued, not listened to and unable to communicate. Some organizations remain locked in the *tell* and *sell* mode; others are working hard to move into buy and buy in.

Box 7.1   Language of the 'It' phase

- Internal focus: 'Make it' (driven by production)
- Customer interface: 'Make it available' (driven by distribution/retail)
- External focus: 'Make you want it' (driven by selling/promotion).

'You' – a focus on the customer

From a focus and language based on 'it' the product, organizations began shifting their concentration onto 'you'. Why? Because customers started to speak up. They created their own culture by speaking their own language. 'I want this – *now*, and I want it *right*'. The ever-increasingly sophisticated consumer had arrived as a force to be reckoned with. So how did organizations respond? By moving up the timeline into the communication and marketing modes of *buy* and *buy in*. For the *internal focus*, this meant 'meeting the needs of you, the external customer'. The only way to produce it for you '*now*' and '*right*' was by total quality.

A new language of quality sprang up: 'Right first time', 'the customer is King', 'zero defects', 'continuous improvement' and, the most important of all in quality language, 'meet the customer needs now, and for the future'. 'You' had arrived as the product had to meet customer expectations, not the manufacturer's expectations. The quality movement spawned the need for people to work together, collaborate together, learn together. This required a completely new set of processes. More importantly, it needed a new language to get the internal customer to reach the heights of 'buy' and 'buy in' and help the organization to deliver the ever increasingly stiff goals set by the customer.

Communication throughout the supply chain was also needed as organizations tried to meet the hugely demanding and changing needs of the outside world. The *customer interface* was driven by marketing. The language of 'target markets', 'segmentation', 'promotions', 'advertising', 'research', 'brands', 'the competition' and 'market share' became common in organizations. The reason may well be more to do with the fear factor. 'If we don't market ourselves we are dead!' Wow, this is a positive motivator! This would make you excited about the next promotion wouldn't it?

The marketing revolution did take hold (it had to) and marketing professionals began to take their seat on boards. Yet while the interface between the organization and the customers became marketing, the marketing department was, and still is all too often, more externally focused than internally. It is to my never-ending surprise and regret that less than 6% of marketing departments in the UK are responsible, or get involved in internal marketing and communication. This will change – soon!

Although marketing has imbued organizations with its language, this has been used almost exclusively for the external customer only, and has often only permeated the upper echelons of companies. When was the last time you heard anyone say 'I must target this e-mail'? Is it more likely you will hear. 'Send this out to everyone – I think it's important they know about it'. Yes, but do the customers on the receiving end think it's important?! If a marketing- and customer-based language is rife in you organization, and everyone has the processes of marketing to deliver internal customer satisfaction then you are truly on your way to becoming 'marketing driven'. Otherwise you may simply be 'marketing department driven'.

If marketing processes, like research, targeting, design, promotion, are only used externally and the language only applied to external customers, then the culture cannot become marketing-driven. If marketing isn't in the processes and language of everyone, then asking people to focus on customers is going to be difficult. How can people even begin to think in terms of customers if they were being treated like employees? If you aren't marketing to me, the internal customer, why should I be worried about what the organization wants?

With the focus on quality happening internally, and marketing serving as the interface, something different was happening externally. The *external focus* of organizations was to do things 'for' the customer. Organizations began to recognize that customer loyalty and retention could be achieved by creating 'happy' customers in any face-to-face encounter. The language was one of 'have a nice day', 'how may I help you', and 'you're welcome'.

Marketing and customer service were therefore seen as two different things, run by different departments with different processes. Marketing would use research techniques to ask customers what they thought. Customer service would find out if good service was occurring through pretending to be customers and having 'mystery shoppers'.

Yet while marketing and quality changed the external focus of organizations, there was a problem internally. Employees were still being controlled in a top-down way. The language was supposed to be side-to-side to enable continuous improvement;

the culture was supposed to be empowered and team-based. Who was responsible for the management of these changes? Managers.

With marketing processes and language being divorced from customer service, the cultural shift to a marketing- and customer-focused organization was difficult. According to Bryan Gladstone, managers met the needs of an external focus with an updated version of what they already knew, which he calls Managerial Fordism: 'Production had moved beyond Fordism but management has not done so. Such management is characterized by overly technical definition of management roles and the use of numerical measures of achievement to the virtual exclusion of all else.'

Once again, organizations were stuck with language and communication processes that belong in the 50s and 60s. So all too often, customer service was treated as an instruction: 'Thou shalt smile, and answer the phone in three rings'. I know: I pioneered many of the campaigns in the 80s and was asked to help repair the damage of many well-intentioned programs (see Box 7.2).

But external marketing itself, whether to mass groups or even niche markets was being overtaken on the timeline. The paradigm shift to relationships was about to hit in the 90s and beyond to the next millennium. It would soon become plain that *everyone* would need to be in the marketing department, *everyone* would need to be in PR, *everyone* would need to be a brand ambassador, and *everyone* would need to be a brand manager. Why? Because *everyone* has customers of one, inside and outside of their organization.

How can an individual or a whole organization take on board two decades of changes in external marketing techniques in order to adopt a much more sophisticated approach of relationship and one-to-one marketing? With enough of a 'What's in it for me?' I believe it can be accomplished. Everyone can be given marketing principles and tools to meet the needs of customers, inside and out. But we need to get out of the 'You' phase and into the 'We' phase.

Box 7.2   Language of the 'You' phase

- Internal focus: 'Meeting the needs of you, the customer' (driven by total quality)
- Customer interface: 'Targeting messages to you' (driven by marketing)
- External focus: 'Doing things for you' (driven by customer service).

The 'We' phase – a focus on relationships

Today customers are highly sophisticated and, in some cases, almost totally jaded by a bombardment of promotional, brand, corporate and advertising imagery. They are also profoundly affected by the huge societal and technological changes. Against this backdrop, something new is needed to maintain customers' interest. Database, then relationship marketing on the 'one to one' customer has arrived. But what about the internal changes in process and language to meet the even higher levels of sophistication required on the outside?

Now we have scientific management practices ruling a new art form: the pleasures and pain of dealing with fickle customers. Gladstone describes the new focus as Post-Fordism. He writes that this approach recognizes the need to refocus on social interaction as the core management function. It recognizes that flexible technology does not necessarily create flexible organizations and is more likely to do the opposite if inadequate attention is given to the social needs of the people. In this phase, the marketing and quality revolution has done its job. Now the language is no longer 'more, better, faster, cheaper'. In Frederick

Hertzberg's terms these benefits, as well as price and availability, are simply 'hygiene factors'. This means that consumers *assumes* they will get good quality, competitive prices, good advertising and great customer service. What they now want is to see, hear and touch things that are 'new, new, new'.

'What's new?' demands the increasingly sophisticated and bored customer. So the *internal focus* is on innovation. In 3M, for example, everyone is given creative time to develop new ideas. Good on them. But beware introducing innovation when the processes, language and therefore the culture of the organization is not ready for it.

If an organization is to survive by producing things that are new, then it will do so by involving everyone. We have talked about the innovation *process*. There is also an innovation *language*. Innovation requires 'Yes ...and', and is killed by 'No ... but'. Innovation demands 'I feel this might work and I don't know why', not 'That won't work' or 'Prove it!' Innovation requires a completely different language as well as a process to allow the ideas to permeate through the organization. It demands a language of marketing where needs can be identified, concerns met, products trialed and researched, and a huge sense of freedom to *fail*.

Once again we come back down the timeline with a crash. Is everyone in the organization talking the same language as the customer, never mind imaging what they may want in the future? Is everyone talking the same language as those in Research & Development? If not, then a process of innovation will be difficult to instill, and an innovative culture will be even more difficult to create.

If innovation is now the external driving force that motivates customers to buy, who is matching the needs of the demanding customer to the abilities and skills of the organization? The *customer interface* with the internal organization is not being driven by traditional marketing techniques – 'customers of one' have arrived.

Relationship marketing has had to develop to cope with the needs of today's customer. Customers of one need to be spoken to in one language only – their language. This is the task of relationship marketing, to create lifetime relationships and one-to-one dialogue. How will this be achieved? By knowing what every customer thinks, feels, believes, values and therefore what they say and do as a result.

A whole new method of talking to customers is developing. A whole new way of using individual customer data is enabling organizations to have one-to-one conversations. Who should be involved in these one-to-one conversations? Everyone. In order to do this everyone will need to understand the needs, wants and desires of the customer, together with their psychographic and demographic profiles.

The information technology revolution has given businesses databases and information management of unbelievable power. The Internet, the World Wide Web and electronic communication have also given us unlimited access to talk to someone through call centers, or other electronic access, including TV, PC and PCTV. Everyone is literally in a geographic frame where they could be 'next door'. As a result, not only will do we need to know each customer well, the *external focus* of every organization is to be accessible to each customer 'anywhere, anyplace, anytime'.

Technology has allowed the communication and relationship marketing modes to see each other as *friends* (for now), and ideally *best friends* (for life, if we can make it happen). The good thing is that this is not a one-way, 'big brother' approach. You the customer lead such busy lives that you are happy to have us help you. We don't have an 'us and them' situation like we did in the manufacturing or consumerist days. More and more organizations are recognizing through internal measures like the Balanced Scorecard and a focus on the stakeholder that they want to survive in this world by going with the flow, not against it or even for it. We have what can be called a 'we' situation where there is joint benefit in joint relationships. The language moves from adversarial (as in manufacturing power or consumer power), to one where *both organization and customer* are looking for things to be mutually beneficial. It doesn't stop there. It is now in both party's interest to have lifetime relationships. Customers just don't have the time, or energy to 'shop around', so if they can have their needs met then it is worth them investing time to give you data *about* them to make life easier *for* them.

Now the approach is to work *with* customers, both internal and external. Now the implications for organizations are even greater. Working with someone requires a new way of doing business. It requires new methods of communication and marketing. It requires new processes like innovation and integration. It requires a new language; a language of customer intimacy where lifetime relationships are the goal, as shown in Box 7.3.

Box 7.3   Language of the 'We' phase

- Internal focus: 'We need to be different to meet the ever-changing needs of the customer' (driven by innovation)
- Customer interface: 'Getting close to our individual customer needs, now and for a lifetime' (driven by lifetime relationship marketing)
- External focus: 'Being available 24 hours a day for our customers (driven by total accessibility).

A word about words

When looked at in this light, it is amazing to see how quickly the focus of organizations has changed over the last 50 years, as has the language of business leaders, managers and change specialists. But has the language of the *whole* organization kept pace and changed in the same way? Detailed analysis of the different words, meanings and understandings among people at the top and bottom of organizations reveals that very little of the new language tends to reach very far down the organization. Truth is, we find many organizations are *still* stuck in the 50s and 60s. How do we know? Firstly they tell us. The timeline has revealed to many organizations where they are. Secondly we just listen. Listen to the words people say and you can place them on the timeline pretty easily.

Box 7.4 Inside and out – do the two meet in your organization?

Ask yourself: what is the focus of our organization internally as well as externally – do they tally? Then, complete this quick table – tick which language people use – inside and out.

	External focus	Internal focus
'It' phase		
Manufacturing	❏	❏
Selling	❏	❏
Distribution	❏	❏
'You' phase		
Quality	❏	❏
Marketing	❏	❏
Customer service	❏	❏
'We' phase		
Innovation	❏	❏
Lifetime relationships	❏	❏
Total accessibility	❏	❏

Words, words, words ... money, money, money

Does this approach to changing cultures present a total solution in the changing of process and language? Yes... and no! We have seen many, many successes in changing culture through changing language *but* – and it is a big but – we have yet to see a totally integrated approach where any organization is using all the elements of the new P&L, the processes and language of the six *I*s, and no wonder. We are talking here of covering half a century of change, and adapting this to the new model. It is, after all, only recently that businesses have begun to contemplate the management of intellectual capital, never mind the management of emotional capital. It is only recently that organizations have seen, through total quality, that there is an internal customer, and a customer-supplier chain. So it is no wonder that the new approach of using customer-driven principles of marketing are still catching up.

The question is, does an integrated approach make sense? If it does make sense, and something needs to be done to deliver hearts and minds, then what is there to lose? The rewards are incalculable (well, for the moment anyway).

The purpose of this skim across the surface of the languages in organizations is to point the way to a powerful lever for change changing the climate and the day-to-day way of doing business. Words are a powerful currency. Properly used and traded they add tremendous value to the organization, its customers and stakeholders.

Currently words are perceived to have little value except as a part of intellectual property. In the next millennium, if ALL physical assets are outsourced, it may well be that words, and the language they create, are the only 'capital' worth valuing – for it is words that create intellectual and emotional capital. This is where we look in the next and final chapter.

My notes on climate, language and culture

'If you want to change your life change your thinking.' So advises Brian Tracy, the self development expert. Let's make that more specific, and targeted to organizations: If you want to change your culture change your language. Why? Because what we say — our language, combined with what we do — our processes create the climate within which we operate, and a sustained climate creates the basis for a new culture. Culture, as with each of the other outputs on the wheel in our model is a result not a driver.

This chapter has looked how each of the time phases has produced three types of focus, which in turn produce three types of language. The mismatch comes when one part of the organization is saying one thing, like 'we need one-to-one relationships with customers', while another is saying 'we need to get product out of the door'. So we have seen three phases, from a focus on 'it', making and getting the product sold, to 'you' the all important customer, to 'we' the lifetime relationship with every customer by meeting their needs all day every day.

Thought provokers for the future

So now we have some fundamental questions: just what are you talking about!

Go around your organization and listen to what people are discussing. Which phase are you in? Where is the focus, is it internal, is it about the interface with the customer, is it on what is going on outside the organization?

- '<u>It</u>' — <u>the product</u>: How many 'it' conversations are people having?
- '<u>You</u>' — <u>the customer</u>: How many marketing-type conversations are people having about 'you' and 'meeting your needs as a customer'?
- '<u>We</u>' — <u>the relationship</u>: How many conversations involve the word 'we', such as 'If we work together on this we both win by ...', 'If we know this about them we will be able to this to create lifetime relationships'?

Your notes

C H A P T E R 8

The New Financial Model – from Volume to Value to Vision

Overview

This chapter covers:

- how business strategy has followed the marketing and communication timeline
- the new financial model that is emerging to reflect the true value of businesses
- strategies and processes for measuring the total worth of a business, including emotional capital.

EIGHT

The New Financial Model – from Volume to Value to Vision

Just like James T. Kirk and his crew, we have seen how our captains of industry and their followers have moved along the marketing and communication timeline over the last 50 years on their evolving business missions and strategies. Many have moved from a 1950s two-dimensional strategy of communicating with their customers and (sometimes) employees in a 'top-down', *tell* mode to a 1990s strategy of one-to-one relationships helped by the use of external marketing, and (sometimes) internal marketing – though they may not have called it that at the time – to get us to the phases of *buy-in* and *best friends*.

The aim of this chapter is to consider the implications of what we have explored so far and put these strategic changes in hard business terms. How? By first exploring how business strategy has followed the movement of the marketing and communication timeline. We will then analyze how the fundamental paradigm shifts that occurred affect not just what is said and done, but more importantly the profit and loss statements of businesses. Finally, we'll look at the new financial model that is emerging to reflect the true value of emotional and intellectual capital in the balance sheet, so that book value and market value start to equate. We will call it 'Triple A Accounting'.

Once this accounting model has been outlined, the final section of this chapter will outline a new approach to valuing businesses and the processes and tools that are needed to support it.

From volume to value to vision – an overview

Each element of business strategy, and the tactical executions that go with it, along the timeline has affected the methods used to generate income, save costs and increase profitability within businesses. As we have already seen they have also helped shape the way businesses operate.

Broadly speaking, there have been three distinct and very different phases in the way that businesses have identified, maximized and valued their physical, intellectual and emotional assets. We have already met these in one guise under the business focus and the language this created. We considered the business focus as a soft issue, now we meet it in the P&L, a hard issue. I have dubbed these phases, in each of the three paradigms as volume, value and vision.

The first phase which concentrated on **volume** was in the 'Product'-led phase. The volume-based strategy led to the drive of increasing revenue, as the main P&L goal. This was done through maximizing output, increasing distribution and generating sales volume. For the balance sheet, it meant an emphasis on the physical assets and measuring returns produced by volumes.

The second phase on adding **value** to meet the needs of the 'Customer'-led revolution of the time, the language was 'you'. Here the key drivers moved from manufacturing to quality; from distribution to marketing and from sales to customer service. The new approaches drove businesses to focus, through total quality type programs on cutting costs, cutting faults, returns, etc.; maximizing returns on advertising and marketing costs; while

ensuring repeat purchase by delivering good service. The assets
(but not yet accounted for in 'the books') were similarly affected
by a move to put the increasingly valuable knowledge into the
intellectual property base of the business.

The third phase business strategy uses **vision.** This comes in
the 'Relationship' phase, which we are in today and the language is of 'we'. This vision is a twofold one; first, the ability to
clearly 'see' which customers to target; and secondly to understand and anticipate both what they want now and in the future.
Both require tremendous insight in today's highly complex, fragmented and hugely changing global market. The revenue figures
can now be seen to be affected by the power of the corporate
and brand values placed on them by the customer. The business
strategy changes as the drivers change, from quality to innovation; from marketing to technology and from customer service
to lifetime relationships. The balance sheet is slowly adopting to
the recognition of emotional capital with the starting point being adding brand value to the asset base of the business.

The relationship between the marketing and communication
strategy and the business strategy is illustrated in the Blueprint
model -see end of chapter. This shows how each of the hori-
zontal and vertical axes impact on each other in the time period
they each relate to. What now follows is each phase in more
detail, showing (as with the previous chapter on 'language') the
three ways of achieving the *business strategy* of the time with
what occurred (1) internally, (2) at the interface with the customer and (3) externally. We then go on to show the impact of
all this on the P&L and balance sheet.

1950s–1960s: volume, volume, volume

During the *tell* and *sell* periods of the 50s and 60s, the concentration of organizations was simple – create revenue. How? The
answer was volume, volume, volume. It was achieved in three
ways:

1   **Manufacturing** (the internal part of the business strategy).
     Here the goal of increasing revenues is simply to make
     enough to satisfy demand. This required organizations to
     develop mass production techniques.

2   **Distributing** (the interface part of the business strategy).
     Here the goal is to 'move' enough stock to fulfill the de-
     mand. This caused organizations to develop distribution
     channels, ranging from physically moving goods in trucks,
     to owning or creating retail/mail order outlets.

3   **Selling** (the external part of the business strategy). Here
     the goal is to 'push' enough product into the customers
     (often gullible) arms. . This caused organizations to de-
     velop mass selling techniques to 'close that sale'. They may
     have opted for large sales forces, telesales, or simply trained
     shop assistants to 'sell, sell, sell'.

The external focus in these businesses was on generating volume to improve the top line, this was delivered by an internal
focus on making and distributing enough of the product to create economies of scale. Revenue through selling volume was
the target. Profit through maximizing production and distribution was the goal.

As we have seen this volume-based strategy had a direct influence on how management was perceived. Typically,
organizations took a scientific, mechanical approach to management, ranking 'people issues' alongside other manufacturing
techniques. Manufacturing was king in every sense. Accordingly,
the focus on profit and loss was to generate enough volumes to
ensure the maximum benefit was leveraged from mass production techniques.

The volume-based strategy affected how organizations viewed
their employees. For many companies, their people were cogs
in a large manufacturing machine. The employees were there
simply to deliver whatever management wanted.

The organization's most significant assets were perceived to be physical assets, anything that made things or helped distribute or sell the product. Investing and expanding these physical assets such as plant, machinery, vehicles for distribution, and retail property was of paramount importance in order to allow more manufacturing and distribution to take place. If an organization invested in these, if it sold enough products to cover the costs of making and distributing the goods, then the return on capital employed was obvious.

Return on investment and its variants is therefore a key measure in the volume-based business model. Asset-based accounting becomes a fine art. What gets measured gets done, and measurement of physical assets and the volumes of product produced meant that organizations concentrated on delivering against these measures.

Communication strategy and business strategy – a merger in the offing

Now we come to the link with communication. In volume-led businesses, communication tended to be top-down. The process of setting and communicating goals was straightforward – managers told workers what their goals were and then measured their output against those goals.

Any bottom-up techniques of communication were applied as part of a scientific management approach tempered with the humanistic approach such as the *X and Y theory* of Douglas McGregor, where X was effectively top-down control of 'the lazy so-and-sos', and Y was basically bottom-up, treating people like thinking, feeling, caring beings. However, McGregor himself admitted that the consequence of X and Y assumptions-led managers to rely on 'rewards, promises, or threats and other coercive devices'.

Many companies used time-and-motion studies alongside piece rates to measure and motivate employees. How times change … or do they? A recent book reviewing the thinking of management gurus, called appropriately *Management Gurus* by Andrzej A. Huczynski, suggests not: under the entry, *scientific management*, the author comments: 'This [approach] focused on the shop floor and upon the techniques that could be used to maximize the productivity of manual workers. Scientific management principles continue to be widely applied today.' Oh dear …

1970s–1980s: value-added

This phase marked a move away from the business strategy based on production, revenue and volume focus, towards a more customer-driven approach. Marketing, total quality and customer service became the new creeds, leading to marked differences in the way organizations reached their customers, structured their operations, generated revenue and ultimately, valued their assets.

In this next phase, the ingrained attitudes of managing as a science still prevailed and the 'top-down' communication remained the internal modus operandi; however, the external environment was changing. Thanks to increasing competition and a more discerning 'consumer', (the user, in marketing terms) organizations had to move into the next paradigm, of marketing. Businesses now had to concentrate on looking after the 'customer' (the buyer) and to focus on improving the product, using the concept and techniques of total quality.

Employees began to play a more important role; to provide both quality and 'excellent' service to the individual customer in any face-to-face encounters.

The paradigm shift started with fairly crass approaches to quality, marketing and customer service, characterized for example by the ubiquitous 'Right first time', 'Buy one get one free' and 'Have a nice day' catch phrases of the day. Increased competition and customer sophistication in the 80s led to companies taking more sophisticated approaches. The concentration on quality moved from simply making the product 'better', to making sure the product precisely met customers needs.

Quality in its numerous guises became the main driving force for maximizing effectiveness – replacing the production-led goals of maximizing efficiency. The Total Quality movement arrived from Japan and was soon followed by more sophisticated approaches like Kaizen and JIT (Just In Time manufacturing). Quality Assurance arrived from Britain with BS5750, out of which came the international standard of ISO 9000.

Marketing had arrived too, but much more as an external force. Marketing departments mainly tackled issues relating to the external environment and the business' target markets. (And we've already seen the problems that have been caused by divorcing external marketing from internal issues, particularly traditional employee communications.)

Although quality ruled internally, marketing was seen to have primary responsibility for the interface with the customer. In its heyday, marketing ruled (for a while) in the boardroom as the 'black arts' of marketing were seen to be the savior of organizations who really only understood production, and hadn't quite got a handle on these strange creature called customers. Following the rapid ascent of marketing to the board table Human Resource people came in favor as they understood the issues like culture, and were able to get hold of the 'mission critical' strategy of improving customer service. This became the 'pet' issue of the CEO in the 80s.

This paradigm shift led to a profound difference in how organizations structured their operations. Companies began to realize that their traditional functions were no longer sufficient to meet the new challenges. Manufacturing had learned to be efficient in the 50s, but in times of increasing competition and specialization, more was needed. Although distribution had learned to get product out there, either physically or through a sales force, and sales had learned to sell, this still wasn't enough to engage a more discerning and more diverse groups of customers.

Organizations rose to the new challenges by creating additional departments and functions:

1   **Marketing** (the interface part of the business strategy). Marketing delivered customers by defining the 'targets' to aim for and by creating perceptions of 'added value' in the target customers' minds.
2   **Quality** (the internal part of the business strategy). Quality created effectiveness and produced savings; it also helped meet customer expectation, reduce the number of defects, and improve customer retention rates.
3   **Customer service** (the external part of the business strategy). Customer service became the human face of the organization, , and the manifestation of the marketing focus on 'you' the customer, helping to make customers feel more 'welcome' – so they spent more.

Each of these departments or specialties was intended to do one thing – have an impact on the profit and loss account.

1. Marketing

Mass marketing was the first to arrive in the new phase, so we'll cover this first. It was later to be allowed by the more narrow targeting of niche marketing. Marketing added value to the business by finding, attracting and retaining those fickle customers hidden away in one target group or another, or one niche or another. Marketing was also adding value in the consumer's mind for the brand. If brands were special they could command a number of benefits:

- increased price
- increased market share
- increased customer retention
- increased customer loyalty
- lower costs in attracting new customers
- improved margins on repeat business
- leverage into new areas
- more efficient return on marketing
- higher return on capital
- higher return on revenues
- higher share price
- greater shareholder value.

All these benefits were seen to affect the top and bottom line and also to add value to customers and shareholders.

During this phase it was just fine for the 'experts' to be doing the marketing – so marketing departments were created with ever increasing numbers of specialists and support services like advertising, promotions, brand identity, etc.. However, this 'specialist' mentality meant that whilst the marketing function had a direct impact on the bottom line through marketing and advertising activity this was their only focus. They rarely, if ever got involved with the internal customer, or on the way the business was run internally. Quality, when it arrived became the internal strategy, something very separate to the external strategy.

2. Quality

Total quality programs were introduced to ensure that the whole organization worked on solving problems and improving production and business processes in order to cut costs, to increase profit and maximize revenue.

The initial focus of these quality programs was an extension of scientific management thinking, as the following quote from quality guru Crosby reveals: 'Quality management is a systematic way of guaranteeing that organized activities happen the way they are planned. It is a management discipline concerned with preventing problems from occurring by creating the attitudes and controls that make prevention possible.'

Quality programs had a sharp profit-and-loss focus. Organizations wanted quality to help them meet customer needs and expectations. They wanted a quality product to make customers come back for more. Quality was expected to make a difference to the revenue and add value. By concentrating on producing 'zero defects', and spreading cost containment along the customer and supplier chain, quality was used to help contain and minimize costs.

Total Quality (TQ) ran its course for a time, but eventually organizations came to see that it was no longer enough to keep global competitors at bay. Here is a candid admission from the CEO of BMW the 'quality icon' of German engineering. During a speech about the mains trends determining the world markets for car, given at the Geneva motor show, Bernd Pischetsrieder commented: 'Quality and reliability are no longer a mark of distinction. Quality is simply taken for granted, differentiation is now only possible at the highest level of value.'

So after quality came further cost cutting and efficiency programs such as business process re-engineering, downsizing, rightsizing and, when taken too far, capsizing.

People matter

As organizations looked more and more closely at how they could achieve competitive differentiation, the focus begun to switch to employees. Businesses began to realize that their brains and creativity were the vital ingredients that gave life, energy and ultimately, success, to initiatives like Total Quality, Just in Time and the like.

Suddenly, in order to maximize revenue and minimize costs, worker participation was important. Suddenly it was critical to get everyone to 'buy-in' to being involved, being part of a team, being in a quality circle, being interested in suggestion schemes and being empowered to deliver whatever was needed to 'get it right first time' (the favorite incantation of quality gurus).

All these changes occurred against a backdrop where, according to Tom Peters, there was a 'surplus of everything' and capturing any greater degree of market share had become difficult. The logic propelling business was that unless they followed the principles embodied in 'business transformation' strategies such as 'Excellence', Business Process Reengineering, The Malcolm Baldridge Awards, The European Foundation for Quality Management (EFQM), etc.., then they would be unable to compete and deliver value.

By this stage, however, organizations were beginning to define value more broadly. The concept of 'shareholder value', for example, was beginning to creep into the organizational psyche. The concentration on improving profitability was moving therefore from a simple quality and costs focus to what was going on, in and around the organization.

3. Customer service

Customer service was the 'toothpaste grin' of the 70s and 80s. It did its job of ensuring the customer got the organizational 'feel good' factor. The smile, three ring telephone pick up, and 'Have a nice day' did wonders, with stores like Nordstroms building their business around it.

Good service added to the top line and underpinned all the marketing goals of retention and improved margins on repeat business. But a paradigm shift occurred again because of the need to differentiate. If everyone is delivering good service how will that differentiate competitors? What will organizations do when margins are falling and so are customers levels of loyalty? Ever more competition, ever more sophistication and – oh no! – ever more advanced technology adds up to one unpalatable truth. Businesses have less and less ability to control what is going on in their markets. Time to look for another way of valuing and organizing the business.

1990s and beyond: the vision thing

Shareholder value really took hold in the 1990s as BMW's description of itself on the worldwide web reveals: 'The company is built on trust: trust based on honesty, dependability, and commitment (yet more of the dynamic emotions); trust that provides a constant source of orientation, one which guides the employee in assessing the value of his actions, and the shareholder in the investment of his capital.' (www.bmw.com)

As companies began to look at processes and people, hard and soft management issues, and the wider needs of the shareholder, another profound shifting in thinking took place. Organizations began to think about the power of a balanced approach – to all the issue they faced, not just those that mattered to shareholders. In the early 1990s, the 'Balanced Scorecard' began pointing the way to looking after the hard and soft issues.

Today, adding value is not enough. What has become critical, both for now and the future, is meeting your customer's every wish. The issues for organizations are translating the ability to meet customers' needs into one-to-one relationships and then into producing innovative products and services that keep those relationships alive. The glue that holds the organization and the customer together becomes communication.

The profit and loss focus is now on three new areas. Once again, massive changes are occurring inside organizations in order to deliver the cultures and behaviors needed to strengthen the P&L. Organizations have to concentrate on the following capabilities if they are to maximize the value of customer relationships:

1   **Innovation** (the internal part of the business strategy). Innovation today is the basis of an organization's strategy for tomorrow. Innovation is about creating the revenue for 'the day after next' (the 'new future'). It is all about creating the vital differences that create and maintain market positioning. This positioning will   come from the way the organization markets itself and its new products, targeted to a customer's exact needs. A new vision also will help create and sustain the innovation process itself so that a flow of new products will keep bored customers excited, and excited customers committed.

2   **Lifetime relationship** (the interface part of the business strategy). This involves developing the one-to-one contacts that benefit both the organization and the individual in a symbiotic relationship where *everyone* benefits.

3   **Technology** (the external part of the business strategy). The advent of 24 hour access through increasingly sophisticated electronic media – like call centers and the Internet allows to get closer than ever to the customer and his or her ever changing needs. With billions of customers worldwide and instant access to them becoming possible, only technology can create the tools to deliver the next need – from database marketing to one-to-one relationships for life

These capabilities will drive the revenue of today's and tomorrow's organizations. Vision will be all. Organizations will need a clear vision of their customers. Customers will have a vision of the organization, delivered to them by the brand and corporate identity. These identities will, of course, be delivered by communication and marketing. This 'customer vision' will be like a mirror to customers and other stakeholders, reflecting what the people in an organization believe to be their values, behaviors, lifestyle, needs and likes.

These two types of vision – that of the organization and of the customer – help ensure customers and organizations remain face-to-face and ideally, fascinated with one another! The technological revolution is helping more and more customers to develop a vision of the organizations that are now part of their daily lives. Can your customer see you clearly and is their view positive or negative? Is the value your organization delivers clear and visible 24 hours a day? If not, another competitor will be.

Box 8.1 shows how Coca-Cola Chairman and CEO Roberto C. Goizueta (before his death in 1997) believed the company's success springs from its dedication to creating value for all its shareholders and stakeholders. The Coke vision is being shared on the World Wide Web to ensure everyone sticks with 'the real thing' so that it stays 'the real thing' into the next millennium.

Relationships are it!

Coca-Cola is telling shareholders and us that the whole company is working to deliver shareholder value through a thirst *to reach more consumers in more places with more of our products, creating more value for you.* How? Through knowing the customer. Coca-Cola believes, and its research tells it, that relationship marketing has a direct link to the generation of more revenue.

Box 8.1 Creating value at Coca-Cola

In a letter to shareholders, Chairman and CEO Roberto C. Goizueta writes:

'Even after another rewarding year, The Coca-Cola Company is still unquenchably thirsty – thirsty for more ways to reach more consumers in more places with more of our products, creating more value for you.

'We have worked hard to make that unending craving one of the trademarks that define us as a Company, like our contour bottle and our script logo. It defines the way we work; we have long been successful, but we have always remained discontented *[wow what a dynamic emotional driver]*. That's the way we are today.

'And we were honored again this month as *Fortune's* annual ranking proclaimed us: 'America's Most Admired Company' for the second year in a row. ...we also know that in business, admiration *[another emotional driver]* is born of creating value, and we have great confidence that the system we have built will continue to do just that for decades to come.

Reasons for success

'In candid employee sessions, in our Company magazine, even in the hallways of our offices around the world, we talked at length about our mission, which remains to create value for our share owners on a long-term basis. It only makes sense that if we are to achieve success together, we need a common understanding of what success is. At The Coca-Cola Company, we know: It is creating value for the people who have entrusted *[another one]* their assets to us.

'We work hard to remember that the wonderful things our Company is capable of – serving customers and consumers, creating jobs, positively impacting society, supporting communities – happen only as long as we fulfil our mission of creating value for you. We strongly believe that, and I have included a few further personal thoughts on this important subject.

'Our people remain intensely committed to creating value for you over the long term, capturing our virtually infinite growth opportunities.

'Our people know that the only way to increase further the value of our Company is not to idly hope the market thinks even more highly of us, but to earn that higher valuation by taking the intelligent long-term steps necessary to maintain our excellent returns, increase our earnings, market our brands effectively and sell more of our products....

'We know that amid all the trades in the frenzied stock market are real investors – real people with real hopes and dreams *[this is the essence of 'emotional capitalism']*, investing their hard-earned money in the future of our Company. I assure you that being the stewards of your investment in our Company, for whatever length of time you hold that investment, is a responsibility we take most seriously, and we appreciate your continued confidence.'

Paul Allaire, the CEO of Xerox, has a similar view, saying: 'If we do what's right for the customer, our market share and return on assets will take care of themselves'.

Coca-Cola clearly has vision. Xerox has a vision.

Their ability to know what the customer is like and what they want, and to know them better than anyone else, tangibly adds to the revenue of the organization.

Brands are it!

Leading companies like Coca-Cola and General Motors are concentrating on looking after their brand and corporate reputations by looking after all their relationships – *in order to deliver shareholder value*. Now we can say that brand values create revenues.

In a letter to its shareholders, General Motors says the following about the importance and value if its brand: 'To enhance the value of our brands, we are forming clear and distinct strategies for each of our car and truck brands and have appointed Brand Managers to direct our initiatives in the marketplace. They will be focused on building the long-term equity of each brand – equity is what the brand means to the customer.'

The value of brands like General Motors and Coca-Cola is almost measureless because they are emotional, unique, living. This is how Jim Taylor and Watts Wacker, authors of *The 500 Year Delta*, describe brands: 'Great brands are more than just names. They are mission statements, they are value, they are language, they are even nonsense, because no rational explanation can wholly account for them.' (See Box 8.2.)

Taylor and Wacker go on powerfully to make the point that in a world saturated with products, brands constitute the lifeblood of a company's prosperity and future. Surprise, surprise the Coke brand name gets mentioned again. The authors say: 'When the market has become supersaturated with products, when customers have taken control of the marketing equation, how do you create and sustain a business? How do you put a product in the store and have it succeed? Two ways (and they are deeply intertwined): by fostering brand latency and by earning customer loyalty.

Box 8.2   A question

If you were to be given the choice of being presented with (1)
all the assets of the Coca-Cola Co., including the formulas for
the drinks but not the name, or (2) only the name, which would
you take? Think hard about it, and if you picked (1), think seriously about a career in the arts. Why is the name Coca-Cola so
valuable, more valuable than the entire assets of the company
itself? Because Coca-Cola has brand latency. It has the implicit
power to continue to sustain a market well into the future simply because it is what it is.'

Source: *The 500 Year Delta*, Jim Taylor and Watts Wacker.

Stakeholders add value, too

Brands are important, customers are important, shareholders are
important – but so too are other stakeholders. Whether members of the local community, industry sector groups, the media
or environmentalists, all have an impact on the business. Their
feelings and opinions about a business have a direct influence
on customers. Companies have to manage their reputations, just
as much as they manage their brands. The greater the brand and
corporate reputation, the more it will increase the value of the
brand. The more the brand value increases, the greater likelihood that customers will pay a higher price, buy more, remain
loyal to the brand and deliver greater returns.

The most valuable asset an organization can have and the
most potent thing it can do is to maximize the brand and corporate reputation. This will deliver sustained revenue, because
relationships are less costly to create and maintain. The financial model is therefore no longer simply about making it (volume),
or making it better (value), it is about these *and* one-to-one
relationships with *all* stakeholders, not just customers (vision).

Levi Strauss is a shining example of a global business that
recognizes the value of its stakeholders. Even when it is having

a tough time it is still perceived as 'generous' to its people, as the downsizing in 1997 has shown.

Box 8.3   Striving for success at Levi Strauss

'The mission of Levi Strauss & Co. is to sustain responsible commercial success as a global marketing company of branded apparel.... We will conduct our business ethically and demonstrate leadership in satisfying our responsibilities to our communities and to society. Our work environment will be safe and productive and characterized by fair treatment, teamwork, open communication, personal accountability and opportunities for growth and development.

'We will strive to achieve responsible commercial success in the eyes of our constituencies, which include stockholders, employees, consumers, customers, suppliers, and communities.

'Our success will be measured not only by growth in shareholder value, but also by our reputation, the quality of our constituency relationships, and our commitment to social responsibility.'

Source: Levi Strauss & Co.'s Web site – www.levistrauss.com

The new balance sheet

The messages from all these marketing experts and world-class companies are the same – the value of today's business lies in its ability to forge one-to-one relationships with all its stakeholders, and the power of its brand identity and corporate reputation. Look at the logic that is beginning to emerge:

- more revenue is generated from loyal, committed customers, who cost less to keep than it costs to keep finding new customers
- as costs become proportionality lower, profits go up.

Profitability is further enhanced by creating customers who are loyal to a brand:

1   a strong brand enables the business to obtain a premium on the price (although even this is being reduced through intense 'own label' competition)
2   strong brand loyalty enables an even higher retention rate for customers, making them less likely to leave and also less costly to keep
3   higher price, higher margins and lower costs obviously have a highly beneficial impact on the bottom line.

As we move to a new era of relationship marketing and where brands, shareholders and stakeholders are of paramount importance, traditional balance sheets begin to look incomplete and outdated.

Take the example of McKinsey's definition of how to evaluate a business. In *Valuation, Measuring and Managing the Value of Companies,* the company makes the following statement: 'The first step in valuing a business is analyzing its historical performance. A sound understanding of the company's past performance provides an essential perspective for developing and evaluating forecasts of future performance ... The rate of return on invested capital is the single most important value driver.'

Is this correct? Is this a vision or a vision of the past? The historical analysis we conducted earlier in this chapter will tell you where a company is best measured – not on its past but on its future and vision of its products, quality processes and relationships.

Contrast the traditional method of evaluation with the vibrant and forward-looking approach of Rogers and Peppers. In *Enterprise One-to-One,* they argue: 'The ideal expression of actual valuation is customer lifetime value (LTV), the stream of expected future profits, net of costs, on a customer's transactions, discounted at some appropriate rate back to its current net present value.

'Remember however, that the profit on a customer's relationship with a firm is not necessarily derived just from future purchases the customer makes. Customers also give a firm other benefits, such as referrals of other customers, knowledge of other customers' tastes and preferences (as well as their own), and help in deciding new products or services.'

Who is right? Are accountants correct when they say that only factories and other assets create products, which create revenue, and which therefore should be put into the balance sheet?

What about the quality experts who argue that it is only reliable products that meet customers expectations which create and sustain revenues? They believe strongly that focusing on quality will create revenue and improve profitability.

Who is right? Both of them. Businesses need to concentrate on their physical and financial assets, their quality processes and their brand reputation in order to generate revenue, cut costs and improve profitability. *But* – and it is a big but – it is the emotional and intellectual capital that are the most important assets. Virtually all other assets of a business can be almost instantly duplicated or replaced with something else. So why aren't more of these intangible (and invaluable) assets included in more financial statements?

The fact is that most accounting measures are only there as emotional crutches for people who are trying to measure the unmeasurable. Without knowing the strength of emotions in a business, or the real worth of its knowledge, how can you measure its value? The best guide seems to be the historical one of what it has made so far, with perhaps a 'stab in the dark' based on the next quarter's forecast. All well and good, for the next quarter, but, horror of horrors, something terrible is about to happen ... the CEO is about to quit for a better job.

If the resignation of a chief executive can slash the stock value and badly affect future profits, what use are the rest of the figures? What use are those wonderful accounting measures like discounted cash flow? Of more use would be discounting the cash flow and counting the emotional capital. It is not the cash flow that is the problem, it's the flow of emotions.

If people did not ultimately affect the value of a business, accounting measures would be enough. But the opposite is true – Steve Job's return to Apple in the US *did* make a huge impact, Bill Gates *is* who he is, John Harvey-Jones in the UK *did* put his stamp on the bureaucratic giant that was ICI. Just think what would happen if *everyone* in *every* firm could add their emotional capital. The technical term is, '*Wow!*'

The search for the Holy Grail

Viewed in this way, one-to-one relationship marketing with customers inside and out impacts business performance in ways never recognized before. Yet for marketing and communication practitioners, measuring the hard impact of 'soft' issues is the search for the holy grail!

Knowledge strategists such as Paul Strassman are already applying pressure for intellectual capital to be formally quantified in some way. Strassman does not mince his words when he says: 'There is no company – with some minor exceptions – that is willing to put on its annual report a verifiable number that is recognized as Knowledge Capital.

'Companies say 'people are our most valuable assets'. The fact is that when they report their statistics, they are still reporting Return-on-Equity, Return-on-Investment or Return-on-Assets. What they say and what they do does not hang together.'

Strassman goes on to argue: 'In so far as the contributions of people, information and knowledge are concerned, the financial statistics remain silent because none of these contributions to creating greater economic value are recognized in generally accepted accounting principles.'

Another influential thinker, Frederick Reicheld in 'The Loyalty Effect' (Harvard Business) is just as critical of the omission of what he calls 'human capital', but which encapsulates emotional and intellectual capital. He says: 'The vast majority of the auditable measures used to run a modern company are embodied in the income statement, which shows only one dimension of the business – this year's profits. And the balance sheet, which tries to summarize the firms long term value, is increasingly useless, especially in service businesses, because it ignores the company's most important asset – human capital. The result is that business leaders are like airline pilots with nothing but an airspeed indicator to tell them how they are doing.'

With such strong arguments being made, more and more work is being done to putting real financial figures and percentages on the value of emotional and intellectual capital and the benefits of relationship marketing. Box 8.4 includes an extract from an article in the customer magazine of one of our strategic partners Ward Dutton Partnership. As well as heading the consultancy, Peter Ward is Technical Director of the Coca-Cola Retailing Research Group. The findings in this survey, presented at the Food Marketing Institute Conference in Phoenix, Arizona, gives some fascinating insights into the true value of relationship marketing.

Box 8.4   The end of the 'average customer'

'Retailers will achieve a substantial competitive advantage by moving away from traditional mass marketing (the concept of the "average" customer) toward a more focused approach', according to *Knowing your customer, how customer information will revolutionize food retailing*, a report on loyalty marketing programs conducted by the Coca-Cola Retailing Research Group, Europe.

'Retailers claim margin gains of 1–2% (according to various sources), increased retention rates of up to 11%; reduced advertising costs; more visits of up to 10–20%; and market share gains due to loyalty programs.

'Food retailers who choose simply to follow the leaders and launch a basic loyalty program without exploiting the customer data are bound to achieve a mediocre financial return at best.

'For those prepared to go the distance, the ultimate stage of a loyalty marketing program is the transformation from a product-based organization to a truly customer-based organization.'

Source: *Knowing Your Customer: How Customer Information Will Revolutionize Food Retailing*, Coca-Cola Retailing Research Group, extract taken from the *Food Marketing Institute Issues Bulletin*, January 1997.

Building the new financial model

Clearly it is important to value the *whole* of a business, not just the past, or the present, or the future, or the tangible assets, or the profits and losses, or the intellectual assets, or the emotional assets – all of the assets.

Knowledge and emotions are your most vital corporate assets. They have a value. Not only can you measure knowledge and emotions when you have them, but as Price Waterhouse has discovered with their K Factor, you can also measure them when you are losing it. The UK government has just announced in the national press that the value of intellectual property rights (like the copyright on the Beatles' songs!) should be included in the UK's balance sheet. Too right. They provide a source of long-term revenue to the nation.

The new balance sheet is beginning to look something like this:

1   **Business (or physical/tangible) assets.** These create revenue; but remember, these can be leased so that a company need not have any. Service industries and knowledge-based industries also have few assets, so how are they really valued? By what they and the people in and around them know and feel, not just what they own.

2   **Brand and corporate value assets.** These assets are the external manifestation of intellectual and emotional assets, These new assets deliver a proposition the customer wants, needs and believes is right for them. These are the real differentiators; but who delivers this? Not just marketing. The people in and around the business. This brings us to the next source of value.

3   **Intellectual and emotional assets**. The assets listed above are important, yet it is people who are making, delivering, selling and *living* the brand. People are fulfilling the one-to-one relationships and making the most of the assets, be they physical, intellectual or emotional. People are the only true differentiator that a business has.

Did you know that the market value of the average organization is *three* times the balance sheet value. Charles Handy, the eminent 'business philosopher' and Professor at the London Business

School, says this is the value of companies in the UK. This is identical to the Fortune 500 figures. This multiplier can only be the brand and corporate value, and intellectual capital and emotional capital tied up, in and around the organization. Figures ranging from 3 times to 20 times can be quoted in many companies of note today, with a number of the high tech companies off the scale!. It is worth saying again that if the value of Microsoft is (currently) at $891 billion, it is not three times the balance sheet value (or assets) but ten times the value. Everyone in Microsoft is contributing to the additional $791 billion of worth to the stockholders. What Microsoft 'knows' and 'believes' creates the stock market value; not the value of a number of buildings dotted here and there, or indeed even the PCs inside them – although they do help!

General Motors is a another powerful example of a global business that incorporates all three assets of quality, brands and customer/stakeholder relationships (see Box 8.5).

Two new assets – intellectual and emotional capital

GM listened but they listened to what? They listened to the words of the customer. Two things emerge. Firstly, they used a marketing process. Listening is research. Secondly, they listened to the language, words, thoughts and feelings of the customer. They listened in order to gain intellectual and emotional capital. What they heard was valuable. What the customer gave them was valuable. It was part of a relationship building exercise to create customers for life. Customers for life create value for a business.

The GM team had to create continuous improvement and innovation through following a number of processes. They had

---

Box 8.5   General Motors: building a global corporation through teamwork

In its annual report, General Motors stated the following: 'General Motors is changing – moving from a multinational corporation to one that integrates its global operations and rationalizes all vehicle design, engineering, manufacturing, and marketing resources and talents worldwide

The company pursued this theme in a letter to its shareholders. It talked of the 'GM vision'. This is 'to be the world leader in transportation products and related services. We will earn our customers' enthusiasm through continuous improvement driven by the integrity, teamwork, and innovation of GM people.

'We also recognize rising expectations regarding the impact of our products on the environment and our responsibility as an employer in the communities in which we operate. We are working hard to become a leader in meeting those expectations.

'One of the biggest factors in GM's turnaround in recent years has been that we have listened — more than ever before —to what our customers tell us about their needs. We are applying this market-driven approach to developing new products for the marketplace of the future.'

Source: General Motors' web site – www.gm.com

---

to use the intellectual and emotional capital, both of the customer and their own people to create value. Processes, allied to the human assets of emotions and using the intellect, all create revenue for businesses.

The only way Xerox and Coca-Cola could create value was to communicate. How? By talking the customers' language. Businesses gain an understanding of their customers through using their words and language inside the organization. Then comes another new language – the language of the employee, the business' internal customer. Understanding the language of the *whole* customer supplier chain gets everyone close to the needs of both internal and external customers.

Think of it this way:

Process × *Language* = *Profit and Loss.*

In other words:

What You Do × *What You Say* = *What You Get.*

This is a 'symbolic formula', shown here to demonstrate the power of words (language) to build or destroy processes and deliver real business results.

It's a pretty straightforward formula with a pretty obvious way of describing how it works. First people get together (do); they talk about how they will satisfy a customer's demand (say); they do it (do); they tell customers about it (say); they deliver it (say); and so on.

But then it gets difficult; everyone keeps doing and saying the wrong things at the wrong time, in the wrong way. For example, someone comes up with a great idea; someone else says it won't work. And as your innovation goes out the window, so does your revenue, reputation and stock price.

Words, words, words, value, value, value

A new concept is emerging. If language is important throughout the organization, it is words that create tremendous value because they drive the process of getting the product to the customer. A value can be put on words – every one of them, a capital value that can be accounted for. This is true not just for those words with a copyright or a registered trade mark, but for every word written or spoken in organizations. The opposite is also true – just as every word can add value, it can also destroy value.

If we view words as having a value that can be traded along the customer-supplier chain, then we can go further than just saying they are important. We can treat words as the new organizational 'currency'. If I am a knowledge worker then the words I give the customer have value. Why? Customers pay me for them. They are what I give back in return. Words, the intellectual capital, are the medium of exchange. I give them to customers in return for what they give me.

Words have value because they convey knowledge – but more importantly, they convey emotions. Emotions have tremendous value because they drive the intellect which drives the revenue production. And if emotions have value, a capital value can be put on them too. Just like words, emotions can either add or destroy value.

Emotions are the source of emotional capital. Emotions are the business' ' hidden reserves', a source of potential revenue hidden in the hearts of everyone in and around the business. Both internal and external customers have a mine of emotional resources such as commitment, loyalty and passion, that are well worth 'digging for'.

Emotional capital creates revenue that *can* be added to the balance sheet. These asset needs to be mined in everyone in and around the organization. How? Take one example – why do customers pay specialists on the basis of time spent on working when what is really important is their output, not their input?

Take the example of this book. Book writers are paid for the thoughts and emotions they create from the words on the page – not the time at their desk. How much is this page worth to you? Doubtless, the time that I spent in creating, testing, polishing and editing the words is irrelevant to you, the customer. Is it not worth at least the time that you decide to invest in order to read this page? But its real worth is how it influences you or your organization. Will you come back for more? Will we work with you to raise your organizations level of emotional and intellectual capital? If so, the page also has a worth for generating future revenue – for *both* our organizations. If words are the basis of intellectual capital they have measurable value. If emotions are the basis of emotional capital they have measurable value. This value can be determined. How? By the worth to the customer, be they internal or external. A final word from PepsiCo. In the company's 1991 annual report, under the title *The value imperatives* they comment: 'PepsiCo's incredible returns have not gone unnoticed by its employees, as the company has been a leader in linking their rewards to shareholder value'. To accomplish this, PepsiCo implemented in 1989 a program called *SharePower*. This awarded stock options to all 300,000 full time employees.

Wayne Calloway, Chairman and Chief Executive of PepsiCo, states in his letter to shareholders: 'Since we began *SharePower*, PepsiCo people have stepped forward with thousands of ideas to increase the financial performance of your company'.

PepsiCo people came up with their currency of words to create intellectual capital. Together with their 'hidden resource' of emotions, they generated innovation and commitment. A proportion of these assets were paid back to employees through the form of financial reward. Ideas and suggestions to PepsiCo were valuable; the currency traded was words; the asset used was emotions, the payback was a share in PepsiCo. And via the web, PepsiCo let the shareholder know what they are doing, so that they value the company at a higher level and will pay a higher price for its stock.

Internal communication and marketing is therefore more than just about creating a higher level of internal emotional capital, it is about creating a higher level of emotional capital around the product, quality and brand. Everyone must be able to use their vision of customers, new products and the shape of the future. Once everyone in an organization is delivering against these visions, the revenues, costs and profits are more likely to be maximized. What next?

Managing and measuring the new assets

So far we have taken the first steps of defining 'why' emotional capital and intellectual capital figure into an organization's financial performance and should be measured. We have covered the 'how to' manage the internal marketing and corporate communication to help build it and grow it. The next part of this chapter will outline how to measure and monitor it.

Let me preface this section by saying that there is much more work to be done in this area. I have identified a new way of valuing and measuring a business that I've called 'Triple A Accounting', which is covered *in outline only*. For now, what I am doing is putting up a 'Straw Man' (something to be knocked down and built up again – even better than before). It may not give us the full answer; however, it will give us food for thought and debate.

However, let's first outline what we mean by the intellectual and emotional capital we are going to put into the Triple A Accounting. The best way to do that? A picture tells a thousand words. We will build the story around these new models as we begin to explore how to measure emotional capital in the future. First let's look at knowledge, and see how it links to the communication/s needed to make it available and understood in organizations (Fig. 8.1).

When it comes to emotions, feelings, and beliefs, people naturally tend to use words to describe something hidden, such as 'deep seated emotions' and 'feelings running deep'. Contrast this the high-flung aspirational words that tend to be used for knowledge, like 'higher levels of understanding' and 'higher education'.

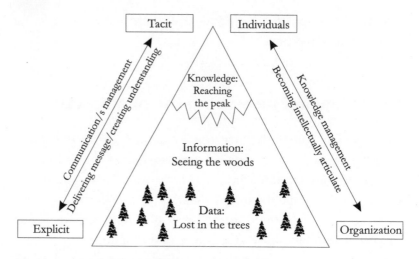

Fig. 8.1 Climbing the knowledge mountain.

The language of using 'higher' and 'deeper' allows us to demonstrate the various 'levels' of intellect or emotions – which is why my simple model is of a mountain and a mine. It is a model which when the two are joined together shows us how to manage the processes of marketing and communication around the various 'levels' of knowledge and emotions.

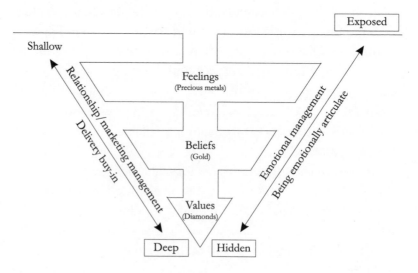

Fig. 8.2 Mining the emotional mine

This understanding of what organizations are trying to do is essential in a relationship marketing environment where everyone is responsible for hearts and minds.

Within each of these two models are three levels of intellectual capital and three levels of emotional capital. The three 'heights' of *intellectual capital* are:

- knowledge
- information
- data.

The three 'depths' of *emotional capital* are:

- feelings
- beliefs
- values.

I put them together in Fig. 8.3, with some simple definitions to show how they add value to an organization. The Knowledge Mountain and Emotional Mine shows *two* sorts of value: 'usable assets' and 'valuable capital'. The 'usable assets' means that they can be utilized to create something of value, e.g. a product or service; 'valuable capital' means they have value in their own right; therefore they can be bought or sold. This means they can now be added to the balance sheet. These new emotional and intellectual assets show what we are going to use to drive organizations forward in the future. As importantly they show how the assets will turn into items of capital value and be included in the accounts.

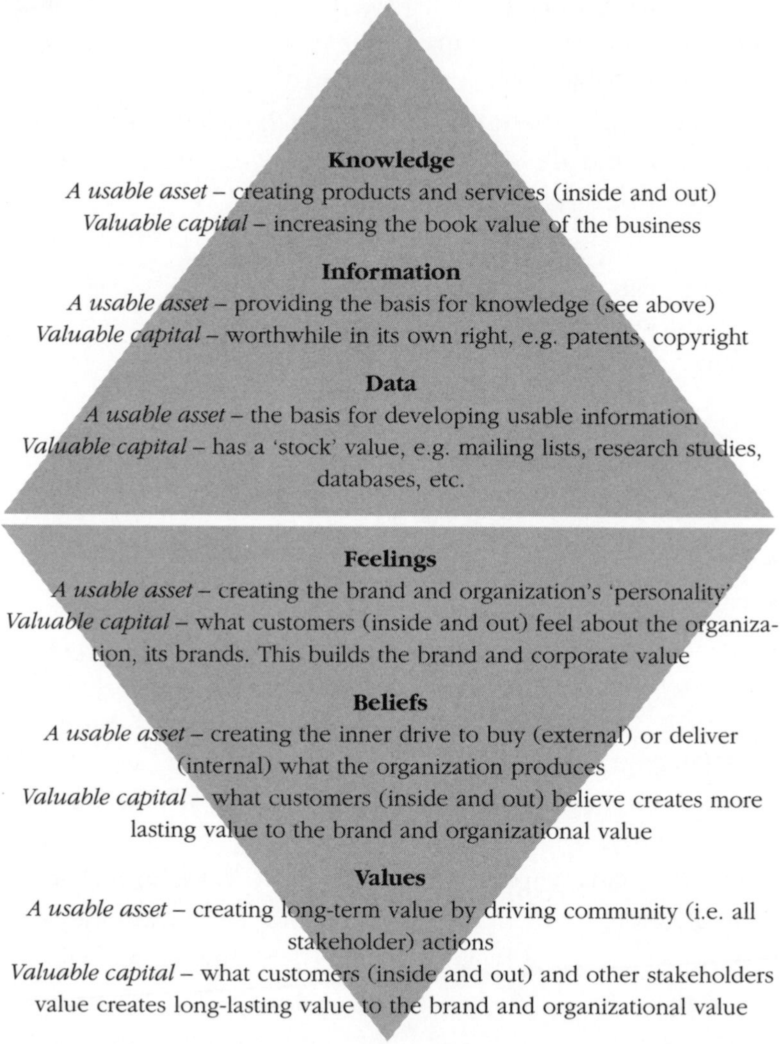

Knowledge
A usable asset – creating products and services (inside and out)
Valuable capital – increasing the book value of the business

Information
A usable asset – providing the basis for knowledge (see above)
Valuable capital – worthwhile in its own right, e.g. patents, copyright

Data
A usable asset – the basis for developing usable information
Valuable capital – has a 'stock' value, e.g. mailing lists, research studies, databases, etc.

Feelings
A usable asset – creating the brand and organization's 'personality'
Valuable capital – what customers (inside and out) feel about the organization, its brands. This builds the brand and corporate value

Beliefs
A usable asset – creating the inner drive to buy (external) or deliver (internal) what the organization produces
Valuable capital – what customers (inside and out) believe creates more lasting value to the brand and organizational value

Values
A usable asset – creating long-term value by driving community (i.e. all stakeholder) actions
Valuable capital – what customers (inside and out) and other stakeholders value creates long-lasting value to the brand and organizational value

Fig. 8.3 Valuing the new assets and capital.

Now we have begun to define the layers of knowledge and emotions we get down to the 'real' business issue. What exactly is going to be put in the books, or more precisely what is going to be measured in the new financial model.

Triple A accounting: Assessing the true value of a business

Without labeling them (overtly) as the Triple As, we have defined throughout this book the three categories that are now going to be shown in the new 'books' of the next millennium. Triple A stands for Assets, Achievements and Accounts. The big difference between the current books, including the P&L and the balance sheet, and the new books is that ALL the information about a company will be visible – not just the figures. So how will the information be presented – here is my version of the future – Triple A accounting. Here is a summary of what these will include.

Assets

The first of the Triple As is Assets. Assets will comprise intellectual capital, emotional capital and business capital. These are best understood as hearts, minds and tangible assets.

- *Emotional capital* (hearts): The feelings, beliefs and values
- *Intellectual capital* (minds): The data, information and knowledge
- *Business capital* (physical and financial): What it owns in terms of inventory, materials, equipment, cash, etc.

In simple terms, like tangible assets, these could have a 'For Sale' sign on them.

Achievements

The second of the Triple As is Achievements. Achievements will comprise the improvements in processes, language and organizational results. These are best understood as the words and deeds that drive the business, and the payoffs that result.

- **Process or Actions:** What improvements are there in the 'how, when, where, who and what' an organization does, such as delivering a new product on time or using processes that are part of Total Quality. Achievements under many process initiatives could be included here like Business Process Reengineering, or indeed successful, or failed mergers and acquisitions.
- **Language or Words:** What improvements are there in the intellectual and emotional assets held in what an organization says and how it says it. This would be demonstrated in the number of articles published (information), attitude surveys or customer research (involvement), number and quality of suggestions (best practice), number of new ideas generated and innovations brought to market, new adverts and campaigns (innovation), awards from external bodies, press comment, successful – or failed – shareholder meetings (integration) as well as the actual language used.
- **Results or Payoffs:** What improvements are there in what an organization delivers. The above lists showing the words and deeds can then be translated into a list of business results in hard deliverables, e.g. for new processes or mergers what are the cost savings and other efficiencies; for articles published what are the leads for new business generated; for suggestion schemes, what are the cost savings; for the number of innovations, what are the revenues generated and % increase/decrease of total revenue and margins; for press comment, what are the increased sales, awareness, stock price.

In simple terms these could be demonstrated as % improvements. It is worth saying that many of these examples are being included in much of the work done in the knowledge management field. Leif Edvinsson and Michael Malone, in their book

Intellectual Capital, includes some 150 areas for inclusion in the intellectual assets of organizations; Karl Erik Sveiby includes an 'Intangible asset Monitor' in his book *The New Organizational Wealth*, listing key areas of employee competence, internal structures and external structures, highlighting areas within each of growth/renewal, efficiency and stability. These knowledge management models are great ... and they would benefit by adding two things – the value of emotions, and a way of presenting them that makes them exciting and accessible to everyone. The two are of course tied in.

My reason for summarizing the examples I have given in the way I have given it under Triple A format is twofold:

1   the measures need to be defined simply, clearly and in a way which *everyone* can understand
2   to create a format in which traditional accounting, knowledge management measures of intellectual capital and management reporting can all be combined with the new concept of emotional capital to present a *total* picture of the actions and worth of an organization.

To show how the actions of a business affect the results it delivers in terms of the top and bottom line we now need to add the accounts.

Accounts

The last of the Triple As is Accounts. Accounts will comprise the figures in the income account, the P&L. This will highlight in overall terms the revenues and profits (or margins) from all its externally focused activity, the savings from business effectiveness efforts, and the feelings or added value from brand and corporate image. I have listed these simply as the financial, the facts, and the feelings. Why? Once again to show to everyone in the organization the simple and direct links between what they say, do, think, feel and believe have a *direct* and measurable link to the results of the business.

- **Financial:** The figures from 'top to bottom line' from buying in, making, distributing and selling its products and services.
- **Facts:** The results of efforts to produce savings, increase productivity and cut cost. These figures can come from examining best practice, benchmarking and the like.
- **Feelings:** The marketing and corporate communication adding value to the brand and the image. Delivering extra revenue from the current customer from providing 'perceived worth', e.g. in premium pricing, increased market share, delivering savings from producing 'lifetime' customer value.

'2Q Analysis' – percentages and perceptions

We now have a three part way of measuring success, but what sort of figures are going into the measures. How can you really measure feelings, in percentages? The 2Q Concept is put forward as the only real way to get to understanding the basis of emotions; that is, to measure what goes on inside us, as well as the results we can see on the outside. We can *only* do this by using both qualitative *and* qualitative measurement methods together. Call them Percentages and Perceptions – both are critical.

The traditional method of valuing a business has been with quantitative data: revenue, profits (or margins), costs, percentage market share. Yet for a long time marketing has been using qualitative data to get into the hearts and minds of customers. If the information is available it should be usable to add to an organizations assets, such as by adding brand value to the asset register. Qualitative and quantitative data are critical to brand value.

Now, the problem internally is that too often only soft issues are measured, and most of the measurement is done through quantitative surveys. For example, '68% of people thought this, or that' in the latest attitude survey. So what! *Why* did that individual think it? What would change their mind? Qualitative measures such as focus groups and feedback forms are used far less frequently than quantitative feedback – a missed opportunity, since such qualitative data could form as much a part of an organization's value as external brand perceptions. But times are changing. Perceptions, such as customer perceptions of a brand are beginning to be used as hard measures of the value of an organization.

In future the percentages will be seen to be part of a bigger picture that is incomplete without the perceptions. Quantitative and qualitative measures will *both* be a part of the balance sheet. Hence the concept of '2Q Analysis'. And by the next millennium qualitative and quantitative date will be *equally* used, as tools for valuing both 'soft' and 'hard' issues, both inside and out. Is this radical? Yes. How many report and accounts contain perception data? How many contain emotional data on for example the desire of an organization to innovate? Not many – yet.

Nearing the end ... and the beginning

Do we have all the answers to the way forward with linking hearts and minds with the top and bottom line – and from there putting them onto the balance sheet? Clearly not. From the outset, this book has been designed to help organizations define (in outline) and manage their emotional capital – often in a simple, visual, easy to understand way. The whole area of defining and measuring emotional capital is one that requires significantly more study and development – and will be subject for my next book! I have had many promises of help from the accountancy, financial and academic professions, as well as our many clients, and contacts in professional organizations. So as we near the end of this book, it's important to know that it really is only the beginning.

Meanwhile, where has this chapter taken us? The focus of this chapter has been to show the effect on the P&L, and balance sheet as we've traveled along the marketing and communication timeline. We have seen the impact of 'soft' issues on the 'hard' issues on profit and loss. We have seen how the strategies of organizations have changed to generate revenue and cut costs.

The bottom line is that the bottom line, the top line and the costs in the middle, are all driven by people. This means that their 'hearts and minds' are as much an asset – in fact, more of an asset – than the buildings, plant and so on. These are the assets that drive the revenue.

We're ready to take one final look at the 'top of the jigsaw box' – the integrated model that forms the hub and wheel of emotional capital.

Building the blueprint: the new financial model

The new accounting
Triple A Accounting will measure *assets*, what is owned, *achievements*, what is said and done and *accounts*, what creates value

The new business focus
Building the 'Knowledge Mountain', mining the 'Emotional Mine' and marketing and communicating throughout the entire customer, supplier and stakeholder chain

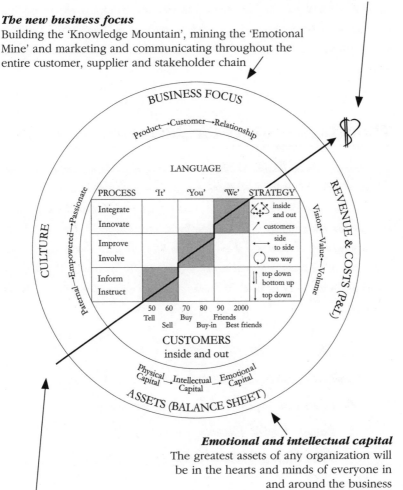

Emotional and intellectual capital
The greatest assets of any organization will be in the hearts and minds of everyone in and around the business

The new measurement
2Q Analysis – Success will be measured not just by the 'numbers' but by perceptions. Both qualitative and quantitative measures will be seen as the basis for measuring the value of organizations

My notes on the new financial model

So there we have it. Is there a lot left to be said? Yes, but not for this book. The future is now clearer in terms of what's going to happen. Why? Because it already is happening. And surprise, surprise it has been happening all along. Every organization lives off what it knows, feels and owns — always has done, always will. It is only now that we are beginning to put the life back into what has clearly been alive and kicking anyway. Recognizing, nurturing, measuring and growing the intellectual, emotional and tangible assets together is surely a better way to improved business results than the old reliance on what was owned and made.

Thought provokers for the future

So I leave you with one thought. See this as the beginning of Emotional Capital 2 — The Sequel! If emotional capital is the driving force of knowledge; if its worth is greater than knowledge, which on its own may actually be useless; and if emotions can build or destroy businesses then can we factor it into any equation as more important? Try this, my own 'symbolic equation'. Let me know if you can apply this to the value of your business. If it doesn't work out mathematically (and we may need to factor the figures to get it 'right') does it work emotionally — let me know. My contact details are in the section called 'About the author'.

$$EC \times IC + BC = TBV$$

Emotional Capital (what we feel, believe, value)

$\times$ Intellectual Capital (what we think and know)

$+$ Business Capital (tangible, physical assets)

$=$ Total Business Value (Market Value)

Your notes

A Final Word
(and a Glimpse into
the Future)

Think back to the time line starting at 'tell' and 'sell'. We have moved rapidly through the timeline and visited the new marketing world of 'buy' and 'buy-in', and moved into a new universe of one-to-one customer relationships with 'best friends'.

We have seen how intellectual capital and emotional capital will impact on every organization in the next millennium; how it will be defined, as a mountain and mine; how it will be assessed, as Triple A Accounting.

The lingering question is how it will be measured. Clearly, all the 'soft' issues we visited impact on the hard issues of revenue, productivity, and profitability, – in every which way we looked at them. We intuitively know that they all impact on each other. Of course they do!

Yet many have told me that quantifying the link between the hard and soft issues is the 'holy grail' of human resources, marketing and communication. I have deliberately chosen in this book to focus on nurturing and mining emotional capital; however, I have already embarked on the quest for this 'holy grail'. It promises to make it an exciting focus for my next book.

Where will this all end? I say again what I said at the beginning: I see a future in which organizations take an integrated approach to managing knowledge and emotions in business and around its stakeholders.

Ultimately, the future will take us well beyond integrated marketing into what I call 'community marketing'. Everyone will look after each other. Everyone will use the new currency of words to add value to our intellectual capital. More importantly I passionately believe everyone will tap into the new assets of emotional capital, to help build better futures for us all.

Glossary of Terms

These definitions (in a logical rather than alphabetical order) are my own definitions, and serve to explain the ways in which we can dissect what organizations and the people in them do, say, think and feel in a way that makes simple sense – and allows people to manage each of them in an appropriate way. But dissecting any living organism however, will no longer give a whole, living entity, so beware. The challenge for now will be to develop a set of working definitions around intellectual and emotional capital, which help in their development, and business development overall.

Intellectual capital – for using as the basis for any business

Intellectual capital goes beyond the asset of intellectual property to include *all* the data, information *and* the knowledge that is held in an organization, and is used by it, to create products, services, revenue, customer satisfaction, wealth and profit. The most important part of intellectual capital is knowledge, which is the usable data and information held in peoples heads. It is the sum total of the information and knowledge needed to run an organization and deliver its products and services now and into the future.

As an asset intellectual capital is either adding to the value of the organization or it is being wasted. Its value goes beyond its worth in its own right – see *intellectual property*. Its value is in when it is being used to add value to what the organization does. This is a value which can be translated into potential future earnings and therefore can be included in the market value of an organization. The more that the intellectual capital is turned from 'tacit knowledge' to 'explicit information' the more it can be also be valued as an item of intellectual property.

(Intellectual capital has been depicted (by Stewart *et al.*) as human, system, and customer capital. This definition falls short by assuming emotional capital is a part of intellectual capital. See *Emotional capital*.)

Intellectual property – for owning or selling

Intellectual property (sometimes shortened to IP) is best defined as the facts, figures and formulae that an organization owns. It will be written down in one form or another. It can be assigned a value especially if it is patented, copyright or, in the case of a visual identity, trademarked. As its term implies it is the mental equivalent of a building – a tangible artefact, be it on paper or in a PC. Intellectual property – just like a building – does not need to be used. It's value is in owning it, and as a potential part of the 'stock' of an organization that could be sold (e.g. a database). In this way it should (but often doesn't) form part of the physical or tangible assets of a business.

Emotional capital – for building and sustaining a business

Like intellectual capital, emotional capital is an asset for using to add value to a business. Its value lies in its power to maximize what an organization knows, its intellectual capital. It is the stock of emotions, feelings, beliefs and values that are held in and around an organization. This stock can be added to or destroyed, and therefore the value of the organization can be affected by how much is held, and what type. It can be invested in to help it grow, which in turn will impact on the value it adds to the business. It cannot be translated into a property item with an independent value, but the holders of it, people, can trade it in the marketplace for their own benefit, as well as the organizations. In this way it may be seen as a liability (borrowed from others) or an asset (owned and created by the organization). Held by customers it is beginning to be put into the balance sheet as part of brand or corporate value.

Business capital, physical capital, tangible capital – for putting on the balance sheet

These are all the same thing. These are the 'observable' traditional assets that a company puts on the balance sheet like property, working capital, machinery, stocks, work in progress, etc. Sadly they are less and less likely to reflect the value of a company as expressed by its market value. So the actual business value stated on the books is in general can be between 3 and 20 times *less* than its market value.

Total business value – for assessing the true worth of an organization

I have called the overall business value (not the market value, but potentially its true worth) in the symbolic asset formula the 'Total Business Value'. If an organization could demonstrate its 'total value', i.e. its physical, intellectual and emotional capital combined it would be much more likely to be able to align this to the value placed on it by a fickle market, often unaware of its true worth.

The knowledge mountain – for depicting levels of information usefulness

This is a model to describe (in simple terms) the difference between three forms of facts, figures of formulae. These are data, information and knowledge. The knowledge mountain demonstrates that 'the higher you climb' from data to information to knowledge the greater the value of the information held. Its components are:

1   **Data** – facts and figures which are of limited use until they are used to create information.
2   **Information** – which is data that provides usable material which forms part of the way an organization runs its business (unlike data which just sits there!). But it is how that information is best used to add more value which is where people come in and turn this usable material into knowledge.
3   **Knowledge** – the 'know how, know when, know who, know what to do, know where to do it' using information as the basis for moving forward and adding value.

Explicit and tacit knowledge – for getting out, and putting back into peoples heads

- **Explicit** – it's written down (somewhere – but finding it is another issue)
- **Tacit** – it's in someone's head (somewhere – but getting it out into the open is even more difficult)
- **Tacit to explicit to tacit** – The *two* tricks of getting data, information and knowledge out of peoples heads, into print and back into other heads. This is where communication and marketing can play a huge part in knowledge management.

Knowledge management – for creating and sustaining the asset of intellectual capital

A whole new management discipline, just waiting, or currently leaping into the breach to take over from the fads of the past and become a core part, like TQM, of the management systems of the future.

The emotional mine – for depicting levels of emotional make-up of an organization

This adds to the model of the knowledge mountain and demonstrates that underneath the knowledge mountain it is emotions which make the data, information and knowledge more valuable; by a multiple factor – see the symbolic formulae. It comes in three core types: as feelings, beliefs and values, which become more 'deep rooted' and therefore more valuable, yet more difficult to 'mine' or to change. These are held in three symbolic places:

1   **Feelings** are held in our bodies (like our gut, or in a smile or frown), these comprise a range of emotions which drive us in ways which may be short lived, yet may be extremely powerful. 'I feel great today – lets go for it'. They may be held long term like 'I feel passionate about this place'. They can be changed more easily and rapidly than beliefs.

2   **Beliefs** are best described as held in hearts. They form the basis for actions of a sustained nature like how important are customers, profit, ideas, etc.

3   **Values** are held in our souls. They are 'valuable' to us as the bedrock on which we build our lives and our organizations, as in honesty, integrity, environmental concern, etc. We give them away, or sell them at our peril.

Top ten dynamic and deadly emotions – for assessing an organization's personality and prioritizing which emotions to build or eradicate

This is an initial 'stake in the ground' to depict positive and negative emotions as part of a mix of an organization's personality.

Emotional mix – for managing as part of the internal marketing mix

The emotional mix can be used to describe what needs to be done to deliver an organizations corporate and brand values.

Emotionally and intellectually articulate – for expressing what you and the organization feels and thinks in a way everyone can feel comfortable expressing, as well as understanding

Having the right words and language to allow people and indeed the whole organization to talk about what it feels – emotionally articulate – in what it knows – intellectually articulate, so that it can make the most of its emotional and intellectual assets.

Emotional climate – for assessing the 'temperature' of an organization

The current state of an organization's way of 'doing things around here'. This is assessed in two ways – what it says (its language) and what it does (its processes). Together the processes and language form the new P&L.

The new P&L – for changing processes and language

By changing what an organization does and says, i.e. its climate, you can begin to affect its culture. The new P&L changes the processes, like involving people and innovating, and changes how it speaks to itself, like going from 'No … but', to 'Yes … and'. The core P&L changes in internal marketing and communication are depicted under the six *I*s.

The six Is – for changing the climate to create a new culture

These are the core marketing and communication processes which allow organization to move from 'tell and sell', through to gaining 'buy and buy-in' and ultimately getting customers, inside and out to become 'friends' and 'best friends' – for life. These processes, which contain a new language as part of the way of operating are Instruction, Information, Involvement, Improvement, Innovation and Integration. These are part of an overall approach to dealing with customers, inside and out under an overall banner of 'internal marketing and communication'.

Internal marketing and communication – for gaining understanding and buy-in from internal customers

Internal marketing goes beyond 'employee communication' to use the philosophy of marketing to deal with internal customers. Its basic approach is to 'match' the needs of the individual to the needs of the organization to create the desire in every individual to deliver better business results. It uses the strategy of developing the six dimensions – the six *Ds* – of marketing and communication, working in an integrated way to ensure all stakeholders and customers in and around the organization are aligned as much as possible.

The six Ds – for aligning all the six dimensions of communication in and around an organization

The six *Ds* serve to show to everyone in an organization that communication strategy is not difficult to understand. It is simply about who talks to who and making sure it happens in a way that meets the needs of each of the dimensions. These are:

Three dimensions internally

Top-down – to allow the 'message makers' in an organization to get their messages across

Bottom-up – for the internal customers to have a 'voice' and give feedback 'up' the organization

Side-to-side – for the individuals, teams, departments, divisions, companies to talk to each other

Three dimensions externally

Customers – to allow *everyone* in the organization and its customers to interface in all those 'moments of truth'

Stakeholders – to allow those around the organization who are affected by its existence to interface in all its activities that affect it as part of the community, like the shareholders, government, local community, unions, potential recruits, etc.

Strategic Alliances/Suppliers – to allow a customer supplier chain to work whether or not people or organizations are part of the organization or are separate to it, e.g. being 'outsourced', a straight supplier, a partner in a project, a joint venture, etc.

The holy grail of business – the link between the soft issues and the hard business results

The quest of the people responsible for the soft, often seen as 'touchy feely', issues has been how to show the operators, the financial 'bean counters' and the board how an investment in people impacts on the bottom line and (even better) on the balance sheet. Have we found it? The next phase in the development of emotional capital will be not to show that they are linked (of course they are, it is people that make businesses) but how and by just how much. How? By measurement of not just the traditional accounts and the tangible assets, but of the actions of the people, and the values of the intellectual and emotional assets. These can be depicted as Triple A Accounting.

Triple A accounting – the measurement of everything a business owns, knows and feels

Everything from customer loyalty: the emotional capital held by an organization in its brand value to its intellectual and emotional capital in all six dimensions of its relationships can be measured. The question is how much will be used to asses the true value of the business and be shown in the books in the next millennium? Time will tell.

Recommended Reading List

Basadur, Min, *The Power of Innovation* (London: FT Pitman, 1995).

Brandon, Michael C., 'From the three Bs to the high Cs', *Communication World*, April/May 1997.

Brown, A., *Organisational Cultures* (London: Pitman Publishing, 1997).

Bryan, Jerry, *Business Process Reengineering – Myth and Reality* (London: Kogan Page, 1994).

Collins, James and Porras, Jerry, *Built to Last* (London: HarperBusiness Publishing, 1995).

Cooper, R. and Sawaf, A., *Executive EQ. How to Develop the Four Cornerstones of Emotional Intelligence for Success in Life and Work* (London: Orion, 1996).

Copeland, T., Koller, T. and Murrin, J., *Valuation – Measuring and Managing the Value of Companies* (Chichester: John Wiley & Sons, 1995).

Anderson, W.C., Stageberg, N.C. and Coulter, P., 'A merger is nothing but a planned crisis', *Communication World*, April/May 1997.

Covey, S., 'Whole New Ball Game', *Executive Excellence*, **13** (8), August 1996.

Crainer, Stuart, 'Brands: what's happening to them?' *Corporate Communications Handbook* (London: Kogan Page, 1997).

Cram, Tony, *The Power of Relationship Marketing* (London: FT Pitman, 1994).

Crosby, P., *Quality is Free* (Aberdeen: Mentor, 1979).

Cryer, Bruce, 'Turning knowledge into wisdom through heart intelligence', *Time* magazine, 2 October 1995.

Deshpande, S., 'The impact of ethical climate types on facets of job satisfaction: an empirical investigation', *Journal of Business Ethics*, **15** (6), June 1996.

Diamond, Beth, 'It's the bottom line, stupid', *Communication World*, April/May 1997.

Dickson, T., 'An oilman refines his strategy', *The Review, Financial Times*, May 1997.

Drucker, Peter, *Managing for the Future* (Oxford: Butterworth Heinemann, 1990).

Elvy, B. Howard, *Marketing Made Simple* (Oxford: Butterworth Heinemann, 1991).

Ernst & Young, *Perspectives on Business Innovation*, **1**, 1997.

Fineman, S., *Organisations as Emotional Arenas: Emotion in Organisations* (London: Sage, 1993).

Flam, H., 'Fear, loyalty and greedy organisation', *Emotion in Organisations* (London: Sage, 1993).

Fulop, L. and Rifkin, W., 'Representing fear in learning organisations', *Management Learning*, **28** (1), pp. 13–25, 1997.

de Geus, Arie 'The Living Company', *Growth Learning and Longevity in the Business World* (London: Nicholas Brealey, 1997).

Gibbs, Nancy 'The EQ factor', *Time* magazine, **146** (14), October 1995.

Gibson, R., *Rethinking the future* (London: Nicholas Brealey, 1997).

Goleman, D., *Emotional Intelligence* (London: Bloomsbury, 1996).

Gorman, Carol Kinsey, 'Energizing a restructured workforce', *Communication World*, April/May 1997.

Goold, M., Campbell, A. and Alexander, M., *Corporate Level Strategy* (Chichester: John Wiley, 1994).

Grates, Gary F., 'Why the coveted top spot is losing its allure',

Communication World, April/May 1997.

Halal, Prof. William, Geranmeyeh, Dr Ali and Pourdehnad, John, *Internal Markets, Bringing the Power of Free Enterprise Inside Your Organisation* (Chichester: John Wiley, 1993).

Harrison, R.J., *Organisation Culture and Quality of Service* (ed. Cunningham, I.), originally published as *Organisation Culture and Quality of Service: A Strategy For Releasing Love in the Workplace* (London: Association for Management Education and Development, 1987)

Harrison, R.J., *The Collected Papers of R. J. Harrison* (London: McGraw Hill).

Hobson, Neville, 'Internal communication the on-line way – are we there yet?' *Corporate Communications Handbook* (London: Kogan Page, 1997).

Hofstede, G., *Cultures and Organisations* (London: HarperCollins, 1991).

Hochschild, A.R., *The Managed Heart: Commercialization of Human Feeling* (Berkeley, CA: University of California Press, 1985).

Hornick, Lee, 'Developing a 21st century corporate image', *Communication World*, August 1995.

Huczynski, A., *Management Gurus* (London: Routledge, 1993).

Ind, N., *The Corporate Brand* (London: Macmillan, 1997).

Johnson, Mark, 'Battling information overload', *Communication World*, April/May 1997.

Jones, Bondi, 'Global Happiness Ratings', *Management Review*, **85** (7) July 1996.

Knobil, M. and Stewart, C., 'Superbrands – an insight into fifty of the world's superbrands', *Creative & Commercial Communications*, London, 1996.

Kanter, R.M., *When Giants Learn to Dance* (London: Routledge, 1992).

Kochan, N., *The World's Greatest Brands, Interbrand* (London: Macmillan Business, 1996).

Kotler, P. and Armstrong, G., *Principles of Marketing* (London: Prentice Hall, 1991).

Marken, Andy, 'The corporate ladder', *Communication World*, February/March 1997.

McTaggart, J., Kontes, P. and Mankins, M. *The Value Imperative* (London: The Free Press, 1994).

Moore, Tom, 'Building credibility in a time of change', *Communication World*, September 1996.

Morgan, Gareth, *Images of Organisations* (London: Sage, 1996).

Morrison, D.E., 'Psychological contracts and change', *Human Resource Management*, **33** (3), Fall 1994.

Nemec, Richard, 'The art of feedback', *Communication World*, February/March 1997.

Payne, Adrian, Martin, Christopher and Ballantyne, David, *Relationship Marketing* (Oxford: Butterworth Heinemann, 1993).

Payne, Adrian (ed.) *Advances in Relationship Marketing* (The Cranfield Management Series. London: Kogan Page, 1997).

Peppers, D. and Rogers, M. *Enterprise One-To-One – Tools for Building Unbreakable Customer Relationships in the Interactive Age* (London: Piatkus, 1997).

Peppers, D. and Rogers, M., *The One-To-One Future – Building Business Relationships One Customer at a Time* (London: Piatkus, 1994).

Pettit *et al.*, 'An examination of organisational communication as a moderator of the relationship between job performance and job satisfaction', *Journal of Business Communication*; **34** (1), pp. 81–98, January 1997.

Prahalad, C.K. and Hamel, G., *Competing for the Future* (Harvard Business School, 1994).

Rappaport, A., *Creating Shareholder Value* (London: The Free Press, 1986).

Robinson, Sandra, 'Trust and breach of the psychological contract', *Administrative Science Quarterly*, **41**, pp. 574–99, 1996.

Sanchez, Paul, 'Agents for change', *Communication World*, April/

May 1997.

Schneider, Benjamin, Brief, Arthur P. and Guzzo, Richard, 'Creating a climate and culture for sustainable organisational change', *Organisational Dynamics*, Spring 1996.

Smith, Steve, *The Quality Revolution – Best Practice from the World's Leading Companies* (Gloucester: Management Books 2000, 1994).

Sparrow, P., 'Transitions in the psychological contract: some evidence from the banking sector', *Human Resource Management*, **6** (4), pp. 75–92, 1996.

St. John, Diane, 'How's the weather inside your organization?' *Communication World*, March 1996.

Stewart, T., *Intellectual Capital* (New York: Doubleday, 1997).

Taylor, J. and Wacker, W., *The 500 Year Delta* (Oxford: Capstone, 1997).

Thomas, A.P., 'The effects of organisational cultures on choices of accounting methods' *Journal of Accounting and Business Research*, **19** (76), Autumn 1989.

Thomson, Kevin, *The Employee Revolution: The Rise Of Corporate Internal Marketing* (Pitman, London, 1990).

Thomson, Kevin and Whitwell, Kathy, *Managing Your Internal Customers* (London: FT Pitman, 1993).

Thomson, Kevin, 'Internal Marketing', *Financial Times Handbook of Management* (ed. Stuart Crainer. London: FT Pitman, 1995).

Thomson, Kevin, 'Meeting today's audience expectations', *CBI Handbook of Corporate Communication* (London: Kogan Page, 1997).

Warren, C., 'Corporate loyalty: loyalty as an organisational virtue', *Business Ethics*, **1** (3), July 1993.

Wiersema, Fred, *Customer Intimacy* (London: HarperCollins, 1997).

Wileman, A. and Jary, M., *Retail Power Plays* (London: Macmillan, 1997).

Wolfe Morrison, Elizabeth and Robinson, Sandra, 'When employees feel betrayed: a model of how psychological contract violation develops', *Academy of Management Review*, **22** (1), pp. 226–56, January 1997.

Worcester, Robert M., 'Tomorrow's company is the company you keep', *Journal of Communication Management*, February 1997.

About the Author

Kevin Thomson has pioneered internal marketing and organizational communication for more than a decade. He is Chairman of The Marketing & Communication Agency Ltd (MCA), the first European internal marketing and communication consulting firm. He has an extensive marketing and operational background in a wide range of industries including finance, leisure, manufacturing, retail, catering and consulting.

The leading authority on applying external marketing concepts internally, Thomson has developed strategies and processes that have proven highly effective in blue-chip organizations in the private and not-for-profit sectors. His approach enables companies to meet and exceed their objectives through their own people, by generating commitment and enthusiasm for business goals. He has earned the prestigious standing of Accredited Business Communicator from the International Association of Business Communicators (IABC) and is currently President-Elect of IABC UK.

A dynamic speaker, Thomson has addressed international conferences and seminars hosted by organizations such as the Chartered Institute of Marketing, Business Intelligence, the Institute of Personnel and Development, IABC and The International Quality and Productivity Centre. He has facilitated corporate conferences and workshops for companies such as KPMG, British Airways, SAAB, Oracle, Ernst & Young, Novell, ICI Paints and many others.

Thomson has published numerous articles and is author of several management books including *The Employee Revolution* and *Managing Your Internal Customers* – the first books of their kind on the subject of internal marketing and communication. He also contributed to the chapter on internal marketing in the *Financial Times Handbook of Management,* which brings together the latest thinking from the world's top management gurus in one volume. His latest book, *Passion At Work* (Capstone Publishing, 1998), shows how to unlock the six secrets for personal success in the workplace, using internal marketing techniques at an individual level.

To find out more about Kevin Thomson or MCA (The Marketing and Communication Agency), call MCA's UK headquarters on +44(0) 1628 473217.

To add your voice, thoughts and feelings on the subject of emotional capital, and contribute to developing the concept and that of internal marketing in the future visit the Web site at www.mca-group.com

Index